An Essay on the Principle of Population

An Essay on the Principle of Population

Volume–2

Thomas Malthus

Introduction by

R.N. Ghosh

ATLANTIC

PUBLISHERS & DISTRIBUTORS (P) LTD

Published by

ATLANTIC

PUBLISHERS & DISTRIBUTORS (P) LTD

7/22, Ansari Road, Darya Ganj,
New Delhi-110002
Phones : +91-11-40775252, 23273880, 23275880, 23280451
Fax : +91-11-23285873
Web : www.atlanticbooks.com
E-mail : orders@atlanticbooks.com

Branch Office
5, Nallathambi Street, Wallajah Road,
Chennai-600002
Phones : +91-44-64611085, 32413319
E-mail : chennai@atlanticbooks.com

ISBN 978-81-269-1520-0 (Vol. 2)
978-81-269-1521-7 (Set)

Printed in India at Nice Printing Press, A-33/3A, Site-IV, Industrial Area, Sahibabad, Ghaziabad, U.P.

Preface

Thomas Robert Malthus's *An Essay on the Principle of Population* stands as a milestone in the history of economic thought. The theory of population in the *Essay* has perhaps created more polemics in the literature than any other economic theory over the last two hundred years.

I have used my lecture notes that I used to regularly deliver to my students at the University of Western Australia in writing my introduction to Malthus's *Essay*. My former students helped me a lot in clarifying my own ideas on Malthus. I would particularly like to mention the names of John Wood, Michael Harvey-Phillips and Michael McLure, all of whom have inspired me in different ways. Ken Clements, the present Head of Economics Discipline in the Business School at the University of Western Australia has also always taken a keen interest in my research activity.

Dr. K.R. Gupta, Honorary Advisor, Atlantic Publishers & Distributors (P) Ltd., New Delhi, who is himself a very good economist, has been my friend over many years. He asked me to finish my introduction to Malthus and persisted until I finished the job. I have a debt of gratitude to all my friends and colleagues; and I hope they will all be pleased to see the finished product.

As always, I would like to thank my wife, Surekha, who, despite her being physically unwell, encouraged me to write my paper on Malthus. Her patience over years with my researches has been a source of my inspiration.

Finally, a word of dedication to the memory of my Professor Terence Wilmot Hutchison, who kindled my interest in the History of Economic Thought, and, my interest, in particular in the writings of T.R. Malthus. Terence passed away a couple of years ago at the mature age of 96. I wish he were still alive to see my paper on Malthus.

Business School,
The University of
Western Australia

R.N. Ghosh

Preface to the Second Edition

The Essay on the Principle of Population, which I published in 1798, was suggested, as is expressed in the preface, by a paper in Mr. Godwin's Inquirer. It was written on the impulse of the occasion, and from the few materials which were then within my reach in a country situation. The only authors from whose writings I had deduced the principle, which formed the main argument of the Essay, were Hume, Wallace, Adam Smith, and Dr. Price; and my object was to apply it, to try the truth of those speculations on the perfectibility of man and society, which at that time excited a considerable portion of the public attention.

In the course of the discussion I was naturally led into some examination of the effects of this principle on the existing state of society. It appeared to account for much of that poverty and misery observable among the lower classes of people in every nation, and for those reiterated failures in the efforts of the higher classes to relieve them. The more I considered the subject in this point of view, the more importance it seemed to acquire; and this consideration, joined to the degree of public attention which the Essay excited, determined me to turn my leisure reading towards an historical examination of the effects of the principle of population on the past and present state of society; that, by illustrating the subject more generally, and drawing those inferences from it, in application to the actual state of things, which experience seemed to warrant, I might give it a more practical and permanent interest.

In the course of this inquiry I found that much more had been done than I had been aware of, when I first published the

Essay. The poverty and misery arising from a too rapid increase of population had been distinctly seen, and the most violent remedies proposed, so long ago as the times of Plato and Aristotle. And of late years the subject has been treated in such a manner by some of the French Economists; occasionally by Montesquieu, and, among our own writers, by Dr. Franklin, Sir James Stewart, Mr. Arthur Young, and Mr. Townsend, as to create a natural surprise that it had not excited more of the public attention.

Much, however, remained yet to be done. Independently of the comparison between the increase of population and food, which had not perhaps been stated with sufficient force and precision, some of the most curious and interesting parts of the subject had been either wholly omitted or treated very slightly. Though it had been stated distinctly, that population must always be kept down to the level of the means of subsistence; yet few inquiries had been made into the various modes by which this level is effected; and the principle had never been sufficiently pursued to its consequences, nor had those practical inferences drawn from it, which a strict examination of its effects on society appears to suggest.

These therefore are the points which I have treated most in detail in the following Essay. In its present shape it may be considered as a new work, and I should probably have published it as such, omitting the few parts of the former which I have retained, but that I wished it to form a whole of itself, and not to need a continual reference to the other. On this account I trust that no apology is necessary to the purchasers of the first edition.

To those who either understood the subject before, or saw it distinctly on the perusal of the first edition, I am fearful that I shall appear to have treated some parts of it too much in detail, and to have been guilty of unnecessary repetitions. These faults have arisen partly from want of skill, and partly from intention. In drawing similar inferences from the state of society in a number of different countries, I found it very difficult to avoid some repetitions; and in those parts of the inquiry which led to conclusions different from our usual habits of thinking, it appeared to me that, with the slightest hope of producing conviction, it was necessary to present them to the reader's mind at different times, and on different occasions. I was willing to sacrifice all pretensions to merit of composition, to the chance of making an impression on a larger class of readers.

The main principle advanced is so incontrovertible, that, if I had confined myself merely to general views, I could have intrenched myself in an impregnable fortress; and the work, in this form, would probably have had a much more masterly air. But such general views, though they may advance the cause of abstract truth, rarely tend to promote any practical good; and I thought that I should not do justice to the subject, and bring it fairly under discussion, if I refused to consider any of the consequences which appeared necessarily to flow from it, whatever these consequences might be. By pursuing this plan, however, I am aware that I have opened a door to many objections, and, probably, to much severity of criticism: but I console myself with the refection, that even the errors into which I may have fallen, by affording a handle to argument, and an additional excitement to examination, may be subservient to the important end of bringing a subject so nearly connected with the happiness of society into more general notice.

Throughout the whole of the present work I have so far differed in principle from the former, as to suppose the action of another check to population which does not come under the head either of vice or misery; and, in the latter part I have endeavoured to soften some of the harshest conclusions of the first Essay. In doing this, I hope that I have not violated the principles of just reasoning; nor expressed any opinion respecting the probable improvement of society, in which I am not borne out by the experience of the past. To those who still think that any check to population whatever would be worse than the evils which it would relieve, the conclusions of the former Essay will remain in full force: and if we adopt this opinion we shall be compelled to acknowledge, that the poverty and misery which prevail among the lower classes of society are absolutely irremediable.

I have taken as much pains as I could to avoid any errors in the facts and calculations which have been produced in the course of the work. Should any of them nevertheless turn out to be false, the reader will see that they will not materially affect the general scope of the reasoning.

From the crowd of materials which presented themselves, in illustration of the first branch of the subject, I dare not flatter myself that I have selected the best, or arranged them in the most perspicuous method. To those who take an interest in moral and political questions, I hope that the novelty and importance of the subject will compensate the imperfections of its execution.

London, June 8, 1803.

Preface to the Fifth Edition

This Essay was first published at a period of extensive warfare, combined, from peculiar circumstances, with a most prosperous foreign commerce.

It came before the public, therefore, at a time when there would be an extraordinary demand for men, and very little disposition to suppose the possibility of any evil arising from the redundancy of population. Its success, under these disadvantages, was greater than could have been reasonably expected; and it may be presumed that it will not lose its interest, after a period of a different description has succeeded, which has in the most marked manner illustrated its principles, and confirmed its conclusions.

On account, therefore, of the nature of the subject, which, it must be allowed is one of permanent interest, as well as of the attention likely to be directed to it in future, I am bound to correct those errors of my work, of which subsequent experience and information may have convinced me, and to make such additions and alterations as appear calculated to improve it, and promote its utility.

It would have been easy to have added many further historical illustrations of the first part of the subject; but as I was unable to supply the want I once alluded to, of accounts of sufficient accuracy to ascertain what part of the natural power of increase each particular check destroys, it appeared to me that the conclusion which I had before drawn from very ample evidence of the only kind that could be obtained, would hardly receive much additional force by the accumulation of more, precisely of the same description.

In the two first books, therefore, the only additions are a new chapter on France, and one on England, chiefly in reference to facts which have occurred since the publication of the last edition.

In the third book I have given an additional chapter on the Poor-Laws; and as it appeared to me that the chapters on the Agricultural and Commercial Systems, and the Effects of increasing Wealth on the Poor, were not either so well arranged, or so immediately applicable to the main subject, as they ought to be; and as I further wished to make some alterations in the chapter on Bounties upon Exportation, and add something on the subject of Restrictions upon Importation, I have recast and rewritten the chapters which stand the 8th, 9th, 10th, 11th, 12th, 13th, in the present edition; and given a new title, and added two or three passages, to the 14th and last chapter of the same book.

In the fourth book I have added a new chapter to the one entitled Effects of the Knowledge of the Principal Cause of Poverty on Civil Liberty; and another to the chapter on the Different Plans of Improving the Poor; and I have made a considerable addition to the Appendix, in reply to some writers on the Principles of Population, whose works have appeared since the last edition.

These are the principal additions and alterations made in the present edition. They consist, in a considerable degree, of the application of the general principles of the Essay to the present state of things.

For the accommodation of the purchasers of the former editions, these additions and alterations will be published in a separate volume.

East-India College,
June 7th, 1817

Advertisement to the Sixth Edition

The additions to the present edition chiefly consist of some further documents and inferences relating to the state of the population in those countries, in which fresh enumerations, and registers of births, deaths and marriages, have appeared since the publication of my last edition in 1817. They refer principally to England, France, Sweden, Russia, Prussia, and America, and will be found in the chapters which treat of the population of these countries. In the chapter on the Fruitfulness of Marriages an additional table has been given, (vol. i. p. 498.) which, from the percentage increase of population in the interval between those decennial enumerations which are now taking place in some countries, shows the period of their doubling, or the rate at which they are increasing. At the end of the Appendix my reasons for not replying to the late publication of Mr. Godwin are shortly stated. In other parts of the work some inconsiderable alterations and corrections have been made which it is unnecessary to specify; and a few notes have been added, the principal of which is one on the variations in the price of corn in Holland under a free trade, and the error of supposing that the scarcity of one country is generally counterbalanced by the plenty of some other.—Vol. ii. p. 207.

Contents

BOOK II—OF THE CHECKS TO POPULATION IN THE DIFFERENT STATES OF MODERN EUROPE

VOLUME–2

BOOK III—OF THE DIFFERENT SYSTEMS OR EXPEDIENTS WHICH HAVE BEEN PROPOSED OR HAVE PREVAILED IN SOCIETY, AS THEY AFFECT THE EVILS ARISING FROM THE PRINCIPLE OF POPULATION

BOOK IV—OF OUR FUTURE PROSPECTS RESPECTING THE REMOVAL OR MITIGATION OF THE EVILS ARISING FROM THE PRINCIPLE OF POPULATION

Introduction

Life

Thomas Robert Malthus (known by his middle name as Robert Malthus) was born near London on 13 February, 1766. His father Daniel Malthus was a learned country gentleman, who was a good friend of both David Hume and Jean-Jacques Rousseau. Robert Malthus had his early education at home under his father and a number of tutors. He entered Jesus College, Cambridge, in 1784 and was ordained a minister of the Church of England in 1788. He took the M.A. degree in 1791, and was elected a Fellow of Jesus College, Cambridge two years later.

Robert Malthus was a tall and good-looking person but born with a harelip and cleft palate. The cleft palate affected his speech: in particular, he had difficulty in speaking the alphabet 'l'. Apparently, such birth defects were known to have happened amongst his relatives. Because of his harelip and the consequent embarrassment, it is said that Malthus refused to have his portrait painted until 1833, i.e. a year before his death.

Malthus married his cousin, Harriet, on 12 April, 1804. It was a happy marriage. They had three children: Henry, Emily and Lucy.

In 1805, Malthus became a Professor of Political Economy at the East India Company College at Haileybury in Hertfordshire. He became a Fellow of the Royal Society in 1818.

Malthus became famous after the publication of *An Essay on the Principle of Population, as it affects the Future*

Improvement of Society, with remarks on the Speculations of Mr. Godwin, M. Condorcet and Other Writers, in 1798.

Other major works by Malthus included:

1. *An Investigation of the Cause of the Present High Price of Provisions*, 1800.
2. *A Letter to Samuel Whitbred, Esq., M.P. on his proposed bill for the amendment of the Poor Laws*, 1807.
3. *Observations on the Effects of the Corn Laws*, 1814.
4. *An Inquiry into the Nature and Progress of Rent, and the Principles by which it is regulated*, 1815.
5. *Principles of Political Economy: Considered with a view to their practical applications*, 1820.
6. *The Measure of Value*, 1823.
7. *"Population" in Encyclopaedia Britannica*, 1824.
8. *A Summary View of the Principle of Population*, 1830.

Malthus was a close friend of David Ricardo, the eminent economist who dominated economic thinking in Britain in the 19th century. The two friends disagreed on many theoretical issues: Ricardo was an abstract theorist who was concerned with the long-run equilibrium of a capitalist economy, but Malthus was a practical economist who focused his attention on the short-run fluctuations of economic activity. Yet the friendship between Malthus and Ricardo continued and reached a rare intellectual level in their discussions in the Political Economy Club of London and in their correspondence.

Malthus died on 23 December, 1834 at Bath, England.

A part of the epitaph of Malthus in Bath Abbey reads:

> "Sacred to the memory of the Rev Thomas Robert Malthus, long known to the lettered world by his admirable writings on the social branches of political economy, particularly by his essay on population."

As an economist, Malthus was respected but his views were not shared by his contemporary fellow economists. David

Ricardo dominated economic thinking. But Malthus was very influential as a social scientist. Those who came to be known as "evolutionary biologists" were influenced by Malthus's theory of population. Charles Darwin and Alfred Russel Wallace derived their idea of 'natural selection' from Malthus. Even today Malthus remains a very influential and controversial thinker.

An Essay on the Principle of Population

The origin of the *Essay* (1798) is very interesting. Malthus's father, Daniel Malthus, was a friend and disciple of the great French thinker, Jean-Jacques Rousseau who was a firm believer in the continuous future improvement of human society.

Rousseau's ideas reflected the general trend in philosophical thinking in the late eighteenth century. William Godwin (1756-1836) (whose daughter, Mary Shelley was married to the famous poet, Percy Shelley) and Marquis de Condorcet (1743-1794) wrote in support of the general optimistic thinking at that time. In his book entitled *An Enquiry Concerning Political Justice* (1793), Godwin expressed his optimism in these words: "Myriads of centuries of ever increasing population may pass, and yet the earth would still not be wanting to supply them with the means of subsistence." Godwin fully subscribed to the notion of "perfectibility of human beings".

A similar position to that of Godwin was taken by the French thinker, Condorcet who was perhaps even more optimistic about the future of human society than Godwin. Condorcet expressed his optimism regarding the future of human society in his book called *Outlines of a Historical View of the Progress of the Human Mind* (1795). Condorcet wrote his book while he was hiding and was under a death sentence. He had been active and influential in the early phases of the French Revolution. But later on he alienated himself from the Jacobin extremists by saying that the king should not be executed and that the Republic ought to abolish death sentence.

Two of the fundamental ideas underlying the optimistic philosophy in the eighteenth century Europe were derived from the medieval Christian theology. These ideas were: (1) God is good; or, in other words, Nature itself is benevolent. It is the attempt of human beings to interfere with nature that causes a deviation from a beneficial natural order. (2) Man is God's most perfect creation. After all, according to the scriptures (the Old Testament), God created man "in his own image". From these two fundamental ideas would follow the necessary conclusion that sex being natural, the consequences of sex leading to procreation cannot be harmful.

Daniel Malthus accepted the above optimistic philosophy and preached it to his son, Robert Malthus, who was unable to accept it and rejected it angrily. Then, Robert proceeded to publish his famous *Essay* in 1798 in which he developed his much debated population theory.

Malthus's theory itself is based on two assumptions: (1) That food is necessary to the existence of humans. This is a (natural) physical law, because it is not made by man. (2) That the passion between man and woman is natural and will always lead to sexual activity. Again, this is a biological law, and it has nothing to do with any substitution of human activity for a natural order. Now, Malthus noted an incompatibility between the physical law and the biological law in the long-run. He argued that, in the absence of checks to population growth, population would always have a tendency to grow faster than the supply of food necessary for its subsistence. Thus, Malthus observed an element of inconsistency in the so-called natural order. He argued: "The power of population is indefinitely greater than the power in the earth to produce subsistence for man." He went on to say that population, when its growth is unchecked, increases in a geometrical progression, such as, 1, 2, 4, 8, 16, 32, and so on, in each successive generation. This means that starting from a base of 1, population in the next generation, i.e. after, say, 25 to 35 years, will increase to 2 (or, double itself), and this process will continue from one generation to the next when it will increase from 2 to 4, and so on. The food supply, on the other hand, increases, according to Malthus, in arithmetic progression, i.e. 1, 2, 3, 4, 5, etc. Hence, from an initial equilibrium position, population growth would far outstrip the supply of food to maintain that additional population within a few years.

However, as population cannot increase beyond available subsistence, it would be held in check by either 'positive checks' or 'preventive checks', or both. 'Positive checks' increase the death rate by causing a higher level of mortality in a given population than normal by way of famines, wars, and deaths due to malnutrition. The operation of 'positive checks' is a clear sign of human misery and suffering.

'Preventive checks', on the other hand, would tend to reduce the birth rate; and such checks would include abortion, contraception, unnatural sex, and any other check that would reduce the birth rate. As in a closed society that is not exposed to emigration or immigration, the growth of population was the excess of the births over deaths, the operation of 'preventive checks' and 'positive checks' would eliminate the excess and bring population growth to an end. However, the operation of 'preventive checks', according to Malthus, indicated the moral decay in a society and was a sign of human vice.

Thus Malthus emerged as a great pessimist, who saw the future of a human society as one that would be caught between either 'vice', or 'misery', or both. This was Malthus's position in 1798, in the first edition of his *Essay*.

It is possible that Malthus took the position of a pessimist par excellence in the first edition of his *Essay* because of his attitude to sex and marriage at the time of writing the book. Because of his harelip and cleft palate from his birth, Malthus did not find it easy to find a woman who was willing to marry him. This perhaps led to Malthus's frustrations and a negative attitude to human sexuality. However, he married a distant cousin in 1804, at the age of 38, and had three children by her. In anticipation of this marriage, Malthus began to soften his views on sex, and when in 1803, he produced the second edition of his *Essay* (which was a much bigger volume than what was the first edition), he introduced a second type of 'preventive checks' and called it 'moral restraint'. So, by 1803, 'preventive checks' to reduce the birth rate were divided into two types:

(1) contraception, abortion, etc. leading to 'vices' and (2) 'moral restraint' involving late marriages, celibacy and voluntary sexual control within the wedlock.

So far, Malthus's ideas can be summarized as below:

In a closed society, population growth = excess of births over deaths. Hence population growth can be reduced by reducing the birth rate through 'preventive checks' and/or by increasing the death rate through 'positive checks'. 'Positive checks' were indicative of human misery, while 'preventive checks' were indicative of human 'vices' unless these were the result of 'moral restraint'. As has been stated before, setting a fair example of 'moral restraint', Malthus himself did not marry until the age of 38 and had then only three children when it was common for an average family in Britain to end up with 10 or 12 children.

The above can be stated as below:

Checks to Population Growth

- Preventive Checks
  - Vice
  - Moral Restraint
- Positive Checks
  - Misery

Diagrammatically, it is shown below:

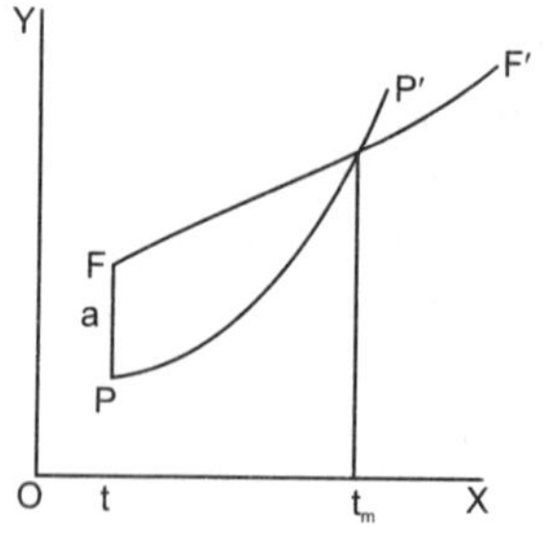

Fig. 1: Population Growth and the Supply of Food.

OX-axis shows "time".

OY-axis shows both (a) the growth of population (PP′) and (b) the supply of food (FF′).

At time t, there is 'a' — surplus of food is available.

The supply of food increases along the line FF′.

The growth of population takes place along the curve PP′.

Food surplus is exhausted and the supply of food just balances population at time t_m. Beyond t_m, there is over-population, as the tendency of population to increase beyond t_m is held in check by the shortage of food.

Malthus was definitely opposed to any artificial method of birth control. He looked upon the use of contraceptive devices as a signal for human vices.

Malthus was initially not taken very seriously by the British public, perhaps, because of the Napoleonic Wars, which led to an unprecedented demand for labour in the army and navy, thereby causing a shortage of labour and a situation of full employment. Any talk of overpopulation at a time of full employment was unlikely to have an impact on the public opinion.

However, at the end of the Napoleonic Wars in 1815, when the war-time boom in the labour market came to an end, and unemployment and pauperism became real social problems, there was a new interest in Malthus and his population theory. The failure of potato crops (the staple food of the Irish people at that time) in two successive years in Ireland led to widespread famines and appalling poverty in Ireland in 1815-1816. There was then a general recognition that Malthus's remedy for overpopulation by way of 'moral restraint' was unlikely to solve the problem of poverty and misery of the Irish people.

Faced with the real life social and economic problems in Britain in the years immediately after the Napoleonic wars, Malthus produced the famous fifth edition of his *Essay* in 1817. In this new edition, Malthus introduced another remedy for overpopulation. He said that emigration of surplus population from an overpopulous and old country like Ireland, could offer a temporary solution for overpopulation. But such temporary solution had to be supplemented by more permanent measures, as otherwise 'the vacuum' in population created by emigration would soon be filled up again by a fresh increase of population.

There were six editions of the *Essay* during Malthus's lifetime. The final (sixth) edition appeared in 1826. However, Malthus did not introduce any major new idea in the sixth edition of his *Essay*.

There were two fundamental ideas which Malthus never abandoned throughout his life. The first idea was that any attempt to reduce the birth rate by using contraceptive methods was morally wrong and should be avoided. Educating the labouring classes would be a better method to solve the problem of overpopulation in the longer-term.

A second idea that runs through all of Malthus's writings is that there was a positive correlation between a worker's real income and his family size in the short-term. A fall in the level of unemployment, associated with rising real wages, would tend to stimulate population growth by means of higher numbers of births and bigger family-size. Malthus remained critical of the English Poor Laws which linked (after the Speenhamland Convention of 1795) parish allowances to the poor people with the cost of living expenses. According to Malthus, any generous parish allowances would lead to rapid increases in the number of poor people in Britain.

Intellectual Reactions to Malthus's *Essay*

Malthus's *Essay on Population* generated intense reactions which have continued till even today. These reactions can be conveniently divided into five broad categories. In the first category are those critics who totally rejected Malthus's ideas. They argued that Malthus was wrong in assuming that the supply of foodgrains could not keep pace with population growth, and that he had underestimated man's ingenuity to overcome diminishing returns on land. It was claimed by these critics that the application of science and technology could improve productivity of land and could increase output indefinitely in the long-run.

A second group of critics accepted the Malthusian theory of population but rejected Malthus's 'moral restraint' as a remedy for overpopulation. According to these critics, it was not realistic to rely on the ability of ordinary people to exercise moral restraint to check family size. These critics broke away with the orthodox Malthusians and preached artificial birth control to restrict population growth. This marked the beginning of the so-called neo-Malthusian movement led by Francis Place. The neo-Malthusians openly advocated the need for widespread use of contraceptive practices as the only practical means of slowing down the growth of population.

Francis Place (1771-1854) can be regarded as the founder of the neo-Malthusian birth control movement in the early nineteenth century. Unlike Malthus, James Mill and David Ricardo, who all had an upper middle class and well-to-do family background, Place was brought up in the midst of poverty and had a very unhappy childhood. But he had a very happy marriage and his wife bore him as many as 15 children. There was no doubt that Place resented Malthus's 'moral restraint' as a remedy for overpopulation. To one of his friends known as Ensor, he wrote: "Between James Mill, you and I, we have 35 children. Do we have any right to preach moral restraint to the working class?"

The leading Classical economists at that time opposed Francis Place's birth control movement. Malthus's opposition to artificial birth control was well known. What was Ricardo's attitude? Ricardo was a personal friend of Place, and had read Place's manuscript entitled *Illustrations and Proofs of the Principle of Population*, in which he had forcefully argued the case for birth control through contraception. But Ricardo was reluctant to support Place openly. It is possible that Ricardo thought it would be imprudent to openly support an explosive topic of birth control at that time. J.R. McCulloch, who was another leading Classical economist, wrote about the birth control movement as "atrocious and disgusting". He argued that the artificial techniques of birth control would destroy "the most effective stimulus to exertion". However, James Mill was the only famous fellow economist who was willing to offer qualified support to the neo-Malthusian movement.

A third group of intellectuals became thoroughgoing Malthusians, and accepted the Malthusian theory, with its 'moral restraint', without asking any further questions. These followers of Malthus argued that if people had foresight, they would practise voluntary (sexual) self-control, restrict the family size and improve their standards of living. This argument was extended to support much (the then existing) social injustice. It was argued that the poor people must blame themselves for their poverty and the consequent misfortune, because of their own inability to exercise self-control.

A fourth type of intellectual reaction to Malthus led to the intense emigration and colonization campaigns in the first half of the nineteenth century. As has been stated earlier, in the fifth edition of his *Essay* (1817), Malthus argued that emigration could offer a temporary solution to the problem of overpopulation in a country like Ireland.

Two of the leading advocates of emigration as a solution for overpopulation were Edward Gibbon Wakefield (1796-1862) and Robert John Wilmot-Horton (1784-1841). Although Wakefield and Wilmot-Horton had major disagreement about specific plans for colonizing Australasia and Canada, both of them agreed that the emigration of surplus population from Britain to the relatively uninhabited parts of the world could be a permanent solution for the problem of overpopulation.

A final major reaction to Malthus was to empirically test the Malthusian theory. Malthus himself based his theory of population (1798) on *a priori* reasoning, and failed to offer any empirical proof or evidence to support his theory. This was a major weakness of Malthus's own formulation, and had to be tested statistically by facts and figures. Malthus was himself aware of this weakness of his theory which was solely based on deductive reasoning and did not rely on real-life evidence to validate it. Therefore, he made his famous Continental trip in 1799 to be able to get some factual proof for his theory. But his travel diaries were lost for a very long time. When eventually

Patricia James found Malthus's diaries and published it in the 1960s, it became obvious that Malthus had not found any adequate empirical proof to establish his population theory.

Theory of the Demographic Transition

In an attempt to get empirical verification of the Malthusian theory of population, demographers and economists collected statistical information regarding the nature of population growth (or, decline) in different countries of the world. Two of the famous American demographers, Warren Thompson (1929) and Frank Notestein (1945) are particularly well known for their efforts to empirically check the Malthusian theory of population, and thereby contributing to the development of the modern theory of the demographic transition as a general theory of population behaviour.

The theory of the demographic transition states that there are three distinct stages in the historical growth of population in any society.

First stage: It is characterised by high birth and high death rates, and hence a relatively stationary population, because both high birth and death rates tend to balance each other. This situation of high birth and high death rates prevails in all pre-industrial and primitive societies.

Second stage: This stage is characterised by a high birth rate but a rapidly slowing death rate, and hence a situation of positive population growth that accelerates in the first phase of this second stage, and then having reached a peak begins to slow down in the second phase. Effectively, then, the second stage is itself divided into two *phases:* (1) a period of widening 'demographic gap' (defined as the excess of births over deaths) followed by (2) a narrowing of the gap between the two vital rates. This second stage is generally applicable (historically) to developing countries.

Third stage: This is a period of low birth rates and low death rates, thereby marking the completion of the process of the demographic transition. This is mostly the situation to be found in developed and industrialised countries.

Diagrammatically, it is depicted below:

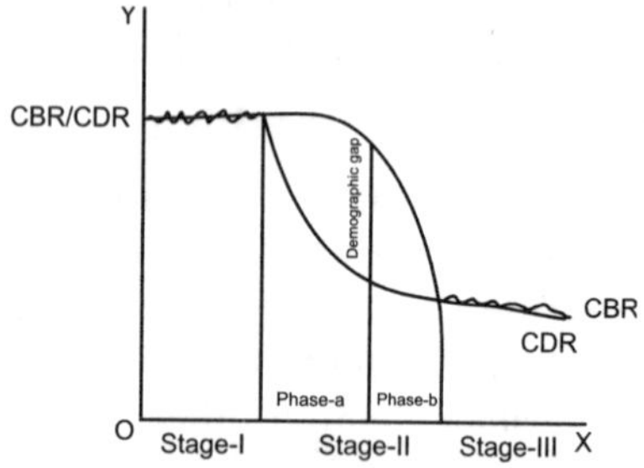

Fig. 2: The Demographic Transition.

CBR=Crude birth rate, defined as $\frac{Bt}{Pmt} \times 1000$ (Bt = live births in time t and Pmt = mean population in time t).

CDR=Crude death rate, defined as $\frac{Dt}{Pmt} \times 1000$ (Dt = deaths in time t and Pmt = mean population in time t).

CDR fluctuates in Stage I, and then sharply declines in Stage-II, and finally stabilises in Stage-III.

"Demographic gap" peaks at the end of Phase-a of Stage-II, and then narrows in Phase-b.

CBR is high in stage I, and then falls and fluctuates in Stage-III.

Now, it can be argued that Malthus, who lived during the first phase (1770–1840) of the Industrial Revolution, experienced rapid population growth in England in his own lifetime, as happens during a period of the initial industrialisation of a country. His population theory is certainly applicable to the second stage of the demographic transition. However, the Malthusian theory does not apply to the first and the third stages of the demographic transition model. It is therefore possible to argue that Malthus was neither right nor wholly wrong but that his population theory is only a special case of a more general theory of the demographic transition.

Modernization and Population Growth

All empirical evidence points towards an inverse long-term relationship between modernization and population growth. Now, the important question is, why should the birth and the death rates fall to low levels in mature and industrialised countries?

The decline in the death rate with modernization and economic development can be explained easily. Modernization would mean a rise in per capita real income. Hence, both governments and households should be able to spend more on health care and public health (including the eradication of epidemic diseases) as a result of economic development. Higher levels of health care expenditures should lower the mortality rate over time. This is reflected in the downward movement in the mortality rate from stage II of the demographic transition model.

However, the impact of economic development on the birth rate is more complex and therefore more difficult to understand. There are two groups of modern fertility theories—macroeconomic and microeconomic theories—which tend to explain the fall in the fertility rate with economic development.

Macroeconomic Analysis of Fertility

Macroeconomic analysis of fertility since Malthus has proceeded along different lines. Two of the main directions are to be found in: (a) Theory of Changing Family Structure, formulated by W.J. Goode in 1963 in his *World Revolution and Family Patterns* and (b) the Theory of Population Balance, formulated by A.H. Hawley in 1950 in *Human Ecology* and O.D. Duncan in 1959 in *The Study of Population* (jointly edited with P.M. Hauser).

Two econometric studies in the 1960s clearly demonstrated how modernization reduced the fertility rate. One study was by Robert Weintraub (*Econometrica,* 1962); and the other study was by Irma Adelman (*American Economic Review*, 1963).

For a sample of 30 nations, including both MDCs and LDCs, Weintraub obtained the partial regression and correlation coefficients of the 1953-54 birth rate on three variables: (a) *mean per capita* income, (b) proportion of population living on farms, and (c) *mean* infant mortality. The second study by Irma Adelman was concerned with the regression of four independent variables (*per capita* income; an index of education; *per cent* of population employed outside agriculture; and population density) on the fertility of women in a sample obtained from 37 countries.

Both the Weintraub and Adelman studies lead to similar results and show a positive correlation between real income and fertility. Hence, they argued that Malthus was right in observing that a rise in the real incomes of the working class families would in the short-term stimulate the growth of population. The "income effect" on population growth is always positive.

However, economic development over a longer period would bring about structural changes in the economy such as urbanisation, low infant mortality, emancipation of women and higher levels of education among the working class. Such structural changes have a negative impact on fertility. When the negative structural change effect more than offsets the positive "income effect", economic development leads to declining fertility in the long-term.

Malthus was unable to foresee how a continuing rising level of real income for the working class families would eventually lead to major structural changes, which would together constitute what is called 'economic development', and how such economic development, in its turn, would inhibit further population growth.

Microeconomic Analysis of Fertility

A second group of theories at the micro-level also look at the question of fertility from the perspective of a family unit. Gary Becker is the most consistent exponent of the modern microeconomic theory of fertility, which is an extension of Harvey Leibenstein's analysis in the 1950s.

In his *Economic Backwardness and Economic Growth* (1957), Harvey Leibenstein argued that parents were able and willing to estimate both costs and benefits of having another child, and that parents would therefore stop having further children when the utility/benefit of an added child was balanced by the cost of rearing that child.

Leibenstein distinguished three types of utility that children give their parents. First, for most parents, a child was a source of pleasure and pride: in other words, children were like consumption goods, *albeit* "durable" consumer goods. Secondly, children could be regarded as "productive agents", because when they would grow up to adulthood, they would be able to contribute to family income; and thirdly, children could be looked upon as providing a social insurance to their parents. They were expected to look after their parents during their old age and sickness. The second and third categories of benefits could be lumped together and could be put under the label of "investment goods". In other words, children were,—in a theoretical sense,—more like "consumer goods" and "investment goods" to their parents.

Gary Becker extended Leibenstein's analysis to examine the human fertility behaviour in different classes in a developed (or mature) country like the United States of America, or Japan, or any other country of Western Europe. Becker's starting point was that in a developed country, children ceased to play any role as "investment goods" to their parents. Developed countries have well-managed schemes of social insurance. Accident, sickness, old age and unemployment benefits are so good in developed countries that couples do not have to depend upon their children for such future benefits. Then, again, in developed countries, children tend to move away from their parental homes as soon as they grow into adults and therefore do not contribute any money to their parents. Hence, Becker concludes that children have only one single role to their parents in developed countries: this is their role as durable "consumer goods", because they can still provide much joy and satisfaction to their parents even in a modern society.

Now, in the case of consumer durables, an increase of income would produce a greater demand for durables such as motor cars, or houses, or refrigerators. This is because the income elasticity of demand for consumer durables is positive. The same would hold true for children if the "income effect" were positive.

But Becker argues that children are like "inferior" consumer goods, because of three reasons: (1) The decision to have a child cannot be revoked at will when the baby is born. (2) The children are not "saleable" in a second-hand market. This is a major disadvantage. Few people would like to buy a durable consumer good that cannot be disposed of. (3) The choice of the quality of children, both physical and intellectual, is restricted by the inherited genes of their parents. For example, black parents cannot have white children, even if they would want it that way.

Because children are like "inferior" consumer goods, any situation of rising real incomes for couples would release a negative income effect against them, thereby leading to a fall in the number of births in affluent households.

For children, the "substitution effect" is also negative, whereas for all normal consumer goods, the "substitution effect" is always positive. The negative substitution effect is caused by the rising cost of rearing up children in families with rising real incomes. There is always a shift from a quantity elasticity to quality elasticity of demand for consumer durables (including children) as real household incomes go upward. Affluent households such as families of medical doctors are expected to spend large sums of money on their children's education and grooming. There is no such social pressure on poor households.

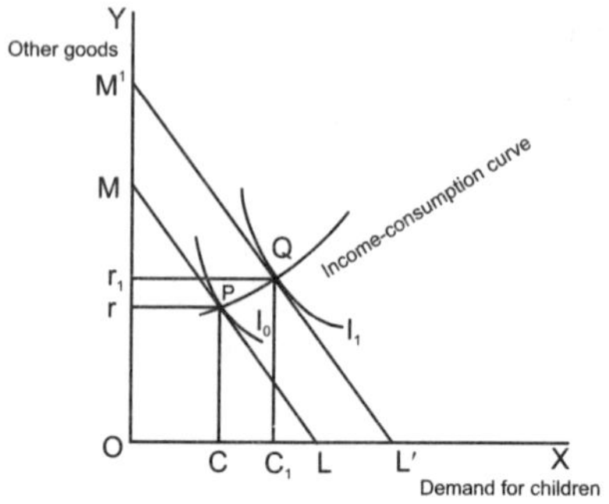

Fig. 3: Income Elasticity of Demand for Children.

OX shows demand for children.

OY shows demand for other goods.

Given the prices of "other goods" and the cost of rearing up children, I_0 shows a couple's choice. I_0 is an indifference curve that is tangential to the price line (ML). When the couple's real income goes up, they are able to move to a higher indifference I_1. If children were "normal" goods, the couple would end up having more children (OC to OC_1) when their income goes up.

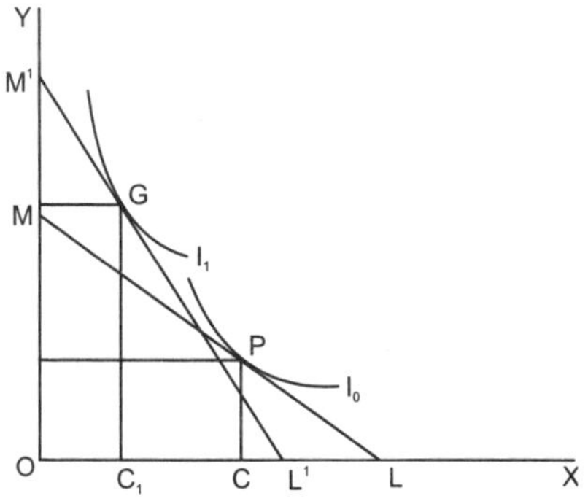

Fig. 4: Children as 'Inferior' Goods.

OX shows demand for children.

OY shows demand for "other goods".

As a couple's real income rises, the couple is faced with a rising cost of bringing up children by way of higher cost of education and related costs. So, the "substitution effect" becomes negative for children. Moreover, as children are looked upon as "inferior" goods, the "income effect" for children is also negative. Hence, rising real income for couples would lead to smaller families, and a decline in the demand for children from OC to OC_1.

Both a negative "income effect" and a negative "substitution effect" for children would cause a dramatic fall in the family size of rich households. Therefore, it can be observed that Malthus was wrong in predicting an exponential population growth, because of an undiminished level of fertility, in any society over time.

A Critical Assessment of the Malthusian Theory of Population

Looked at after this distance of time, it is important to ask whether Malthus has any relevance in the present-day world.

In a totally closed economy that does not have any exports/imports of food and that does not experience any emigration/immigration of population, it is possible that the Malthusian theory of population will hold true. But, in the real world, almost all countries have some interaction among themselves. So, the question is, whether the Malthusian theory has any relevance to the global situation today, where no country is, strictly speaking, a closed society.

The Malthusian theory rests on two variables: the supply of food and the growth of population. It is based on the assumption that population tends to grow exponentially but the production of food grows more and more slowly, that is to say, at a diminishing rate. Now, what are the facts?

The United Nations Food and Agriculture Organization (FAO) keeps regular statistics on world population and food production. The broadest measure used by FAO is an aggregate of all food produced in the world. As this aggregate combines many different types of food, they express this total simply as a percentage of an arbitrarily chosen baseline.

The FAO figures are available from 1961 onwards. The figures for some selected years are given below:

Table 1: Population and Food Production (1961-96)

Year	Population (in millions)	Food Production (index)
1961	3,086	49.5
1966	3,412	56.8
1971	3,777	64.6
1976	4,155	72.6
1981	4,524	81.4
1986	4,933	92.9
1991	5,366	100.8
1996	5,768	115.1

Source: FAO

The above figures are revealing. Since 1961 the global population has been increasing rapidly: indeed, between 1961 and 1996, the world population increased by over 86 per cent. During the same period, however, the world food production has increased, *not* more slowly, but faster and faster. Contrary to what Malthus had predicted in his *Essay on Population*, food production in the world has been increasing, during the period under review, much faster than population: it increased by over 132 per cent.

The dramatic increases in food production since the 1960s became possible because of the application of the new agricultural technology to food production, which came to be known as the "green revolution".

However, in the longer-term, indefinite population growth cannot be sustained, despite modernization of agriculture and the rapid improvement in the supply of food. The risks posed to the environment by both extensive and intensive cultivation (by way of increased use of hybrid seeds and of chemical fertilizers, pesticides and weedkillers, and also irrigated water) to feed an ever increasing population are indeed too great.

The global environment in which human beings live today evolved slowly over millions of years in the shape of a complex and diverse ecology. By multiplying human numbers (and by attempting to feed the increasing population), human beings are trying to simplify the ecology and destroy it. Today, the survival of human beings is at risk because of the continuing population growth and the associated demand by mankind for more food and more material goods leading to an unsustainable ecological demand.

The relevance of Malthus today is to be seen in the context of the modern environmental movement.

R.N. Ghosh
Business School,
The University of Western Australia

SELECTED REFERENCES

1. Becker, Gary, "An Economic Analysis of Fertility" in *Demographic Change in Developed Countries,* Princeton University Press, 1960.
2. Blaug, Mark, *Economic Theory in Retrospect,* Fifth edition, Cambridge University Press, 1997.
3. Bonar, James, *Malthus and His Work*, Allen & Unwin, 1965.
4. Flew, A. (edited), *Malthus: An Essay on the Principle of Population*, Pelican Classics, 1970.
5. Ghatak, Subrata, *An Introduction to Development Economics*, Allen & Unwin, 2003.
6. Ghosh, R.N., *Classical Macroeconomics and the Case for Colonies*, New Age, Calcutta, 1967.
7. Halevy, Elie, *The Growth of Philosophic Radicalism*, Augustus Kelley, New York, 1949.
8. James, Patricia (edited), *T.R. Malthus's An Essay on the Principle of Population*, Cambridge University Press, 2008.
9. Leibenstein, Harvey, *Economic Backwardness and Economic Growth*, Wiley, New York, 1957.
10. Malthus, T.R., *First Essay on Population* (reprints of academic classics), Augustus Kelley, New York, 1965.
11. Pullen, John, "An Index to Malthus's *Essay* on the Principle of Population, 1798", *History of Economics Review*, Vol. 51, 2010.
12. Spengler, J.J., "Malthus' Total Population Theory: A Restatement and Reappraisal" in *Essays in Economic Thought*, edited by J.J. Spengler and W.R. Allen, Rand McNally, Chicago, 1960.
13. Winch, Donald, *Malthus*, Cambridge University Press, 1992.
14. Wood, J.C. (edited), *Thomas Robert Malthus: Critical Assessments* (4 Volumes), Edward Elgar, 1986.

BOOK III

OF THE DIFFERENT SYSTEMS OR EXPEDIENTS WHICH HAVE BEEN PROPOSED OR HAVE PREVAILED IN SOCIETY, AS THEY AFFECT THE EVILS ARISING FROM THE PRINCIPLE OF POPULATION

1

Of Systems of Equality—Wallace, Condorcet

To a person who views the past and present states of mankind in the light in which they have appeared in the two preceding books, it cannot but be a matter of astonishment, that all the writers on the perfectibility of man and of society, who have noticed the argument of the principle of population, treat it always very lightly, and invariably represent the difficulties arising from it as at a great and almost immeasurable distance. Even Mr. Wallace, who thought the argument itself of so much weight as to destroy his whole system of equality, did not seem to be aware that any difficulty would arise from this cause, till the whole earth had been cultivated like a garden, and was incapable of any further increase of produce. If this were really the case, and a beautiful system of equality were in other respects practicable, I cannot think that our ardour in the pursuit of such a scheme ought to be damped by the contemplation of so remote a difficulty. An event at such a distance might fairly be left to Providence. But the truth is, that, if the view of the argument given in this essay be just, the difficulty, so far from being remote, is imminent and immediate. At every period during the progress of cultivation, from the present moment to the time when the whole earth was become like a garden, the distress for want of food would be constantly pressing on all mankind, if they were equal. Though the produce of the earth would be increasing every year, population would have the power of increasing much faster, and this superior power must necessarily be checked by the periodical or constant action of moral restraint, vice, or misery.

M. Condorcet's *Esquisse d'un Tableau Historique des Progrès de l'Esprit Humain* was written, it is said, under the pressure of that cruel proscription which terminated in his death. If he had no hopes of its being seen during his life, and of its interesting France in his favour, it is a singular instance of the attachment of a man to principles, which every day's experience was, so fatally for himself, contradicting. To see the human mind in one of the most enlightened nations of the world, debased by such a fermentation of disgusting passions, of fear, cruelty, malice, revenge, ambition, madness and folly, as would have disgraced the most savage nations in the most barbarous age, must have been such a tremendous shock to his ideas of the necessary and inevitable progress of the human mind, as nothing but the firmest conviction of the truth of his principles, in spite of all appearances, could have withstood.

This posthumous publication is only a sketch of a much larger work, which he proposed should be executed. It necessarily wants therefore that detail and application, which can alone prove the truth of any theory. A few observations will be sufficient to show how completely this theory is contradicted, when it is applied to the real, and not to an imaginary, state of things.

In the last division of the work, which treats of the future progress of man towards perfection, M. Condorcet says that, comparing in the different civilized nations of Europe the actual population with the extent of territory, and observing their cultivation, their industry, their divisions of labour, and their means of subsistence, we shall see that it would be impossible to preserve the same means of subsistence, and consequently the same population, without a number of individuals who have no other means of supplying their wants than their industry.

Having allowed the necessity of such a class of men, and adverting afterwards to the precarious revenue of those families that would depend so entirely on the life and health of their chief,[1] he says very justly, "There exists then a necessary cause of inequality, of dependence, and even of misery, which menaces without ceasing the most numerous and active class of our societies." The difficulty is just and well stated; but his mode of removing it will, I fear, be found totally inefficacious.

By the application of calculations to the probabilities of life, and the interest of money, he proposes that a fund should be established, which should assure to the old an assistance produced in part by their own former savings, and in part by the savings of individuals, who in making the same sacrifice die before they reap the benefit of it. The same or a similar fund should give assistance to women and children who lose their husbands and fathers; and afford a capital to those who were of an age to found a new family, sufficient for the development of their industry. These establishments, he observes, might be made in the name and under the protection of the society. Going still further, he says, that by the just application of calculations, means might be found of more completely preserving a state of equality, by preventing credit from being the exclusive privilege of great fortunes, and yet giving it a basis equally solid, and by rendering the progress of industry and the activity of commerce less dependent on great capitalists.

Such establishments and calculations may appear very promising upon paper; but when applied to real life, they will be found to be absolutely nugatory. M. Condorcet allows that a class of people which maintains itself entirely by industry, is necessary to every state. Why does he allow this? No other reason can well be assigned, than because he conceives, that the labour necessary to procure subsistence for an extended population will not be performed without the goad of necessity. If by establishments upon the plans that have been mentioned, this spur to industry be removed; if the idle and negligent be placed upon the same footing with regard to their credit and the future support of their wives and families, as the active and industrious; can we expect to see men exert that animated activity in bettering their condition, which now forms the master-spring of public prosperity? If an inquisition were to be established to examine the claims of each individual, and to determine whether he had or had not exerted himself to the utmost, and to grant or refuse assistance accordingly, this would be little else than a repetition upon a larger scale of the English poor-laws, and would be completely destructive of the true principles of liberty and equality.

But independently of this great objection to these establishments, and supposing for a moment that they would give no check to production, the greatest difficulty remains yet behind.

If every man were sure of a comfortable provision for a family, almost every man would have one; and if the rising generation were free from the fear of poverty, population must increase with unusual rapidity. Of this M. Condorcet seems to be fully aware himself; and after having described further iinprovements, he says,

"But in this progress of industry and happiness, each generation will be called to more extended enjoyments, and in consequence, by the physical constitution of the human frame, to an increase in the number of individuals. Must not a period then arrive when these laws, equally necessary, shall counteract each other; when, the increase of the number of men surpassing their means of subsistence, the necessary result must be, either a continual diminution of happiness and population—a movement truly retrograde; or at least a kind of oscillation between good and evil? In societies arrived at this term, will not this oscillation be a constantly subsisting cause of periodical misery? Will it not mark the limit, when all further melioration will become impossible, and point out that term to the perfectibility of the human race, which it may reach in the course of ages, but can never pass?"

He then adds,

"There is no person who does not see how very distant such a period is from us. But shall we ever arrive at it? It is equally impossible to pronounce for or against the future realization of an event, which cannot take place but at in era when the human race will have attained improvements, of which we can at present scarcely form a conception."

M. Condorcet's picture of what may be expected to happen, when the number of men shall surpass their means of subsistence, is justly drawn. The oscillation which he describes will certainly take place, and will without doubt be a constantly subsisting cause of periodical misery. The only point in which I differ from

M. Condorcet in this description is with regard to the period when it may be applied to the human race. M. Condorcet thinks that it cannot possibly be applicable but at an era extremely distant. If the proportion between the natural increase of population and of food in a limited territory, which was stated in the beginning of this essay, and which has received considerable confirmation from the poverty that has been found to prevail in every stage of human society, be in any degree near the truth; it will appear, on the contrary, that the period when the number of men surpasses their means of easy subsistence has long since arrived; and that this necessary oscillation, this constantly subsisting cause of periodical misery, has existed in most countries ever since we have had any histories of mankind, and continues to exist at the present moment.

M. Condorcet, however, goes on to say, that should the period which he conceives to be so distant, ever arrive, the human race, and the advocates of the perfectibility of man, need not be alarmed at it. He then proceeds to remove the difficulty in a manner which I profess not to understand. Having observed that the ridiculous prejudices of superstition would by that time have ceased to throw over morals a corrupt and degrading austerity, he alludes either to a promiscuous concubinage, which would prevent breeding, or to something else as unnatural. To remove the difficulty in this way will surely, in the opinion of most men, be to destroy that virtue and purity of manners, which the advocates of equality and of the perfectibility of man profess to be the end and object of their views.

The last question which M. Condorcet proposes for examination is the organic perfectibility of man. He observes, if the proofs which have been already given, and which, in their developement, will receive greater force in the work itself, are sufficient to establish the indefinite perfectibility of man, upon the supposition of the same natural faculties and the same organization which he has at present; what will be the certainty, what the extent of our hopes, if this organization, these natural faculties themselves, be susceptible of melioration?

From the improvement of medicine; from the use of more wholesome food and habitations; from a manner of living, which will improve the strength of the body by exercise, without impairing it by excess; from the destruction of the two great causes of the degradation of man, misery and too great riches; from the gradual removal of transmissible and contagious disorders by the improvement of physical knowledge, rendered more efficacious by the progress of reason and of social order; he infers, that though man will not absolutely become immortal, yet the duration between his birth and natural death will increase without ceasing, will have no assignable term, and may properly be expressed by the word indefinite. He then defines this word to mean either a constant approach to an unlimited extent without ever reaching it; or an increase in the immensity of ages to an extent greater than any assignable quantity.

But surely the application of this term in either of these senses to the duration of human life is in the highest degree unphilosophical, and totally unwarranted by any appearances in the laws of nature. Variations from different causes are essentially distinct from a regular and unretrograde increase. The average duration of human life will, to a certain degree, vary from healthy or unhealthy climates, from wholesome or unwholesome food, from virtuous or vicious manners, and other causes; but it may be fairly doubted whether there has been really the smallest perceptible advance in the natural duration of human life, since first we had any authentic history of man. The prejudices of all ages have indeed been directly contrary to this supposition; and though I would not lay much stress upon these prejudices, they must have some tendency to prove that there has been no marked advance in an opposite direction.

It may perhaps be said, that the world is yet so young, so completely in its infancy, that it ought not to be expected that any difference should appear so soon.

If this be the case, there is at once an end of all human science. The whole train of reasonings from effects to causes will be destroyed. We may shut our eyes to the book of nature, as it will no longer be of any use to read it. The wildest and most improbable conjectures may be advanced with as much certainty, as the most just and sublime theories, founded on careful and reiterated experiments. We may return again to the old mode of philosophizing, and make facts bend to systems, instead of establishing systems upon facts. The grand and consistent theory of Newton will be placed upon the same footing as the wild and eccentric hypotheses of Descartes. In short, if the laws of nature be thus fickle and inconstant; if it can be affirmed, and be believed, that they will change, when for ages and ages they have appeared immutable; the human mind will no longer have any incitements to inquiry, but must remain sunk in inactive torpor, or amuse itself only in bewildering dreams and extravagant fancies.

The constancy of the laws of nature, and of effects and causes, is the foundation of all human knowledge; and if, without any previous observable symptoms or indications of a change, we can infer that a change will take place, we may as well make any assertion whatever; and think it as unreasonable to be contradicted, in affirming that the moon will come in contact with the earth tomorrow, as in saying that the sun will rise at its expected time.

With regard to the duration of human life, there does not appear to have existed, from the earliest ages of the world to the present moment, the smallest permanent symptom or indication of increasing prolongation. The observable effects of climate, habit, diet, and other causes, on length of life, have furnished the pretext for asserting its indefinite extension; and the sandy foundation on which the argument rests is, that because the limit of human life is undefined, because you cannot mark its precise term, and say so far exactly shall it go, and no farther, therefore its extent may increase for ever, and be properly termed indefinite or unlimited. But the fallacy and absurdity of this argument will sufficiently appear from a slight examination of what M. Condorcet calls the organic perfectibility or degeneration of the race of plants and animals, which, he says, may be regarded as one of the general laws of nature.

I have been told that it is a maxim among some of the improvers of cattle, that you may breed to any degree of nicety you please; and they found this maxim upon another, which is, that some of the offspring will possess the desirable qualities of the parents in a greater degree. In the famous Leicestershire breed of sheep, the object is to procure them with small heads and small legs. Proceeding upon these breeding maxims, it is evident that we might go on till the heads and legs were evanescent quantities; but this is so palpable an absurdity, that we may be quite sure the premises are not just, and that there really is a limit, though we cannot see it, or say exactly where it is. In this case, the point of the greatest degree of improvement, or the smallest size of the head and legs, may be said to be undefined; but this is very different from unlimited, or from indefinite, in M. Condorcet's acceptation of the term. Though I may not be able in the present instance to mark the limit, at which further improvement will stop, I can very easily mention a point, at which it will not arrive. I should not scruple to assert, that were the breeding to continue for ever, the heads and legs of these sheep would never be so small as the head and legs of a rat.

It cannot be true therefore, that, among animals, some of the offspring will possess the desirable qualities of the parents in a greater degree; or that animals are indefinitely perfectible.

The progress of a wild plant to a beautiful garden-flower is perhaps more marked and striking than any thing that takes place among animals; yet, even here, it would be the height of absurdity to assert that the progress was unlimited or indefinite. One of the most obvious features of the improvement is the increase of size. The flower has grown gradually larger by cultivation. If the progress were really unlimited, it might be increased *ad infinitum*; but this is so gross an absurdity, that we may be quite sure that, among plants as well as among animals, there is a limit to improvement, though we do not exactly know where it is. It is probable that the gardeners who contend for flower-prizes have often applied stronger dressing without success. At the same time it would be highly presumptuous in any man to say, that he had seen the finest carnation or anemone that could ever be made to grow. He might, however, assert, without the smallest chance of being contradicted by a future fact, that no carnation or anemone could ever, by cultivation, be increased to the size of a large cabbage; and yet there are assignable quantities greater than a cabbage. No man can say that he has seen the largest ear of wheat, or the largest oak, that could ever grow; but he might easily, and with perfect certainty, name a point of magnitude at which they would not arrive. In all these cases, therefore, a careful distinction should be made between an unlimited progress, and a progress where the limit is merely undefined.

It will be said, perhaps, that the reason why plants and animals cannot increase indefinitely in size is, that they would fall by their own weight. I answer, how do we know this but from experience? from experience of the degree of strength, with which these bodies are formed. I know, that a carnation long before it reached the size of a cabbage would not be supported by its stalk; but I only know this from my experience of the weakness and want of tenacity in the materials of a carnation-stalk. There might be substances of the same size that would support as large a head as a cabbage.

The reasons of the mortality of plants are at present perfectly unknown to us. No man can say why such a plant is annual, another biennial, and another endures for ages. The whole affair in all these cases, in plants, animals, and in the human race, is an affair of experience; and I only conclude, that man is mortal, because the invariable experience of all ages has proved the mortality of that organized substance, of which his visible body is made.

"What can we reason but from what we know?"

Sound philosophy will not authorize me to alter this opinion of the mortality of man on earth, till it can be clearly proved that the human race has made, and is making, a decided progress toward an illimitable extent of life. And the chief reason why I adduce the two particular instances from animals and plants was to expose and illustrate, if I could, the fallacy of that argument, which infers an unlimited progress merely because some partial improvement has taken place, and that the limit of this improvement cannot be precisely ascertained.

The capacity of improvement in plants and animals, to a certain degree, no person can possibly doubt. A clear and decided progress has already been made; and yet I think it appears that it would be highly absurd to say, that this progress has no limits.

In human life, though there are great variations from different causes, it may be doubted whether, since the world began, any organic improvement whatever of the human frame can be clearly ascertained. The foundations, therefore, on which the arguments for the organic perfectibility of man rest are unusually weak, and can only be considered as mere conjectures. It does not, however, by any means, seem impossible that, by an attention to breed, a certain degree of improvement similar to that among animals might take place among men. Whether intellect could be communicated may be a matter of doubt; but size, strength, beauty, complexion, and, perhaps, even longevity, are in a degree transmissible. The error does not lie in supposing a small degree of improvement possible, but in not discriminating between a small improvement, the limit of which is undefined, and an improvement really unlimited. As the human race, however, could not be improved in this way, without condemning all the bad specimens to celibacy, it is not probable that an attention to breed should ever become general; indeed I know of no well-directed attempts of this kind, except in the ancient family of the Bickerstaffs, who are said to have been very successful in whitening the skins and increasing the height of their race by prudent marriages, particularly by that very judicious cross with Maud the milkmaid, by which some capital defects in the constitutions of the family were corrected.

It will not be necessary, I think, in order more completely to show the improbability of any approach in man towards immortality on earth, to urge the very great additional weight, that an increase in the duration of life would give to the argument of population.

M. Condorcet's book may be considered not only as a sketch of the opinions of a celebrated individual, but of many of the literary men in France at the beginning of the revolution. As such, though merely a sketch, it seems worthy of attention.

Many, I doubt not, will think that the attempting gravely to controvert so absurd a paradox, as the immortality of man on earth, or, indeed, even the perfectibility of man and society, is a waste of time and words; and that such unfounded conjectures are best answered by neglect. I profess, however, to be of a different opinion. When paradoxes of this kind are advanced by ingenious and able men, neglect has no tendency to convince them of their mistakes. Priding themselves on what they conceive to be a mark of the reach and size of their own understandings, of the extent and comprehensiveness of their views, they will look upon this neglect merely as an indication of poverty and narrowness in the mental exertions of their contemporaries, and only think that the world is not yet prepared to receive their sublime truths.

On the contrary, a candid investigation of these subjects, accompanied with a perfect readiness to adopt any theory warranted by sound philosophy, may have a tendency to convince them that, in forming improbable and unfounded hypotheses, so far from enlarging the bounds of human science, they are contracting it; so far from promoting the improvement of the human mind, they are obstructing it: they are throwing us back again almost into the infancy of knowledge; and weakening the foundations of that mode of philosophizing, under the auspices of which science has of late made such rapid advances. The late rage for wide and unrestrained speculation seems to have been a kind of mental intoxication, arising perhaps from the great and unexpected discoveries, which had been made in various branches of science. To men elate and giddy with such successes, every thing appeared to be within the grasp of human powers; and under this illusion they confounded subjects where no real progress could be proved, with those where the progress had been marked, certain and acknowledged. Could they be persuaded to sober themselves with a little severe and chastised thinking, they would see that the cause of truth and of sound philosophy cannot but suffer, by substituting wild flights and unsupported assertions for patient investigation and well-supported proofs.

NOTE

1. To save time and long quotations, I shall here give the substance of M. Condorcet's sentiments, and I hope that I shall not misrepresent them; but I refer the reader to the work itself, which will amuse, if it do not convince him.

2

Of Systems of Equality—Godwin

In reading Mr. Godwin's ingenious work on political justice, it is impossible not to be struck with the spirit and energy of his style, the force and precision of some of his reasonings, the ardent tone of his thoughts, and particularly with that impressive earnestness of manner which gives an air of truth to the whole. At the same time it must be confessed that he has not proceeded in his inquiries with the caution that sound philosophy requires; his conclusions are often unwarranted by his premises; he fails sometimes in removing objections which he himself brings forward; he relies too much on general and abstract propositions, which will not admit of application; and his conjectures certainly far outstrip the modesty of nature. The system of equality, which Mr. Godwin proposes, is, on a first view of it, the most beautiful and engaging of any that has yet appeared. A melioration of society to be produced merely by reason and conviction gives more promise of permanence than any change effected and maintained by force. The unlimited exercise of private judgment is a doctrine grand and captivating, and has a vast superiority over those systems, where every individual is in a manner the slave of the public. The substitution of benevolence, as the master-spring and moving principle of society, instead of self-love, appears at first sight to be a consummation devoutly to be wished. In short, it is impossible to contemplate the whole of this fair picture, without emotions of delight and admiration, accompanied with an ardent longing for the period of its accomplishment. But alas! that moment can never arrive. The whole is little better than a dream—a phantom of the imagination. These "gorgeous palaces" of happiness and immortality, these "solemn temples" of truth and virtue, will dissolve, "like the baseless fabric of a vision," when we awaken to real life, and contemplate the genuine situation of man on earth.

Mr. Godwin, at the conclusion of the third chapter of his eighth book, speaking of population, says, "there is a principle in human society, by which population is perpetually kept down to the level of the means of subsistence. Thus among the wandering tribes of America and Asia we never find, through the lapse of ages, that population has so increased, as to render necessary the cultivation of the earth."[1] This principle, which Mr. Godwin thus mentions as some mysterious and occult cause, and which he does not attempt to investigate, has appeared to be the law of necessity—misery, and the fear of misery.

The great error under which Mr. Godwin labours throughout his whole work is, the attributing of almost all the vices and misery that prevail in civil society to human institutions, political regulations and the established administration of property are, with him, the fruitful sources of all evil, the hotbeds of all the clinics that degrade mankind. Were this really a true state of the case, it would not seem an absolutely hopeless task, to remove evil completely from the world; and reason seems to be the proper and adequate instrument for effecting so great a purpose. But the truth is, that though human institutions appear to be, and indeed often are, the obvious and obtrusive causes of much mischief to society, they are, in reality, light and superficial, in comparison with those deeper-seated causes of evil, which result from the laws of nature and the passions of mankind.

In a chapter on the benefits attendant upon a system of equality, Mr. Godwin says, "The spirit of oppression, the spirit of servility, and the spirit of fraud, these are the immediate growth of the established administration of property. They are alike hostile to intellectual improvement. The other vices of envy, malice and revenge, are their inseparable companions. In a state of society where men lived in the midst of plenty, and where all shared alike the bounties of nature these sentiments would inevitably expire. The narrow principle of selfishness would vanish. No man being obliged to guard his little store, or provide with anxiety and pain for his restless wants, each would lose his individual existence in the thought of the general good.

No man would be an enemy to his neighbours, for they would have no subject of contention; and of consequence philanthropy would resume the empire which reason assigns her. Mind would be delivered from her perpetual anxiety about corporal support; and be free to expatiate in the field of thought which is congenial to her. Each would assist the inquiries of all."[2]

This would indeed be a happy state. But that it is merely an imaginary picture with scarcely a feature near the truth, the reader, I am afraid, is already too well convinced.

Man cannot live in the midst of plenty. All cannot share alike the bounties of nature. Were there no established administration of property, every man would be obliged to guard with force his little store. Selfishness would be triumphant. The subjects of contention would be perpetual. Every individual would be under a constant anxiety about corporal support, and not a single intellect would be left free to expatiate in the field of thought.

How little Mr. Godwin has turned his attention to the real state of human society, will sufficiently appear from the manner in which he endeavours to remove the difficulty of a superabundant population. He says, "The obvious answer to this objection is, that to reason thus is to foresee difficulties at a great distance. Three-fourths of the habitable globe are now uncultivated. The parts already cultivated are capable of immeasurable improvement. Myriads of centuries of still increasing population may pass away, and the earth be still found sufficient for the subsistence of its inhabitants."[3]

I have already pointed out the error of supposing that no distress or difficulty would arise from a redundant population, before the earth absolutely refused to produce any more. But let us imagine for a moment Mr. Godwin's system of equality realized, and see how soon this difficulty might be expected to press, under so perfect a form of society. A theory that will not admit of application cannot possibly be just.

Let us suppose all the causes of vice and misery in this island removed. War and contention cease. Unwholesome trades and manufactories do not exist. Crowds no longer collect together in great and pestilent cities for purposes of court intrigue, of commerce, and of vicious gratification. Simple, healthy and rational amusements take place of drinking, gaming and debauchery. There are no towns sufficiently large to have any prejudicial effects on the human constitution. The greater part of the happy inhabitants of this terrestrial Paradise live in hamlets and farm-houses scattered over the face of the country. All men are equal. The labours of luxury are at an end; and the necessary labours of agriculture are shared amicably among all. The number of persons and the produce of the island we suppose to be the same as at present. The spirit of benevolence, guided by impartial justice, will divide this produce among all the members of society according to their wants. Though it would be impossible that they should all have animal food every day, yet vegetable food, with meat occasionally, would satisfy the desires of a frugal people, and would be sufficient to preserve them in health, strength and spirits.

Mr. Godwin considers marriage as a fraud and a monopoloy.[4] Let us suppose the commerce of the sexes established upon principles of the most perfect freedom. Mr. Godwin does not think himself, that this freedom would lead to a promiscuous intercourse; and in this I perfectly agree with him. The love of variety is a vicious, corrupt and unnatural taste, and could not prevail in any great degree in a simple and virtuous state of society. Each man would probably select for himself a partner, to whom he would adhere, as long as that adherence continued to be the choice of both parties. It would be of little consequence, according to Mr. Godwin, how many children a woman had, or to whom they belonged. Provisions and assistance would spontaneously flow from the quarter in which they abounded to the quarter in which they were deficient.[5] And every man, according to his capacity, would be ready to furnish instruction to the rising generation.

I cannot conceive a form of society so favourable upon the whole to population. The irremediableness to marriage, as it is at present constituted, undoubtedly deters many from entering into this state. An unshackled intercourse on the contrary would be a most powerful incitement to early attachments; and as we are supposing no anxiety about the future support of children to exist, I do not conceive that there would be one woman in a hundred, of twenty-three years of age, without a family.

With these extraordinary encouragements to population, and every cause of depopulation, as we have supposed, removed, the numbers would necessarily increase faster than in any society that has ever yet been known. I have before mentioned that the inhabitants of the back settlements of America appear to double their numbers in fifteen years. England is certainly a more healthy country than the back settlements of America; and as we have supposed every house in the island to be airy and wholesome, and the encouragements to have a family greater even than in America, no probable reason can be assigned, why the population should not double itself in less, if possible, than fifteen years. But to be quite sure, that we do not go beyond the truth, we will only suppose the period of doubling to be twenty-five years; a ratio of increase, which is slower than is known to have taken place throughout all the United States of America.

There can be little doubt that the equalization of property which we have supposed, added to the circumstance of the labour of the whole community being directed chiefly to agriculture, would tend greatly to augment the produce of the country. But to answer the demands of a population increasing so rapidly, Mr. Godwin's calculation of half an hour a day would certainly not be sufficient. It is probable that the half of every man's time must be employed for this purpose. Yet with such or much greater exertions, a person who is acquainted with the nature of the soil in this country, and who reflects on the fertility of the lands already in cultivation, and the barrenness of those that are not cultivated, will be very much disposed to doubt, whether the whole average produce could possibly be doubled in twenty-five years from the present period. The only chance of success would be from the ploughing up of most of the grazing countries, and putting an end almost entirely to animal food. Yet this scheme would probably defeat itself. The soil of England will not produce much without dressing; and cattle seem to be necessary to make that species of manure, which best suits the land.

Difficult however as it might be to double the average produce of the island in twenty-five years, let us suppose it effected. At the expiration of the first period therefore, the food, though almost entirely vegetable, would be sufficient to support in health the population increased from 11 to 22 millions.[6]

During the next period, where will the food be found to satisfy the importunate demands of the increasing numbers? Where is the fresh land to turn up? Where is the dressing necessary to improve that which is already in cultivation? There is no person with the smallest knowledge of land but would say that it was impossible that the average produce of the country could be increased during the second twenty-five years by a quantity equal to what it at present yields. Yet we will suppose this increase, however improbable, to take place. The exuberant strength of the argument allows of almost any concession. Even with this concession, however, there would be 11 millions at the expiration of the second term unprovided for. A quantity equal to the frugal support of 33 millions would be to be divided among 44 millions.

Alas! what becomes of the picture, where men lived in the midst of plenty, where no man was obliged to provide with anxiety and pain for his restless wants; where the narrow principle of selfishness did not exist; where the mind was delivered from her perpetual anxiety about corporal support, and free to expatiate in the field of thought which is congenial to her? This beautiful fabric of the imagination vanishes at the severe touch of truth. The spirit of benevolence, cherished and invigorated by plenty, is repressed by the chilling breath of want. The hateful passions that had vanished reappear. The mighty law of self-preservation expels all the softer and more exalted emotions of the soul. The temptations to evil are too strong for human nature to resist. The corn is plucked up before it is ripe, or secreted in unfair proportions; and the whole black train of vices that belong to falsehood are immediately generated. Provisions no longer flow in for the support of a mother with a large family. The children are sickly from insufficient food. The rosy flush of health gives place to the pallid cheek and hollow eye of misery. Benevolence, yet lingering in a few bosoms, makes some faint expiring struggles, till at length self-love resumes his wonted empire, and lords it triumphant over the world.

No human institutions here existed, to the perverseness of which Mr. Godwin ascribes the original sin of the worst men.[7] No opposition had been produced by them between public and private good. No monopoly had been created of those advantages which reason directs to be left in common. No man had been goaded to the breach of order by unjust laws. Benevolence had established her reign in all hearts. And yet in so short a period as fifty years, violence, oppression, falsehood, misery, every hateful vice and every form of distress, which degrade and sadden the present state of society, seem to have been generated by the most imperious circumstances, by laws inherent in the nature of man, and absolutely independent of all human regulations.

If we be not yet too well convinced of the reality of this melancholy picture, let us but look for a moment into the next period of twenty-five years, and we shall see that, according to the natural increase of population, 44 millions of human beings would be without the means of support; and at the conclusion of the first century, the population would have had the power of increasing to 176 millions, while the food was only sufficient for 55 millions, leaving 121 millions unprovided for: and yet all this time we are supposing the produce of the earth absolutely unlimited, and the yearly increase greater than the boldest speculator can imagine.

This is undoubtedly a very different view of the difficulty arising from the principle of population from that which Mr. Godwin gives, when he says, "Myriads of centuries of still increasing population may pass away, and the earth be still found sufficient for the subsistence of its inhabitants."

I am sufficiently aware that the redundant millions which I have mentioned could never have existed. It is a perfectly just observation of Mr. Godwin, that "there is a principle in human society by which population is perpetually kept down to the level of the means of subsistence." The sole question is, what is this principle? Is it some obscure and occult cause? Is it some mysterious interference of Heaven, which at a certain period strikes the men with impotence, and the women with barrenness? Or is it a cause open to our researches, within our view; a cause which has constantly been observed to operate, though with varied force, in every state in which man has been placed? Is it not misery and the fear of misery, the necessary and inevitable results of the laws of nature in the present stage of man's existence, which human institutions, so far from aggravating, have tended considerably to mitigate, though they can never remove?

It may be curious to observe, in the case that we have been supposing, how some of the principal laws, which at present govern civilized society, would be successively dictated by the most imperious necessity. As man, according to Mr. Godwin, is the creature of the impressions to which he is subject, the goadings of want could not continue long, before some violations of public or private stock would necessarily take place. As these violations increased in number and extent, the more active and comprehensive intellects of the society would soon perceive that, while the population was fast increasing, the yearly produce of the country would shortly begin to diminish. The urgency of the case would suggest the necessity of some immediate measures being taken for the general safety. Some kind of convention would be then called, and the dangerous situation of the country stated in the stronger terms. It would be observed that while they lived in the midst of plenty, it was of little consequence who laboured the least, or who possessed the least, as every man was perfectly willing and ready to supply the wants of his neighbour. But that the question was no longer, whether one man should give to another that which he did not use himself; but whether he should give to his neighbour the food which was absolutely necessary to his own existence. It would be represented that the number of those who were in want very greatly exceeded the number and means of those who should supply them; that these pressing wants, which from the state of the produce of the country could not all be gratified, had occasioned some flagrant violations of justice; that these violations had already checked the increase of food, and would, if they were not by some means or other prevented, throw the whole community into confusion;

that imperious necessity seemed to dictate that a yearly increase of produce should, if possible, be obtained at all events; that in order to effect this first great and indispensable purpose, it would be advisable to make a more complete division of land, and to secure every man's property against violation by the most powerful sanctions.

It might be urged perhaps by some objectors, that as the fertility of the land increased, and various accidents occurred, the shares of some men might be much more than sufficient for their support; and that when the reign of self-love was once established, they would not distribute their surplus produce without some compensation in return. It would be observed in answer, that this was an inconvenience greatly to be lamented; but that it was an evil which would bear no comparison to the black train of distresses inevitably occasioned by the insecurity of property; that the quantity of food, which one man could consume, was necessarily limited by the narrow capacity of the human stomach; that it was certainly not probable that he should throw away the rest; and if he exchanged his surplus produce for the labour of others, this would be better than that these others should absolutely starve.

It seems highly probable therefore that an administration of property, not very different from that which prevails in civilized states at present, would be established as the best (though inadequate) remedy for the evils which were pressing on the society.

The next subject which would come under discussion, intimately connected with the preceding, is the commerce of the sexes. It would be urged by those who had turned their attention to the true cause of the difficulties under which the community laboured, that while every man felt secure that all his children would be well provided for by general benevolence, the powers of the earth would be absolutely inadequate to produce food for the population which would ensue; that even if the whole attention and labour of the society were directed to this sole point, and if by the most perfect security of property, and every other encouragement that could be thought of, the greatest possible increase of produce were yearly obtained, yet still the increase of food would by no means keep pace with the much more rapid increase of population; that some check to population therefore was imperiously called for; that the most natural and obvious check seemed to be, to make every man provide for his own children; that this would operate in some respect as a measure and a guide in the increase of population, as it might be expected that no man would bring beings into the world for whom he could not find the means of support; that, where this notwithstanding was the case, it seemed necessary for the example of others, that the disgrace and inconvenience attending such a conduct should fall upon that individual, who had thus inconsiderately plunged himself and his innocent children into want and misery.

The institution of marriage, or at least of some express or implied obligation on every man to support his own children, seems to be the natural result of these reasonings in a community under the difficulties that we have supposed.

The view of these difficulties presents us with a very natural reason, why the disgrace which attends a breach of chastity should be greater in a woman than in a man. It could not be expected that women should have resources sufficient to support their own children. When therefore a woman had lived with a man who had entered into no compact to maintain her children, and aware of the inconveniences that he might bring upon himself, had deserted her, these children must necessarily fall upon the society for support, or starve. And to prevent the frequent recurrence of such an inconvenience, as it would be highly unjust to punish so natural a fault by personal restraint or infliction, the men might agree to punish it with disgrace. The offence is besides more obvious and conspicuous in the woman, and less liable to any mistake. The father of a child may not always be known; but the same uncertainty cannot easily exist with regard to the mother. Where the evidence of the offence, was most complete, and the inconvenience to the society, at the same time, the greatest, there it was agreed that the largest share of blame should fall. The obligation on every man to support his children, the society would enforce by positive laws; and the greater degree of inconvenience or labour, to which a family would necessarily subject him, added to some portion of disgrace which every human being must incur who leads another into unhappiness, might be considered as a sufficient punishment for the man.

That a woman should at present be almost driven from society for an offence, which men commit nearly with impunity, seems undoubtedly to be a breach of natural justice. But the origin of the custom, as the most obvious and effectual method of preventing the frequent recurrence of a serious inconvenience to the community, appears to be natural, though not perhaps perfectly justifiable. This origin is now lost in the new train of ideas that the custom has since generated. What at first might be dictated by state necessity is now supported by female delicacy; and operates with the greatest force on that part of the society, where, if the original intention of the custom were preserved, there is the least real occasion for it.

When these two fundamental laws of society, the security of property, and the institution of marriage, were once established, inequality of conditions must necessarily follow. Those who were born after the division of property would come into a world already possessed. If their parents, from having too large a family, were unable to give them sufficient for their support, what could they do in a world where every thing was appropriated? We have seen the fatal effects that would result to society, if every man had a valid claim to an equal share of the produce of the earth. The members of a family, which was grown too large for the original division of land appropriated to it, could not then demand a part of the surplus produce of others as a debt of justice. It has appeared that from the inevitable laws of human nature some human beings will be exposed to want. These are the unhappy persons, who in the great lottery of life have drawn a blank. The number of these persons would soon exceed the ability of the surplus produce to supply. Moral merit is a very difficult criterion, except in extreme cases. The owners of surplus produce would in general seek some more obvious mark of distinction; and it seems to be both natural and just, that, except upon particular occasions, their choice should fall upon those who were able, and professed themselves willing, to exert their strength in procuring a further surplus produce, which would at once benefit the community and enable the proprietors to afford assistance to greater numbers. All who were in want of food would be urged by necessity to offer their labour in exchange for this article so absolutely necessary to existence. The fund appropriated to the maintenance of labour would be the aggregate quantity of food possessed by the owners of land beyond their own consumption. When the demands upon this fund were great and numerous it would naturally be divided into very small shares. Labour would be ill paid. Men would offer to work for a bare subsistence; and the rearing of families would be checked by sickness and misery. On the contrary, when this fund was increasing fast; when it was great in proportion to the number of claimants, it would be divided in much larger shares. No man would exchange his labour without receiving an ample quantity of food in return. Labourers would live in ease and comfort, and would consequently be able to rear a numerous and vigorous offspring.

On the state of this fund, the happiness, or the degree of misery, prevailing among the lower classes of people in every known state at present, chiefly depends; and on this happiness or degree of misery, depends principally the increase, stationariness, or decrease of population.

And thus it appears that a society constituted according to the most beautiful form that imagination can conceive, with benevolence for its moving principle instead of self-love, and with every evil disposition in all its members corrected by reason, not force, would, from the inevitable laws of nature, and not from any fault in human institutions, degenerate in a very short period into a society constructed upon a plan not essentially different from that which prevails in every known state at present; a society, divided into a class of proprietors and a class of labourers, and with self-love for the main-spring of the great machine.

In the supposition which I have made, I have undoubtedly taken the increase of population smaller, and the increase of produce greater, than they really would be. No reason can be assigned why, under the circumstances supposed, population should not increase faster than in any known instance. If then we were to take the period of doubling at fifteen years instead of twenty-five years, and reflect upon the labour necessary to double the produce in so short a time, even if we allow it possible; we may venture to pronounce with certainty, that, if Mr. Godwin's system of society were established, instead of myriads of centuries, not thirty years could elapse before its utter destruction from the simple principle of population.

I have taken no notice of emigration in this place, for obvious reasons. If such societies were instituted in other parts of Europe, these countries would be under the same difficulties with regard to population, and could admit no fresh members into their bosoms. If this beautiful society were confined to our island, it must have degenerated strangely from its original purity, and administer but a very small portion of the happiness it proposed, before any of its members would voluntarily consent to leave it, and live under such governments as at present exist in Europe, or submit to the extreme hardships of first settlers in new regions.

NOTES

1. P. 460, 8vo. 2nd edit.
2. *Political Justice*, b. viii. c. iii. p. 458.
3. *Id.* c. x. p. 510.
4. *Id.*, c. viii. p. 498, et seq.
5. *Id.*, b. vii. c. viii. p. 504.
6. The numbers here mentioned refer to the enumeration of 1800.
7. *Polit. Justice*, b. viii, c. iii, p. 340.

3

Of Systems of Equality (*continued*)

It was suggested to me same years since by persons for whose judgment I have a high respect, that it might be advisable, in a new edition, to throw out the matter relative to systems of equality, to Wallace, Condorcet and Godwin, as having in a considerable degree lost its interest, and as not being strictly connected with the main subject of the *Essay*, which is an explanation and illustration of the theory of population. But independently of its being natural for me to have some little partiality for that part of the work which led to those inquiries on which the main subject rests; I really think that there should be somewhere on record an answer to systems of equality founded on the principle of population; and perhaps such an answer is as appropriately placed, and is likely to have as much effect, among the illustrations and applications of the principle of population, as in any other situation to which it could be assigned.

The appearances in all human societies, particularly in all those which are the furthest advanced in civilization and improvement, will ever be such, as to inspire superficial observers with a belief that a prodigious change for the better might be effected by the introduction of a system of equality and of common property. They see abundance in some quarters, and want in others; and the natural and obvious remedy seems to be an equal division of the produce. They see a prodigious quantity of human exertion wasted upon trivial, useless, and sometimes pernicious objects, which might either be wholly saved or more effectively employed. They see invention after invention in machinery brought forward, which is seemingly calculated, in the most marked manner, to abate the sum of human toil. Yet with these apparent means of giving plenty, leisure, and happiness to all, they still see the labours of the great mass of society undiminished, and their condition, if not deteriorated, in no very striking and palpable manner improved.

Under these circumstances, it cannot be a matter of wonder that proposals for systems of equality should be continually reviving. After periods when the subject has undergone a thorough discussion, or when some great experiment in improvement has failed, it is likely that the question should be dormant for a time, and that the opinions of the advocates of equality should be ranked among those errors which had passed away to be heard of no more. But it is probable that if the world were to last for any number of thousand years, systems of equality would be among those errors, which like the tunes of a barrel organ, to use the illustration of Dugald Stewart,[1] will never cease to return at certain intervals.

I am induced to make these remarks, and to add a little to what I have already said on systems of equality, instead of leaving out the whole discussion, by a tendency to a revival of this kind at the present moment.[2]

A gentleman, for whom I have a very sincere respect, Mr. Owen, of Lanark, has lately published a work entitled *A New View of Society*, which is intended to prepare the public mind for the introduction of a system involving a community of labour and of goods. It is also generally known that an idea has lately prevailed among some of the lower classes of society, that the land is the people's farm, the rent of which ought to be equally divided among them; and that they have been deprived of the benefits which belong to them from this their natural inheritance, by the injustice and oppression of their stewards, the landlords.

Mr. Owen is, I believe, a man of real benevolence, who has done much good; and every friend of humanity must heartily wish him success in his endeavours to procure an Act of Parliament for limiting the hours of working among the children in the cotton manufactories, and preventing them from being employed at too early an age. He is further entitled to great attention on all subjects relating to education, from the experience and knowledge which he must have gained in an intercourse of many years with two thousand manufacturers, and from the success which is said to have resulted from his modes of management. A theory professed to be founded on such experience is, no doubt, worthy of much more consideration than one formed in a closet.

The claims to attention possessed by the author of the new doctrines relating to land are certainly very slender; and the doctrines themselves indicate a very great degree of ignorance; but the errors of the labouring classes of society are always entitled to great indulgence and consideration. They are the natural and pardonable result of their liability to be deceived by first appearances, and by the arts of designing men, owing to the nature of their situation, and the scanty knowledge which in general falls to their share. And, except in extreme cases, it must always be the wish of those who are better informed, that they should be brought to a sense of the truth, rather by patience and the gradual diffusion of education and knowledge, than by any harsher methods.

After what I have already said on systems of equality in the preceding chapters, I shall not think it necessary to enter into a long and elaborate refutation of these doctrines. I merely mean to give an additional reason for leaving on record an answer to systems of equality, founded on the principle of population, together with a concise restatement of this answer for practical application.

Of the two decisive arguments against such systems, one is, the unsuitableness of a state of equality, both according to experience and theory, to the production of those stimulants to exertion which can alone overcome the natural indolence of man, and prompt him to the proper cultivation of the earth and the fabrication of those conveniences and comforts which are necessary to his happiness.

And the other, the inevitable and necessary poverty and misery in which every system of equality must shortly terminate from the acknowledged tendency of the human race to increase faster than the means of subsistence, unless such increase be prevented by means infinitely more cruel than those which result from the laws of private property, and the moral obligation imposed on every man by the commands of God and nature to support his own children.

The first of these arguments has, I confess, always appeared to my own mind sufficiently conclusive. A state, in which an inequality of conditions offers the natural rewards of good conduct, and inspires widely and generally the hopes of rising and the fears of falling in society, is unquestionably the best calculated to develop the energies and faculties of man, and the best suited to the exercise and improvement of human virtue;[3] and history, in every case of equality that has yet occurred, has uniformly borne witness to the depressing and deadening effects which arise from the want of this stimulus. But still, perhaps, it may be true that neither experience nor theory on this subject is quite so decisive as to preclude all plausible arguments on the other side. It may be said that the instances which history records of systems of equality really carried into execution are so few, and those in societies so little advanced from a state of barbarism, as to afford no fair conclusions relative to periods of great civilization and improvement; that, in other instances, in ancient times, where approaches were made toward a tolerable equality of conditions, examples of considerable energy of character in some lines of exertion are not unfrequent; and that in modern times some societies, particularly of Moravians, are known to have had much of their property in common without occasioning the destruction of their industry. It may be said that, allowing the stimulus of inequality of conditions to have been necessary, in order to raise man from the indolence and apathy of the savage to the activity and intelligence of civilized life, it does not follow that the continuance of the same stimulus should be necessary when this activity and energy of mind has been once gained. It may then be allowable quietly to enjoy the benefit of a regimen which, like many other stimulants, having produced its proper effect at a certain point, must be left off, or exhaustion, disease, and death will follow.

These observations are certainly not of a nature to produce conviction in those who have studied the human character; but they are, to a certain degree, plausible, and do not admit of so definite and decisive an answer as to make the proposal for an experiment in modern times utterly absurd and unreasonable.

The peculiar advantage of the other argument against systems of equality, that which is founded on the principle of population, is, that it is not only still more generally and uniformly confirmed by experience, in every age and in every part of the world, but it is so pre-eminently clear in theory, that no tolerably plausible answer can be given to it; and, consequently, no decent pretence can be brought forward for an experiment. The affair is a matter of the most simple calculation applied to the known properties of land, and the proportion of births to deaths which takes place in almost every country village. There are many parishes in England, where, notwithstanding the actual difficulties attending the support of a family which must necessarily occur in every well-peopled country, and making no allowances for omissions in the registers, the births are to the deaths in the proportion of 2 to 1. This proportion, with the usual rate of mortality in country places, of about 1 in 50, would continue doubling the population in 41 years, if there were no emigrations from the parish. But in any system of equality, either such as that proposed by Mr. Owen, or in parochial partnerships in land, not only would there be no means of emigration to other parishes with any prospect of relief; but the rate of increase at first would, of course, be much greater than in the present state of society. What then, I would ask, is to prevent the division of the produce of the soil to each individual from becoming every year less and less, till the whole society and every individual member of it are pressed down by want and misery?[4]

This is a very simple and intelligible question. And surely no man ought to propose or support a system of equality, who is not able to give a rational answer to it, at least in theory. But, even in theory, I have never yet heard any thing approaching to a rational answer to it.

It is a very superficial observation which has sometimes been made, that it is a contradiction to lay great stress upon the efficacy of moral restraint in an improved and improving state of society, according to the present structure of it, and yet to suppose that it would not act with sufficient force in a system of equality, which almost always presupposes a great diffusion of information, and a great improvement of the human mind. Those who have made this observation do not see that the encouragement and motive to moral restraint are at once destroyed in a system of equality, and community of goods.

Let us suppose that in a system of equality, in spite of the best exertions to procure more food, the population is pressing hard against the limits of subsistence, and all are becoming very poor. It is evidently necessary under these circumstances, in order to prevent the society from starving, that the rate at which the population increases should be retarded. But who are the persons that are to exercise the restraint thus called for, and either to marry late or not at all? It does not seem to be a necessary consequence of a system of equality that all the human passions should be at once extinguished by it; but if not, those who might wish to marry would feel it hard that they should be among the number forced to restrain their inclinations. As all would be equal, and in similar circumstances, there would be no reason whatever why one individual should think himself obliged to practise the duty of restraint more than another. The thing however must be done, with any hope of avoiding universal misery; and in a state of equality, the necessary restraint could only be effected by some general law. But how is this law to be supported, and how are the violations of it to be punished? Is the man who marries early to be pointed at with the finger of scorn? is he to be whipped at the cart's tail? is he to be confined for years in a prison? is he to have his children exposed? Are not all direct punishments for an offence of this kind shocking and unnatural to the last degree? And yet, if it be absolutely necessary, in order to prevent the most overwhelming wretchedness, that there should be some restraint on the tendency to early marriages, when the resources of the country are only sufficient to support a slow rate of increase, can the most fertile imagination conceive one at once so natural, so just, so consonant to the laws of God and to the best laws framed by the most enlightened men, as that each individual should be responsible for the maintenance of his own children; that is, that he should be subjected to the natural inconveniences and difficulties arising from the indulgence of his inclinations, and to no other whatever?

That this natural check to early marriages arising from a view of the difficulty attending the support of a large family operates very widely throughout all classes of society in every civilized state, and may be expected to be still more effective, as the lower classes of people continue to improve in knowledge and prudence, cannot admit of the slightest doubt. But the operation of this natural check depends exclusively upon the existence of the laws of property, and succession; and in a state of equality and community of property could only be replaced by some artificial regulation of a very different stamp, and a much more unnatural character. Of this Mr. Owen is fully sensible, and has in consequence taxed his ingenuity to the utmost to invent some mode, by which the difficulties arising from the progress of population could be got rid of, in the state of society to which he looks forward. His absolute inability to suggest any mode of accomplishing this object that is not unnatural, immoral, or cruel in a high degree, together with the same want of success in every other person, ancient[5] or modern, who has made a similar attempt, seem to show that the argument against systems of equality founded on the principle of population does not admit of a plausible answer, even in theory. The fact of the tendency of population to increase beyond the means of subsistence may be seen in almost every register of a country parish in the kingdom. The unavoidable effect of this tendency to depress the whole body of the people in want and misery, unless the progress of the population be somehow or other retarded, is equally obvious; and the impossibility of checking the rate of increase in a state of equality, without resorting to regulations that are unnatural, immoral, or cruel, forms an argument at once conclusive against every such system.

NOTES

1. Preliminary Dissertation to Supplement to the *Encyclopaedia Britannica*, p. 121.
2. Written in 1817.
3. See this subject very ably treated in a work on the Records of the Creation, and the Moral Attributes of the Creator, by the Rev. John

Bird Sumner, not long since published; a work of very great merit, which I hope soon to see in as extensive circulation as it deserves.

4. In the Spencean system, as published by the secretary of the Society of Spencean Philanthropists, it unfortunately happens, that after the proposed allowances have been made for the expenses of the government, and of the other bodies in the state which are intended to be supported, there would be absolutely no remainder; and the people would not derive a single six pence from their estate, even at first, and on the supposition of the national debt being entirely abolished, without the slightest compensation to the national creditors. The annual rent of the land, houses, mines, and fisheries, is estimated at 150 millions, about three times its real amount; yet, even upon this extravagant estimate, it is calculated that the division would only come to about four pounds a head, not more than is sometimes given to individuals from the poor's rates; a miserable provision! and yet constantly diminishing.
5. The reader has already seen in ch. xiii. bk. i. the detestable means of checking population proposed by some ancient lawgivers in order to support their systems of equality.

4

Of Emigration

Although the resource of emigration seems to be excluded from such perfect societies as the advocates of equality generally contemplate, yet in that imperfect state of improvement, which alone can rationally be expected, it may fairly enter into our consideration. And as it is not probable that human industry should begin to receive its best direction throughout all the nations of the earth at the same time, it may be said that, in the case of a redundant population in the more cultivated parts of the world, the natural and obvious remedy which presents itself is emigration to those parts that are uncultivated. As these parts are of great extent, and very thinly peopled, this resource might appear, on a first view of the subject, an adequate remedy, or at least of a nature calculated to remove the evil to a distant period: but when we advert to experience and the actual state of the uncivilized parts of the globe, instead of any thing like an adequate remedy, it will appear but a slight palliative.

In the accounts which we have received of the peopling of new countries, the dangers, difficulties and hardships, with which the first settlers have had to struggle, appear to be even greater than we can well imagine they could be exposed to in their parent state. The endeavour to avoid that degree of unhappiness which arises from the difficulty of supporting a family might long have left the new world of America unpeopled by Europeans, if those more powerful passions, the thirst of gain, the spirit of adventure, and religious enthusiasm, had not directed and animated the enterprise. These passions enabled the first adventurers to triumph over every obstacle; but in many instances, in a way to make humanity shudder, and to defeat the true end of emigration. Whatever may be the character of the Spanish inhabitants of Mexico and Peru at the present moment, we cannot read the accounts of the first conquests of these countries, without feeling strongly, that the race destroyed was, in moral worth as well as numbers, superior to the race of their destroyers.

The parts of America settled by the English, from being thinly peopled, were better adapted to the establishment of new colonies; yet even here, the most formidable difficulties presented themselves. In the settlement of Virginia, begun by Sir Walter Raleigh and established by Lord Delaware, three attempts completely failed. Nearly half of the first colony was destroyed by the savages, and the rest, consumed and worn down by fatigue and famine, deserted the country, and returned home in despair. The second colony was cut off to a man in a manner unknown; but they were supposed to be destroyed by the Indians. The third experienced the same dismal fate; and the remains of the fourth, after it had been reduced by famine and disease in the course of six months from 500 to 60 persons, were returning in a famishing and desperate condition to England, when they were met in the mouth of the Chesapeak bay by Lord Delaware, with a squadron loaded with provisions, and every thing for their relief and defence.[1]

The first puritan settlers in New England were few in number. They landed in a bad season, and were only supported by their private funds. The winter was premature and terribly cold; the country was covered with wood, and afforded very little for the refreshment of persons sickly with such a voyage, or for the sustenance of an infant people. Nearly half of them perished by the scurvy, by want, and the severity of the climate; yet those who survived were not dispirited by their hardships, but, supported by their energy of character, and the satisfaction of finding themselves out of the reach of the spiritual arm, reduced this savage country by degrees to yield a comfortable subsistence.[2]

Even the plantation of Barbadoes, which increased afterwards with such extraordinary rapidity, had at first to contend with a country utterly desolate, an extreme want of provisions, a difficulty in clearing the ground unusually great from the uncommon size and hardness of the trees, a most disheartening scantiness and poverty in their first crops, and a slow and precarious supply of provisions from England.[3]

The attempt of the French in 1663, to form at once a powerful colony in Guiana, was attended with the most disastrous consequences. Twelve thousand men were landed in the rainy season, and placed under tents and miserable sheds. In this situation, inactive, weary of existence, and in want of all necessaries; exposed to contagious distempers, which are always occasioned by bad provisions, and to all the irregularities which idleness produces among the lower classes of society, almost the whole of them ended their lives in all the horrors of despair. The attempt was completely abortive. Two thousand men, whose robust constitutions had enabled them to resist the inclemency of the climate, and the miseries to which they had been exposed, were brought back to France; and the 26,000,000 of livres, which had been expended in the expedition, were totally lost.[4]

In the late settlements at Port Jackson in New Holland, a melancholy and affecting picture is drawn by Collins of the extreme hardships, with which, for some years, the infant colony had to struggle, before the produce was equal to its support. These distresses were undoubtedly aggravated by the character of the settlers; but those which were caused by the unhealthiness of a newly cleared country, the failure of first crops, and the uncertainty of supplies from so distant a mother-country, were of themselves sufficiently disheartening, to place in a strong point of view the necessity of great resources, as well as unconquerable perseverance, in the colonization of savage countries.

The establishment of colonies in the more thinly peopled regions of Europe and Asia would evidently require still greater resources. From the power and warlike character of the inhabitants of these countries, a considerable military force would be necessary, to prevent their utter and immediate destruction. Even the frontier provinces of the most powerful states are defended with considerable difficulty from such restless neighbours; and the peaceful labours of the cultivator are continually interrupted by their predatory incursions. The late Empress Catherine of Russia found it necessary to protect by regular fortresses the colonies which she had established in the districts near the Wolga; and the calamities which her subjects suffered by the incursions of the Crim Tartars furnished a pretext, and perhaps a just one, for taking possession of the whole of the Crimea, and expelling the greatest part of these turbulent neighbours, and reducing the rest to a more tranquil mode of life.

The difficulties attending a first establishment from soil, climate, and the want of proper conveniences, are of course nearly the same in these regions as in America. Mr. Eton, in his Account of the Turkish Empire, says that 75,000 Christians were obliged by Russia to emigrate from the Crimea, and sent to inhabit the country abandoned by the Nogai Tartars; but the winter coming on before the houses built for them were ready, a great part of them had no other shelter from the cold than what was afforded them by holes dug in the ground, covered with what they could procure, and the greatest part of them perished. Only seven thousand remained a few years afterwards. Another colony from Italy to the banks of the Borysthenes had, he says, no better fate, owing to the bad management of those, who were commissioned to provide for them.

It is needless to add to these instances, as the accounts given of the difficulties experienced in new settlements are all nearly similar. It has been justly observed by a correspondent of Dr. Franklin, that one of the reasons why we have seen so many fruitless attempts to settle colonies at an immense public and private expense by several of the powers of Europe is, that the moral and mechanical habits adapted to the mother-country are frequently not so to the new-settled one, and to external events, many of which are unforeseen; and that it is to be remarked that none of the English colonies became any way considerable, till the necessary manners were born and grew up in the country. Pallas particularly notices the want of proper habits in the colonies established by Russia, as one of the causes why they did not increase so fast as might have been expected.

In addition to this it may be observed, that the first establishment of a new colony generally presents an instance of a country peopled considerably beyond its actual produce; and the natural consequence seems to be, that this population, if not amply supplied by the mother-country, should at the commencement be diminished to the level of the first scanty productions, and not begin permanently to increase, till the remaining numbers had so far cultivated the soil, as to make it yield a quantity of food more than sufficient for their own support; and which consequently they could divide with a family. The frequent failures in the establishment of new colonies tend strongly to show the order of precedence between food and population.

It must be acknowledged then, that the class of people, on whom the distress arising from a too rapidly increasing population would principally fall, could not possibly begin a new colony in a distant country. From the nature of their situation, they must necessarily be deficient in those resources, which alone could ensure success; and unless they could find leaders among the higher classes urged by the spirit of avarice or enterprise, or of religious or political discontent; or were furnished with means and support by government; whatever degree of misery they might suffer in their own country from the scarcity of subsistence, they would be absolutely unable to take possession of any of those uncultivated regions, of which there is such an extent on the earth.

When new colonies have been once securely established, the difficulty of emigration is indeed very considerably diminished; yet, even then, some resources are necessary to provide vessels for the voyage, and support and assistance till the emigrants can settle themselves, and find employment in their adopted country. How far it is incumbent upon a government to furnish these resources may be a question; but whatever be its duty in this particular, perhaps it is too much to expect that, except where any particular colonial advantages are proposed, emigration should be actively assisted.

The necessary resources for transport and maintenance are however frequently furnished by individuals or private companies. For many years before the American war, and for some few since, the facilities of emigration to this new world, and the probable advantages in view, were unusually great; and it must be considered undoubtedly as a very happy circumstance for any country, to have so comfortable an asylum for its redundant population. But I would ask, whether, even during these periods, the distress among the common people in this country was little or nothing; and whether every man felt secure before he ventured on marriage, that, however large his family might be, he should find no difficulty in supporting it without parish assistance. The answer, I fear, could not be in the affirmative.

It will be said that, when an opportunity of advantageous emigration is offered, it is the fault of the people themselves, if, instead of accepting it, they prefer a life of celibacy or extreme poverty in their own country. Is it then a fault for a man to feel an attachment to his native soil, to love the parents that nurtured him, his kindred, his friends, and the companions of his early years? Or is it no evil that he suffers, because he consents to bear it rather than snap these cords which nature has wound in close and intricate folds round the human heart? The great plan of Providence seems to require, indeed, that these ties should sometimes be broken; but the separation does not, on that account, give less pain; and though the general good may be promoted by it, it does not cease to be an individual evil. Besides, doubts and uncertainty must ever attend all distant emigrations, particularly in the apprehensions of the lower classes of people. They cannot feel quite secure, that the representations made to them of the high price of labour or the cheapness of land, are accurately true. They are placing themselves in the power of the persons who are to furnish them with the means of transport and maintenance, who may perhaps have an interest in deceiving them; and the sea which they are to pass, appears to them like the separation of death from all their former connections, and in a manner to preclude the possibility of return in case of failure, as they cannot expect the offer of the same means to bring them back. We cannot be surprised then, that, except where a spirit of enterprise is added to the uneasiness of poverty, the consideration of these circumstances should frequently:

"Make them rather bear the ills they suffer,
Than fly to others which they know not of."

If a tract of rich land as large as this island were suddenly annexed to it, and sold in small lots, or let out in small farms, the case would be very different, and the melioration of the state of the common people would be sudden and striking; though the rich would be continually complaining of the high price of labour, the pride of the lower classes, and the difficulty of getting work done. These, I understand, are not unfrequent complaints among the men of property in America.

Every resource however from emigration, if used effectually, as this would be, must be of short duration. There is scarcely a state in Europe, except perhaps Russia, the inhabitants of which do not often endeavour to better their condition by removing to other countries. As these states therefore have nearly all rather a redundant than deficient population in proportion to their produce, they cannot be supposed to afford any effectual resources of emigration to each other. Let us suppose for a moment, that in this more enlightened part of the globe, the internal economy of each state were so admirably regulated, that no checks existed to population, and that the different governments provided every facility for emigration. Taking the population of Europe, excluding Russia, at a hundred millions, and allowing a greater increase of produce than is probable, or even possible, in the mother-countries, the redundancy of parent stock in a single century would be eleven hundred millions, which, added to the natural increase of the colonies during the same time, would more than double what has been supposed to be the present population of the whole earth.

Can we imagine, that in the uncultivated parts of Asia, Africa, or America, the greatest exertions and the best-directed endeavours could, in so short a period, prepare a quantity of land sufficient for the support of such a population? If any sanguine person should feel a doubt upon the subject, let him only add 25 or 50 years more, and every doubt must be crushed in overwhelming conviction.

It is evident, therefore, that the reason why the resource of emigration has so long continued to be held out as a remedy to redundant population is, because, from the natural unwillingness of people to desert their native country, and the difficulty of clearing and cultivating fresh soil, it never is or can be adequately adopted. If this remedy were indeed really effectual, and had power so far to relieve the disorders of vice and misery in old states, as to place them in the condition of the most prosperous new colonies, we should soon see the phial exhausted; and when the disorders returned with increased virulence, every hope from this quarter would be for ever closed.

It is clear, therefore, that with any view of making room for an unrestricted increase of population, emigration is perfectly inadequate; but as a partial and temporary expedient, and with a view to the more general cultivation of the earth, and the wider extension of civilization, it seems to be both useful and proper; and if it cannot be proved that governments are bound actively to encourage it, it is not only strikingly unjust, but in the highest degree impolitic in them to prevent it. There are no fears so totally ill-grounded as the fears of depopulation from emigration. The *vis inertiae* of the great body of the people, and their attachment to their homes, are qualities so strong and general, that we may rest assured they will not emigrate unless, from political discontents or extreme poverty, they are in such a state as will make it as much for the advantage of their country as of themselves that they should go out of it. The complaints of high wages in consequence of emigrations are of all others the most unreasonable, and ought the least to be attended to. If the wages of labour in any country be such as to enable the lower classes of people to live with tolerable comfort, we may be quite certain that they will not emigrate; and if they be not such, it is cruelty and injustice to detain them.

In all countries the progress of wealth must depend mainly upon the industry, skill, and success of individuals, and upon the state and demands of other countries. Consequently, in all countries great variations may take place at different times in the rate at which wealth increases, and in the demand for labour. But though the progress of population is mainly regulated by the effective demand for labour, it is obvious that the number of people cannot conform itself immediately to the state of this demand. Some time is required to bring more labour into the market when it is wanted; and some time to check the supply when it is flowing in with too great rapidity. If these variations amount to no more than that natural sort of oscillation noticed in an early part of this work, which seems almost always to accompany the progress of population and food, they should be submitted to as a part of the usual course of things. But circumstances may occasionally give them great force, and then, during the period that the supply of labour is increasing faster than the demand, the labouring classes are subject to the most severe distress. If, for instance, from a combination of external and internal causes, a very great stimulus should be given to the population of a country for ten or twelve years together, and it should then comparatively cease, it is clear that labour will continue flowing into the market with almost undiminished rapidity, while the means of employing and paying it have been essentially contracted. It is precisely under these circumstances that emigration is most useful as a temporary relief; and it is in these circumstances that Great Britain finds herself placed at present.[5] Though no emigration should take place, the population will by degrees conform itself to the state of the demand for labour; but the interval must be marked by the most severe distress, the amount of which can scarcely be reduced by any human efforts; because, though it may be mitigated at particular periods, and as it affects particular classes, it will be proportionably extended over a larger space of time, and a greater number of people. The only real relief in such a case is emigration; and the subject at the present moment is well worthy the attention of the government, both as a matter of humanity and policy.

NOTES

1. Burke's America, vol. ii. p. 219. Robertson, b. ix. p. 83, 86.
2. Burke's America, vol. ii. p. 144.
3. *Id.* p. 85.
4. Raynal, *Hist. des Indes*, tom. vii. liv. xiii. p. 43. 10 vols. 8vo. 1795.
5. 1816 and 1817.

5

Of Poor-Laws

To remedy the frequent distresses of the poor, laws to enforce their relief have been instituted; and in the establishment of a general system of this kind England has particularly distinguished herself. But it is to be feared, that, though it may have alleviated a little the intensity of individual misfortune, it has spread the evil over a much larger surface.

It is a subject often started in conversation, and mentioned always as a matter of great surprise, that, notwithstanding the immense sum which is annually collected for the poor in this country, there is still so much distress among them. Some think that the money must be embezzled for private use; others, that the churchwardens and overseers consume the greatest part of it in feasting. All agree that somehow or other it must be very ill managed. In short, the fact, that even before the late scarcities three millions were collected annually for the poor, and yet that their distresses were not removed, is the subject of continual astonishment. But a man who looks a little below the surface of things would be much more astonished, if the fact were otherwise than it is observed to be; or even if a collection universally of eighteen shillings in the pound, instead of four, were materially to alter it.

Suppose, that by a subscription of the rich the eighteen pence or two shillings, which men earn now, were made up five shillings: it might be imagined, perhaps, that they would then be able to live comfortably, and have a piece of meat every day for their dinner. But this would be a very false conclusion. The transfer of three additional shillings a day to each labourer would not increase the quantity of meat in the country. There is not at present enough for all to have a moderate share. What would then be the consequence? the competition among the buyers in the market of meat would rapidly raise the price from eight pence or nine pence to two or three shillings in the pound, and the commodity would not be divided among many more than it is at present. When an article is scarce, and cannot be distributed to all, he that can show the most valid patent, that is, he that offers the most money, becomes the possessor. If we can suppose the competition among the buyers of meat to continue long enough for a greater number of cattle to be reared annually, this could only be done at the expense of the corn, which would be a very disadvantageous exchange; for it is well known, that the country could not then support the same population; and when subsistence is scarce in proportion to the number of people, it is of little consequence, whether the lowest members of the society possess two shillings or five. They must, at all events, be reduced to live upon the hardest fare, and in the smallest quantity.

It might be said, perhaps, that the increased number of purchasers in every article would give a spur to productive industry, and that the whole produce of the island would be increased. But the spur that these fancied riches would give to population would more than counterbalance it; and the increased produce would be to be divided among a more than proportionably increased number of people.

A collection from the rich of eighteen shillings in the pound, even if distributed in the most judicious manner, would have an effect similar to that resulting from the supposition which I have just made; and no possible sacrifices of the rich, particularly in money, could for any time prevent the recurrence of distress among the lower members of society, whoever they were. Great changes might indeed be made. The rich might become poor, and some of the poor rich: but while the present proportion between population and food continues, a part of the society must necessarily find it difficult to support a family, and this difficulty will naturally fall on the least fortunate members.

It may at first appear strange, but I believe it is true, that I cannot by means of money raise the condition of a poor man, and enable him to live much better than he did before, without proportionably depressing others in the same class. If I retrench the quantity of food consumed in my house, and give him what I have cut off, I then benefit him without depressing any but myself and family, who perhaps may be well able to bear it. If I turn up a piece of uncultivated land, and give him the produce, I then benefit both him and all the members of society, because what he before consumed is thrown into the common stock, and probably some of the new produce with it. But if I only give him money, supposing the produce of the country to remain the same, I give him a title to a larger share of that produce than formerly, which share he cannot receive without diminishing the shares of others. It is evident that this effect in individual instances must be so small as to be totally imperceptible; but still it must exist, as many other effects do, which, like some of the insects that people the air, elude our grosser perceptions.

Supposing the quantity of food in any country to remain the same for many years together, it is evident that this food must be divided according to the value of each man's patent, or the sum of money which he can afford to spend in this commodity so universally in request. It is a demonstrative truth, therefore, that the patents of one set of men could not be increased in value without diminishing the value of the patents of some other set of men. If the rich were to subscribe and give five shillings a day to five hundred thousand men, without retrenching their own tables, no doubt can exist, that as these men would live more at their ease, and consume a greater quantity of provisions, there would be less food remaining to divide among the rest; and consequently each man's patent would be diminished in value, or the same member of pieces of silver would purchase a smaller quantity of subsistence, and the price of provisions would universally rise.

These general reasonings have been strikingly confirmed during the late scarcities.[1] The supposition which I have made of a collection from the rich of eighteen shillings in the pound has been newly realized; and the effect has been such as might have been expected. If the same distribution had been made when no scarcity existed, a considerable advance in the price of provisions would have been a necessary consequence; but following as it did a scarcity, its effect must have been doubly powerful. No person, I believe, will venture to doubt, that if we were to give three additional shillings a day to every labouring man in the kingdom, as I before supposed, in order that he might have meat for his dinner, the price of meat would rise in the most rapid and unexampled manner. But surely, in a deficiency of corn, which renders it impossible for every man to have his usual share, if we still continue to furnish each person with the means of purchasing the same quantity as before, the effect must be in every respect similar.

It seems in great measure to have escaped observation, that the price of corn in a scarcity will depend much more upon the obstinacy with which the same degree of consumption is persevered in, than on the degree of the actual deficiency. A deficiency of one half of a crop, if the people could immediately consent to consume only one half of what they did before, would produce little or no effect on the price of corn. A deficiency of one-twelfth, if exactly the same consumption were to continue for ten or eleven months, might raise the price of corn to almost any height. The more is given in parish assistance, the more power is furnished of persevering in the same consumption; and, of course, the higher will the price rise before the necessary diminution of consumption is effected.

It has been asserted by some people, that high prices do not diminish consumption. If this were really true, we should see the price of a bushel of corn at a hundred pounds or more, in every deficiency, which could not be fully and completely remedied by importation. But the fact is, that high prices do ultimately diminish consumption; but, on account of the riches of the country, the unwillingness of the people to resort to substitutes, and the immense sums which are distributed by parishes, this object cannot be attained till the prices become excessive, and force even the middle classes of society, or, at least, those immediately above the poor, to save in the article of bread from the actual inability of purchasing it in the usual quantity. The poor who were assisted by their parishes, had no reason whatever to complain of the high price of grain; because it was the excessiveness of this price, and this alone, which by enforcing such a saving left a greater quantity of corn for the consumption of the lowest classes, which corn the parish allowances enabled them to command. The greatest sufferers in the scarcity were, undoubtedly, the classes immediately above the poor; and these were in the most marked manner depressed by the excessive bounties given to those below them. Almost all poverty is relative; and I much doubt whether these people would have been rendered so poor, if a sum equal to half of these bounties had been taken directly out of their pockets, as they were, by the new distribution of the money of the society which actually took place.[2] This distribution, by giving to the poorer classes a command of food so much greater than that to which their degree of skill and industry entitle them, in the actual circumstances of the country, diminished exactly in the came proportion that command over the necessaries of life, which the classes above them, by their superior skill and industry, would naturally possess; and it may be a question, whether the degree of assistance which the poor received, and which prevented them from resorting to the use of those substitutes which, in every other country on such occasions the great law of necessity teaches, was not more than overbalanced by the severity of the pressure on so large a body of the people from the extreme high prices, and the permanent evil which must result from forcing so many persons on the parish, who before thought themselves almost out of the reach of want.

If we were to double the fortunes of all those who possess above a hundred a year, the effect on the price of grain would be slow and inconsiderable; but if we were to double the price of labour throughout the kingdom, the effect in raising the price of grain would be rapid and great. The general principles on this subject will not admit of dispute; and that, in the particular case which we have been considering, the bounties to the poor were of a magnitude to operate very powerfully in this manner will sufficiently appear, if we recollect that before the late scarcities the sum collected for the poor was estimated at three millions, and that during the year 1801 it was said to be ten millions. An additional seven millions acting at the bottom of the scale,[3] and employed exclusively in the purchase of provisions, joined to a considerable advance in the price of wages in many parts of the kingdom, and increased by a prodigious sum expended in voluntary charity, must have had a most powerful effect in raising the price of the necessaries of life, if any reliance can be placed on the clearest general principles confirmed as much as possible by appearances. A man with a family has received, to my knowledge, fourteen shillings a week from the parish. His common earnings were ten shillings a week, and his weekly revenue, therefore, twenty-four. Before the scarcity he had been in the habit of purchasing a bushel of flour a week with eight shillings perhaps, and, consequently, had two shillings out of his ten, to spare for other necessaries. During the scarcity he was enabled to purchase the same quantity at nearly three times the price. He paid twenty-two shillings for his bushel of flour, and had, as before, two shillings remaining for other wants. Such instances could not possibly have been universal, without raising the price of wheat very much higher than it really was during any part of the dearth. But similar instances were by no means unfrequent; and the system itself of measuring the relief given by the price of grain was general.

If the circulation of the country had consisted entirely of specie, which could not have been immediately increased, it would have been impossible to have given such an additional sum as seven millions to the poor without embarrassing, to a great degree, the operations of commerce. On the commencement, therefore, of this extensive relief, which would necessarily occasion a proportionate expenditure in provisions throughout all the ranks of society, a great demand would be felt for an increased circulating medium. The nature of the medium then principally in use was such, that it could be created immediately on demand. From the accounts of the Bank of England, as laid before Parliament, it appeared, that no very great additional issues of paper took place from this quarter. The three millions and a half added to its former average issues were not probably much above what was sufficient to supply the quantity of specie that had been withdrawn from the circulation. If this supposition be true, (and the small quantity of gold which made its appearance at that time furnishes the strongest reason for believing that nearly as much as this must have been withdrawn), it would follow that the part of the circulation originating in the Bank of

England, though changed in its nature, had not been much increased in its quantity; and with regard to the effect of the circulating medium on the prices of all commodities, it cannot be doubted that it would be precisely the same, whether this medium were made up principally of guineas, or of pound-notes and shillings which would pass current for guineas.

The demand, therefore, for an increased circulating medium was left to be supplied principally by the country banks, and it could not be expected that they should hesitate in taking advantage of so profitable an opportunity. The paper issues of a country bank are, as I conceive, measured by the quantity of its notes which will remain in circulation; and this quantity is again measured, supposing a confidence to be established, by the sum of what is wanted to carry on all the money transactions of the neighbourhood. From the high price of provisions, all these transactions became more expensive. In the single article of the weekly payment of labourers' wages, including the parish allowances, it is evident that a very great addition to the circulating medium of the neighbourhood would be wanted. Had the country banks attempted to issue the same quantity of paper without such a particular demand for it, they would quickly have been admonished of their error by its rapid and pressing return upon them; but at this time it was wanted for immediate and daily use, and was, therefore, eagerly absorbed into the circulation. It may even admit of a question, whether, under similar circumstances, the country banks would not have issued nearly the same quantity of paper, if the Bank of England had not been restricted from payment in specie. Before this event the issues of the country banks in paper were regulated by the quantity which the circulation would take up; and after, as well as before, they were obliged to pay the notes which returned upon them in Bank of England circulation. The difference in the two cases would arise principally from the pernicious custom, adopted since the restriction of the bank, of issuing one and two pound notes, and from the little preference that many people might feel, if they could not get gold, between country bank paper and Bank of England paper.

This very great issue of country bank paper during the years 1800 and 1801 was evidently, therefore, in its origin, rather a consequence than a cause of the high price of provisions; but being once absorbed into the circulation, it must necessarily affect the price of all commodities, and throw very great obstacles in the way of returning cheapness. This is the great mischief of the system. During the scarcity, it is not to be doubted that the increased circulation, by preventing the embarrassments which commerce and speculation must otherwise have felt, enabled the country to continue all the branches of its trade with less interruption, and to import a much greater quantity of grain, than it could have done otherwise; but to overbalance these temporary advantages, a lasting evil might be entailed upon the community, and the prices of a time of scarcity might become permanent, from the difficulty of reabsorbing this increased circulation.

In this respect, however, it is much better that the great issue of paper should have come from the country banks than from the Bank of England. During the restriction of payment in specie, there is no possibility of forcing the bank to retake its notes when too abundant; but with regard to the country banks, as soon as their notes are not wanted in the circulation, they will be returned; and if the Bank of England notes be not increased, the whole circulating medium will thus be diminished.

We may consider ourselves as peculiarly fortunate, that the two years of scarcity were succeeded by two events the best calculated to restore plenty and cheapness—an abundant harvest, and a peace; which together produced a general conviction of plenty, in the minds both of buyers and sellers; and by rendering the first slow to purchase, and the others eager to sell, occasioned a glut in the market, and a consequent rapid fall of price, which has enabled parishes to take off their allowances to the poor, and thus to present a return of high prices, when the alarm among the sellers was over.

If the two years of scarcity had been succeeded merely by years of average crops, I am strongly disposed to believe, that, as no glut would have taken place in the market, the price of grain would have fallen only in a comparatively inconsiderable degree, the parish allowances could not leave been resumed, the increased quantity of paper would still have been wanted, and the price of all commodities might by degrees have been regulated permanently according to the increased circulating medium.

If instead of giving the temporary assistance of parish allowances, which might be withdrawn on the first fall of price, we had raised universally the wages of labour, it is evident, that the obstacles to a diminution of the circulation and to returning cheapness would have been still farther increased; and the high price of labour would have become permanent, without any advantage whatever to the labourer.

There is no one that more ardently desires to see a real advance in the price of labour than myself; but the attempt to effect this object by forcibly raising the nominal price, which was practised to a certain degree, and recommended almost universally during the late scarcities, every thinking man must reprobate as puerile and ineffectual.

The price of labour, when left to find its natural level, is a most important political barometer, expressing the relation between the supply of provisions, and the demand for them; between the quantity to be consumed and the number of consumers; and taken on the average, independently of accidental circumstances, it further expresses clearly the wants of the society respecting population; that is, whatever may be the number of children to a marriage necessary to maintain exactly the present population, the price of labour will be just sufficient to support this number, or be above it, or below it, according to the state of the real funds for the maintenance of labour, whether stationary, progressive or retrograde. Instead, however, of considering it in this light, we consider it as something which we may raise or depress at pleasure, something which depends principally upon his Majesty's justices of the peace. When an advance in the price of provisions already expresses that the demand is too great for the supply, in order to put the labourer in the same condition as before, we raise the price of labour, that is, we increase the demand, and are then much surprised that the price of provisions continues rising. In this we act much in the same manner as if, when the quicksilver in the common weather-glass stood at stormy, we were to raise it by some mechanical pressure to settled fair, and then be greatly astonished that it continued raining.

Dr. Smith has clearly shown, that the natural tendency of a year of scarcity is either to throw a number of labourers out of employment, or to oblige them to work for less than they did before, from the inability of masters to employ the same number at the same price. The raising of the price of wages tends necessarily to throw more out of employment, and completely to prevent the good effects, which, he says, sometimes arise from a year of moderate scarcity, that of making the lower classes of people do more work, and become more careful and industrious. The number of servants out of place, and of manufacturers wanting employment during the late scarcities, were melancholy proofs of the truth of these reasonings. If a general rise in the wages of labour had taken place proportioned to the price of provisions, none but farmers and a few gentlemen could have afforded to employ the same number of workmen as before. Additional crowds of servants and manufacturers would have been turned off; and those who were thus thrown out of employment would of course have no other refuge than the parish. In the natural order of things a scarcity must tend to lower, instead of to raise, the price of labour.

After the publication and general circulation of such a work as Adam Smith's, I confess it appears to me strange, that so many men, who would yet aspire to be thought political economists, should still think that it is in the power of the justices of the peace or even of the omnipotence of parliament to alter by a fiat the whole circumstances of the country; and when the demand for provisions is greater than the supply, by publishing a particular edict, to make the supply at once equal to or greater than the demand. Many men who would shrink at the proposal of a maximum, would propose themselves, that the price of labour should be proportioned to the price of provisions, and do not seem to be aware that the two proposals are very nearly of the same nature, and that both tend directly to famine. It matters not whether we enable the labourer to purchase the same quantity of provisions which he did before, by fixing their price, or by raising in proportion the price of labour. The only advantage on the side of raising the price of labour is, that the rise in the price of provisions, which necessarily follows it, encourages importation: but putting importation out of the question, which might possibly be prevented by war, or other circumstances, a universal rise of wages in proportion to the price of provisions, aided by adequate parish allowances to those who were thrown out of work, would, by preventing any kind of saving, in the same manner as a maximum, cause the whole crop to be consumed in nine months, which ought to have lasted twelve, and thus produce a famine. At the same time we must not forget, that both humanity and true policy imperiously require, that we should give every assistance to the poor on these occasions, that the nature of the case will admit. If provisions were to continue at the price of scarcity, the wages of labour must necessarily rise, or sickness and famine would quickly diminish the number of labourers; and the supply of labour being unequal to the demand, its price would soon rise in a still greater proportion than the price of provisions. But even one or two years of scarcity, if the poor were left entirely to shift for themselves, might produce some effect of this kind, and consequently it is our interest, as well as our duty, to give them temporary aid in such seasons of distress. It is on such occasions that every cheap substitute for bread, and every mode of economizing food should be resorted to. Nor should we be too ready to complain of that high price of corn, which by encouraging importation increases the supply.

As the inefficacy of poor-laws, and of attempts forcibly to raise the price of labour, is most conspicuous in a scarcity, I have thought myself justified in considering them under this view; and as these causes of increased price received great additional force during the late scarcity from the increase of the circulating medium, I trust, that the few observations which I have made on this subject will be considered as an allowable digression.

NOTES

1. The scarcities referred to in this chapter were those of 1800 and 1801.
2. Supposing the lower classes to earn on an average ten shillings a week, and the classes just above them twenty, it is not to be doubted,

that in a scarcity these latter would be more straitened in their power of commanding the necessaries of life, by a donation of ten shillings a week to those below them, than by the subtraction of five shillings a week from their own earnings. In the one case, they would be all reduced to a level; the price of provisions would rise in an extraordinary manner from the greatness of the competition; and all would be straitened for subsistence. In the other case, the losses above the poor would still maintain a considerable part of their relative superiority; the price of provisions would by no means rise in the same degree; and their remaining fifteen shillings would purchase much more than their twenty shillings in the former case.

3. See a small pamphlet published in November, 1800, entitled, *An Investigation of the Cause of the Present high Price of Provisions.* This pamphlet was mistaken by some for an inquiry into the cause of the scarcity, and as such it would naturally appear to be incomplete, adverting, as it does, principally to a single cause. But the sole object of the pamphlet was to give the principal reason for the extreme high price of provisions, in proportion to the degree of the scarcity, admitting the deficiency of one-fourth, as stated in the Duke of Portland's letter; which, I am much inclined to think, was very near the truth.

6

Of Poor-Laws (*continued*)

Independently of any considerations respecting a year of deficient crops, it is evident, that an increase of population, without a proportional increase of food, must lower the value of each man's earnings. The food must necessarily be distributed in smaller quantities, and consequently a day's labour will purchase a smaller quantity of provisions. An increase in the price of provisions will arise either from an increase of population faster than the means of subsistence, or from a different distribution of the money of the society. The food of a country which has been long peopled, if it be increasing, increases slowly and regularly, and cannot be made to answer any sudden demands: but variations in the distribution of the money of the society are not unfrequently occurring, and are undoubtedly among the causes which occasion the continual variations in the prices of provisions.

The poor-laws of England tend to depress the general condition of the poor in these two ways. Their first obvious tendency is to increase population without increasing the food for its support. A poor man may marry with little or no prospect of being able to support a family without parish assistance. They may be said, therefore, to create the poor which they maintain: and as the provisions of the country must, in consequence of the increased population, be distributed to every man in smaller proportions, it is evident that the labour of those who are not supported by parish assistance, will purchase a smaller quantity of provisions than before, and consequently more of them must be driven to apply for assistance.

Secondly, the quantity of provisions consumed in workhouses, upon a part of the society that cannot in general be considered as the most valuable part, diminishes the shares that would otherwise belong to more industrious and more worthy members, and thus, in the same manner, forces more to become dependent. If the poor in the workhouses were to live better than they do now, this new distribution of the money of the society would tend more conspicuously to depress the condition of those out of the workhouses by occasioning an advance in the price of provisions.

Fortunately for England, a spirit of independence, still remains among the peasantry. The poor-laws are strongly calculated to eradicate this spirit. They have succeeded in part; but had they succeeded as completely as might have been expected, their pernicious tendency would not have been so long concealed.

Hard as it may appear in individual instances, dependent poverty ought to be held disgraceful. Such a stimulus seems to be absolutely necessary to promote the happiness of the great mass of mankind; and every general attempt to weaken this stimulus, however benevolent its intention, will always defeat its own purpose. If men be induced to marry from the mere prospect of parish provision, they are not only unjustly tempted to bring unhappiness and dependence upon themselves and children, but they are tempted, without knowing it, to injure all in the same class with themselves.

The poor-laws of England appear to have contributed to raise the price of provisions, and to lower the real price of labour. They have therefore contributed to impoverish that class of people whose only possession is their labour. It is also difficult to suppose that they have not powerfully contributed to generate that carelessness and want of frugality observable among the poor, so contrary to the disposition generally to be remarked among petty tradesmen and small farmers. The labouring poor, to use a vulgar expression, seem always to live from hand to mouth. Their present wants employ their whole attention; and they seldom think of the future. Even when they have an opportunity of saving, they seldom exercise it; but all that they earn beyond their present necessities goes, generally speaking, to the ale-house. The poor-laws may therefore be said to diminish both the power and the will to save, among the common people;

and thus to weaken one of the strongest incentives to sobriety and industry, and consequently to happiness.

It is a general complaint among master manufacturers, that high wages ruin all their workmen; but it is difficult to conceive that these men would not save a part of their high wages for the future support of their families, instead of spending it in drunkenness and dissipation, if they did not rely on parish assistance for support in case of accidents. And that the poor employed in manufactures consider this assistance as a reason why they may spend all the wages which they earn, and enjoy themselves while they can, appears to be evident, from the number of families that, upon the failure of any great manufactory, immediately fall upon the parish; when perhaps the wages earned in this manufactory while it flourished, were sufficiently above the price of common country labour, to have allowed them to save enough for their support till they could find some other channel for their industry.

A man who might not be deterred from going to the ale-house from the consideration that on his death or sickness he should leave his wife and family upon the parish, might yet hesitate in thus dissipating his earnings, if he were assured, that in either of these cases his family must starve, or be left to the support of casual bounty.

The mass of happiness among the common people cannot but be diminished, when one of the strongest checks to idleness and dissipation is thus removed; and positive institutions, which render dependent poverty so general, weaken that disgrace which, for the best and most humane reasons, ought to be attached to it.

The poor-laws of England were undoubtedly instituted for the most benevolent purpose; but it is evident they have failed in attaining it. They certainly mitigate some cases of severe distress, which might otherwise occur; though the state of the poor who are supported by parishes, considered in all its circumstances, is very miserable. But one of the principal objections to the system is, that for the assistance which some of the poor receive, in itself almost a doubtful blessing, the whole class of the common people of England is subjected to a set of grating, inconvenient, and tyrannical laws, totally inconsistent with the genuine spirit of the constitution. The whole business of settlements, even in its present amended state, is contradictory to all ideas of freedom. The parish persecution of men whose families are likely to become chargeable, and of poor women who are near lying-in, is a most disgraceful and disgusting tyranny. And the obstructions continually occasioned in the market of labour by these laws, have a constant tendency to add to the difficulties of those who are struggling to support themselves without assistance.

These evils attendant on the poor-laws seem to be irremediable. If assistance be to be distributed to a certain class of people, a power must be lodged somewhere of discriminating the proper objects, and of managing the concerns of the institutions that are necessary; but any great interference with the affairs of other people is a species of tyranny, and in the common course of things, the exercise of this power may be expected to become grating to those who are driven to ask for support. The tyranny of churchwardens and overseers is a common complaint among the poor; but the fault does not lie so much in these persons, who probably before they were in power were not worse than other people, but in the nature of all such institutions.

I feel persuaded that if the poor-laws had never existed in this country, though there might have been a few more instances of very severe distress, the aggregate mass of happiness among the common people would have been much greater than it is at present.

The radical defect of all systems of the kind is that of tending to depress the condition of those that are not relieved by parishes, and to create more poor. If, indeed, we examine some of our statutes strictly with reference to the principle of population, we shall find that they attempt an absolute impossibility; and we cannot be surprised, therefore, that they should constantly fail in the attainment of their object.

The famous 43rd of Elizabeth, which has been so often referred to and admired, enacts, that the overseers of the poor "shall take order from time to time, by and with the consent of two or more justices, for setting to work the children of all such, whose parents shall not by the said persons be thought able to keep and maintain their children: and also such persons, married or unmarried, as, having no means to maintain them, use no ordinary and daily trade of life to get their living by; and also to raise, weekly or otherwise, by taxation of every inhabitant, and every occupier of lands in the said parish, (in such competent sums as they shall think fit), a convenient stock of flax, hemp, wool, thread, iron, and other necessary ware and stuff, to set the poor to work."

What is this but saying, that the funds for the maintenance of labour in this country may be increased at, will, and without limit, by a fiat of government, or an assessment of the overseers? Strictly speaking, this clause is as arrogant and as absurd, as if it had enacted that two ears of wheat should in future grow where one only had grown before. Canute, when he commanded the waves not to wet his princely foot, did not in reality assume a greater power over the laws of nature. No directions are given to the overseers how to increase the funds for the maintenance of labour; the necessity of industry, economy and enlightened exertion, in the management of agricultural and commercial capital, is not insisted on for this purpose; but it is expected that a miraculous increase of these funds should immediately follow an edict of the government used at the discretion of some ignorant parish officers.

If this clause were really and *bonâ fide* put in execution, and the shame attending the receiving of parish assistance worn off, every labouring man might marry as early as he pleased, under the certain prospect of having all his children properly provided for; and as, according to the supposition, there would be no check to population from the consequences of poverty after marriage, the increase of people would be rapid beyond example in old states. After what has been said in the former parts of this work, it is submitted to the reader, whether the utmost exertions of the most enlightened government could, in this case, make the food keep pace with the population; much less a mere arbitrary edict, the tendency of which is certainly rather to diminish than to increase the funds for the maintenance of productive labour.

In the actual circumstances of every country, the prolific power of nature seems to be always ready to exert nearly its full force; but within the limit of possibility, there is nothing perhaps more improbable, or more out of the reach of any government to effect, than the direction of the industry of its subjects in such a manner, as to produce the greatest quantity of human sustenance that the earth could bear. It evidently could not be done without the most complete violation of the law of property, from which every thing that is valuable to man has hitherto arisen. Such is the disposition to marry, particularly in very young people, that, if the difficulties of providing for a family were entirely removed, very few would remain single at twenty-two. But what statesman or rational government could propose that all animal food should be prohibited, that no horses should be used for business or pleasure, that all the people should live upon potatoes, and that the whole industry of the nation should be exerted in the production of them, except what was required for the mere necessaries of clothing and houses? Could such a revolution be effected, would it be desirable? particularly as in a few years, notwithstanding all these exertions, want, with less resource than ever, would inevitably recur.

After a country has once ceased to be in the peculiar situation of a new colony, we shall always find that in the actual state of its cultivation, or in that state which may rationally be expected from the most enlightened government, the increase of its food can never allow for any length of time an unrestricted increase of population; and therefore the due execution of the clause in the 43rd of Elizabeth, as a permanent law, is a physical impossibility.

It will be said, perhaps, that the fact contradicts the theory; and that the clause in question has remained in force, and has been executed, during the last two hundred years. In answer to this, I should say without hesitation, that it has not really been executed; and that it is merely owing to its incomplete execution, that it remains on our statute-book at present.

The scanty relief granted to persons in distress, the capricious and insulting manner in which it is sometimes distributed by the overseers, and the natural and becoming pride, not yet quite extinct among the peasantry of England, have deterred the more thinking and virtuous part of them from venturing on marriage, without some better prospect of maintaining their families than mere parish assistance. The desire of bettering our condition, and the fear of making it worse, like the *vis medicatrix naturae* in physics, is the *vis medicatrix reipublicae* in politics, and is continually counteracting the disorders arising from narrow human institutions. In spite of the prejudices in favour of population, and the direct encouragements to marriage from the poor-laws, it operates as a preventive check to increase; and happy for this country is it, that it does so. But besides that spirit of independence and prudence, which checks the frequency of marriage, notwithstanding the encouragements of the poor-laws, these laws themselves occasion a check of no inconsiderable magnitude, and thus counteract with one hand what they encourage with the other. As each parish is obliged to maintain its own poor, it is naturally fearful of increasing their number; and every landholder is in consequence more inclined to pull down than to build cottages, except when the demand for labourers is really urgent. This deficiency of cottages operates necessarily as a strong check to marriage; and this check is probably the principal reason why we have been able to continue the system of the poor-laws so long.

Those who are not prevented for a time from marrying by these causes, are either relieved very scantily at their own homes, where they suffer all the consequences arising from squalid poverty; or they are crowded together in close and unwholesome workhouses, where a great mortality almost universally takes place, particularly among the young children. The dreadful account given by Jonas Hanway of the treatment of parish children in London is well known; and it appears from Mr. Howlett and other writers, that in some parts of the country their situation is not very much better. A great part of the redundant population occasioned by the poor-laws is thus taken off by the operation of the laws themselves, or at least by their ill execution. The remaining part which survives, by causing the funds for the maintenance of labour to be divided among a greater number than can be properly maintained by them, and by turning a considerable share from the support of the diligent and careful workman to the support of the idle and negligent, depresses the condition of all those who are out of the workhouses, forces more into them every year, and has ultimately produced the enormous evil, which we all so justly deplore; that of the great and unnatural proportion of the people which is now become dependent upon charity.

If this be a just representation of the manner in which the clause in question has been executed, and of the effects which it has produced, it must be allowed that we have practised an unpardonable deceit upon the poor, and have promised what we have been very far from performing.

The attempts to employ the poor on any great scale in manufactures have almost invariably failed, and the stock and materials have been wasted. In those few parishes which, by better management or larger foods, have been enabled to persevere in this system, the effect of these new manufactures in the market must have been to throw out of employment many independent workmen, who were before engaged in fabrications of a similar nature. This effect has been placed in a strong point of view by Daniel de Foe, in an address to parliament, entitled, Giving Alms no Charity. Speaking of the employment of parish children in manufactures, he says, "For every skein of worsted these poor children spin, there must be a skein the less spun by some poor family that spun it before; and for every piece of baize so made in London, there must be a piece the less made at Colchester, or somewhere else."[1] Sir F. M. Eden, on the same subject, observes, that "whether mops and brooms are made by parish children or by private workmen, no more can be sold than the public is in want of."[2]

It will be said, perhaps, that the same reasoning might be applied to any new capital brought into competition in a particular trade or manufacture, which can rarely be done without injuring, in some degree, those that were engaged in it before. But there is a material difference in the two cases. In this the competition is perfectly fair, and what every man on entering into business must lay his account to. He may rest secure that he will not be supplanted, unless his competitor possess superior skill and industry. In the other case the competition is supported by a great bounty; by which means, notwithstanding very inferior skill and industry on the part of his competitors, the independent workman may be undersold, and unjustly excluded from the market. He himself perhaps is made to contribute to this competition against his own earnings; and the funds for the maintenance of labour are thus turned from the support of a trade which yields a proper profit, to one which cannot maintain itself without a bounty. It should be observed in general, that when a fund for the maintenance of labour is raised by assessment, the greatest part of it is not a new capital brought into trade, but an old one, which before was much more profitably employed, turned into a new channel. The farmer pays to the poor's rates, for the encouragement of a bad and unprofitable manufacture, what he would have employed on his land with infinitely more advantage to his country. In the one case, the foods for the maintenance of labour are daily diminished; in the other, daily increased. And this obvious tendency of assessments for the employment of the poor, to decrease the real funds for the maintenance of labour in any country, aggravates the absurdity of supposing that it is in the power of a government to find employment for all its subjects, however fast they may increase.

It is not intended that these reasonings should be applied against every mode of employing the poor on a limited scale, and with such restrictions as may not encourage at the same time their increase. I would never wish to push general principles too far; though I think that they ought always to be kept in view. In particular cases the individual good to be obtained may be so great, and the general evil so slight, that the former may clearly overbalance the latter.

My intention is merely to show that the poor-laws as a general system are founded on a gross error: and that the common declamation on the subject of the poor, which we see so often in print, and hear continually in conversation, namely, that the market price of labour ought always to be sufficient decently to support a family, and that employment ought to be found for all those who are willing to work, is in effect to say, that the funds for the maintenance of labour in this country are not only infinite, but not subject to variation; and that, whether the resources of a country be rapidly progressive, slowly progressive, stationary or declining, the power of giving full employment and good wages to the labouring classes must always remain exactly the same,—a conclusion which contradicts the plainest and most obvious principles of supply and demand, and involves the absurd position that a definite quantity of territory can maintain an infinite population.

NOTES

1. See Extracts from Daniel de Foe, in Sir F. M. Eden's valuable Work on the poor, vol. i. p. 261.
2. Sir F. M. Eden, speaking of the supposed right of the poor to be supplied with employment while able to work, and with a maintenance when incapacitated from labour, very justly remarks, "It may however be doubted, whether any right, the gratification of which seems to be impracticable, can be said to exist," vol. i. p. 447. No man has collected so many materials for forming a judgment on the effects of the poor-laws as Sir F. M. Eden, and the result he thus expresses: "Upon the whole therefore there seems to be just grounds for concluding, that the sum of good to be expected from a compulsory maintenance of the poor will be far outbalanced by the sum of evil which it will inevitably create," vol. i. p. 467—I am happy to have the sanction of so practical an inquirer to my opinion of the poor-laws.

7

Of Poor-Laws (*continued*)

The remarks made in the last chapter on the nature and effects of the poor-laws have been in the most striking manner confirmed by the experience of the years 1815, 1816 and 1817.[1] During these years, two points of the very highest importance have been established, so as no longer to admit of a doubt in the mind of any rational man.

The first is, that the country does not in point of fact fulfil the promise which it makes to the poor in the poor-laws, to maintain and find in employment, by means of parish assessments, those who are unable to support themselves or their families, either from want of work or any other cause.

And secondly, that with a very great increase of legal parish assessments, aided by the most liberal and praiseworthy contributions of voluntary charity, the country has been wholly unable to find adequate employment for the numerous labourers and artificers who were able as well as willing to work.

It can no longer surely be contended that the poor-laws really perform what they promise, when it is known that many almost starving families have been found in London and other great towns, who are deterred from going on the parish by the crowded, unhealthy and horrible state of the workhouses into which they would be received, if indeed they could be received at all; when it is known that many parishes have been absolutely unable to raise the necessary assessments, the increase of which, according to the existing laws, have tended only to bring more and more persons upon the parish, and to make what was collected less and less effectual; and when it is known that there has been an almost universal cry from one end of the kingdom to the other for voluntary charity to come in aid of the parochial assessments.

These strong indications of the inefficiency of the poor-laws may be considered not only as incontrovertible proofs of the fact that they do not perform what they promise, but as affording the strongest presumption that they cannot do it. The best of all reasons for the breach of a promise, is, the absolute impossibility of executing it; indeed it is the only plea that can ever be considered as valid. But though it may be fairly pardonable not to execute an impossibility, it is unpardonable knowingly to promise one. And if it be still thought advisable to act upon these statutes as far as is practicable, it would surely be wise so to alter the terms in which they are expressed, and the general interpretation given to them, as not to convey to the poor a false notion of what really is within the range of practicability.

It has appeared further as a matter of fact, that very large voluntary contributions, combined with greatly increased parochial assessments, and aided by the most able and incessant exertions of individuals, have failed to give the necessary employment to those who have been thrown out of work by the sudden falling off of demand which has occurred during the last two or three years.

It might perhaps have been foreseen that, as the great movements of society, the great causes which render a nation progressive, stationary or declining, for longer or shorter periods, cannot be supposed to depend much upon parochial assessments or the contributions of charity, it could not be expected that any efforts of this kind should have power to create, in a stationary or declining state of things, that effective demand for labour which only belongs to a progressive state. But to those who did not see this truth before, the melancholy experience of the last two years[2] must have brought it home with an overpowering conviction.

It does not however by any means follow that the exertions which have been made to relieve the present distresses have been ill directed. On the contrary, they have not only been prompted by the most praiseworthy motives; they have not only fulfilled the great moral duty of assisting our fellow-creatures in distress; but they have in point of fact done great good, or at least prevented great evil. Their partial failure does not necessarily indicate either a want of energy or a want of skill in those who have taken the lead in these efforts, but merely that a part only of what has been attempted is practicable.

It is practicable to mitigate the violence and relieve the severe pressure of the present distress, so as to carry the sufferers through to better times, though even this can only be done at the expense of some sacrifices, not merely of the rich, but of other classes of the poor. But it is impracticable by any exertions, either individual or national, to restore at once that brisk demand for commodities and labour which has been lost by events, that, however they may have originated, are now beyond the power of control.

The whole subject is surrounded on all sides by the most formidable difficulties, and in no state of things is it so necessary to recollect the saying of Daniel de Foe quoted in the last chapter. The manufacturers all over the country, and the Spitalfields weavers in particular, are in a state of the deepest distress, occasioned immediately and directly by the want of demand for the produce of their industry, and the consequent necessity felt by the masters of turning off many of their workmen, in order to proportion the supply to the contracted demand. It is proposed, however, by some well-meaning people, to raise by subscription a fund for the express purpose of setting to work again those who have been turned off by their masters, the effect of which can only be to continue glutting a market, already much too fully supplied. This is most naturally and justly objected to by the masters, as it prevents them from withdrawing the supply, and taking the only course which can prevent the total destruction of their capitals, and the necessity of turning off all their men instead of a part.

On the other hand, some classes of merchants and manufacturers clamour very loudly for the prohibition of all foreign commodities which may enter into competition with domestic products, and interfere, as they intimate, with the employment of British industry. But this is most naturally and most justly deprecated by other classes of British subjects, who are employed to a very great extent in preparing and manufacturing those commodities which are to purchase our imports from foreign countries. And it must be allowed to be perfectly true that a court-ball, at which only British stuffs are admitted, may be the means of throwing out of employment in one quarter of the country just as many persons as it furnishes with employment in another.

Still, it would be desirable if possible to employ those that were out of work, if it were merely to avoid the bad moral effects of idleness, and of the evil habits which might be generated by depending for a considerable time on mere alms. But the difficulties just stated will show, that we ought to proceed in this part of the attempt with great caution, and that the kinds of employment which ought to be chosen are those, the results of which will not interfere with existing capitals. Such are public works of all descriptions, the making and repairing of roads, bridges, railways, canals, etc.; and now perhaps, since the great loss of agricultural capital, almost every sort of labour upon the land, which could be carried on by public subscription.

Yet even in this way of employing labour, the benefit to some must bring with it disadvantages to others. That portion of each person's revenue which might go in subscriptions of this kind, must of course be lost to the various sorts of labour which its expenditure in the usual channels would have supported; and the want of demand thus occasioned in these channels must cause the pressure of distress to be felt in quarters which might otherwise have escaped it. But this is an effect which, in such cases, it is impossible to avoid; and, as a temporary measure, it is not only charitable but just, to spread the evil over a larger surface, in order that its violence on particular parts may be so mitigated as to be made bearable by all.

The great object to be kept in view, is to support the people through their present distresses, in the hope (and I trust a just one) of better times. The difficulty is without doubt considerably aggravated by the prodigious stimulus which has been given to the population of the country of late years, the effects of which cannot suddenly subside. But it will be seen probably, when the next returns of the population are made, that the marriages and births have diminished, and the deaths increased in a still greater degree than in 1800 and 1801; and the continuance of this effect to a certain degree for a few years will retard the progress of the population, and combined with the increasing wants of Europe and America from their increasing riches, and the adaptation of the supply of commodities at home to the new distribution of wealth occasioned by the alteration of the circulating medium, will again give life and energy to all our mercantile and agricultural transactions, and restore the labouring classes to full employment and good wages.[3]

On the subject of the distresses of the poor, and particularly the increase of pauperism of late years, the most erroneous opinions have been circulated. During the progress of the war, the increase in the proportion of persons requiring parish assistance was attributed chiefly to the high price of the necessaries of life. We have seen these necessaries of life experience a great and sudden fall, and yet at the same time a still larger proportion of the population requiring parish assistance.

It is now said that taxation is the sole cause of their distresses, and of the extraordinary stagnation in the demand for labour; yet I feel the firmest conviction, that if the whole of the taxes were removed tomorrow, this stagnation, instead of being at an end, would be considerably aggravated. Such an event would cause another great and general rise in the value of the circulating medium, and bring with it that discouragement to industry with which such a convulsion in society must ever be attended. If, as has been represented, the labouring classes now pay more than half of what they receive in taxes, he must know very little indeed of the principles on which the wages of labour are regulated, who can for a moment suppose that, when the commodities on which they are expended have fallen one half by the removal of taxes, these wages themselves would still continue of the same nominal value. Were they to remain but for a short time the same, while all commodities had fallen, and the circulating medium had been reduced in proportion, it would be quickly seen that multitudes of them would be at once thrown out of employment.

The effects of taxation are no doubt in many cases pernicious in a very high degree; but it may be laid down as a rule which has few exceptions, that the relief obtained by taking off a tax, is in no respect equal to the injury inflicted in laying it on; and generally it may be said that the specific evil of taxation consists in the check which it gives to production, rather than the diminution which it occasions in demand. With regard to all commodities indeed of home production and home demand, it is quite certain that the conversion of capital into revenue, which is the effect of loans, must necessarily increase the proportion of demand to the supply; and the conversion of the revenue of individuals into the revenue of the government, which is the effect of taxes properly imposed, however hard upon the individuals so taxed, can have no tendency to diminish the general amount of demand. It will of course diminish the demands of the persons taxed by diminishing their powers of purchasing; but to the exact amount that the powers of these persons are diminished, will the powers of the government and of those employed by it be increased. If an estate of five thousand a year has a mortgage upon it of two thousand, two families, both in very good circumstances, may be living upon the rents of it, and both have considerable demands for houses, furniture, carriages, broad-cloth, silks, cottons, etc. The man who owns the estate is certainly much worse off than if the mortgage-deed was burnt, but the manufacturers and labourers who supply the silks, broad-cloth, cottons, etc., are so far from being likely to be benefited by such burning, that it would be a considerable time before the new wants and tastes of the enriched owner had restored the former demand; and if he were to take a fancy to spend his additional income in horses, hounds and menial servants, which is probable, not only would the manufacturers and labourers who had before supplied their silks, cloths and cottons, be thrown out of employment, but the substituted demand would be very much less favourable to the increase of the capital and general resources of the country.

The foregoing illustration represents more nearly than may generally be imagined the effects of a national debt on the labouring classes of society, and the very great mistake of supposing that, because the demands of a considerable portion of the community would be increased by the extinction of the debt, these increased demands would not be balanced, and often more than balanced, by the loss of the demand from the fund-holders and government.

It is by no means intended by these observations to intimate that a national debt may not be so heavy as to be extremely prejudicial to a state. The division and distribution of property, which is so beneficial when carried only to a certain extent, is fatal to production when pushed to extremity. The division of an estate of five thousand a year will generally tend to increase demand, stimulate production, and improve the structure of society; but the division of an estate of eighty pounds a year will generally be attended with effects directly the reverse.

But, besides the probability that the division of property occasioned by a national debt may in many cases be pushed too far, the process of the division is effected by means which sometimes greatly embarrass production. This embarrassment must necessarily take place to a certain extent in almost every species of taxation; but under favourable circumstances it is overcome by the stimulus given to demand compared with supply. During the late war, from the prodigious increase of produce and population, it may fairly be presumed that the power of production was not essentially impeded, notwithstanding the enormous amount of taxation; but in the state of things which has occurred since the peace, and under a most extraordinary fall of the exchangeable value of the raw produce of the land, and a great consequent diminution of the circulating medium, the very sudden increase of the weight and pressure of taxation must greatly aggravate the other causes which discourage production. This effect has been felt to a considerable extent on the land; but the distress in this quarter is already much mitigated;[4] and among the mercantile and manufacturing classes, where the greatest numbers are without employment, the evil obviously arises, not so much from the want of capital and the means of production, as the want of a market for the commodity when produced—a want, for which the removal of taxes, however proper, and indeed absolutely necessary as a permanent measure, is certainly not the immediate and specific remedy.

The principal causes of the increase of pauperism, independently of the present crisis, are, first, the general increase of the manufacturing system and the unavoidable variations of manufacturing labour; and secondly, and more particularly, the practice which has been adopted in some counties, and is now spreading pretty generally all over the kingdom, of paying a considerable portion of what ought to be the wages of labour out of the parish rates. During the war, when the demand for labour was great and increasing, it is quite certain that nothing but a practice of this kind could for any time have prevented the wages of labour from rising fully in proportion to the necessaries of life, in whatever degree these necessaries might have been raised by taxation. It was seen, consequently, that in those parts of Great Britain where this practice prevailed the least; the wages of labour rose the most. This was the case in Scotland, and some parts of the North of England, where the improvement in the condition of the labouring classes, and their increased command over the necessaries and conveniences of life, were particularly remarkable. And if, in some other parts of the country, where the practice did not greatly prevail, and especially in the towns, wages did not rise in the same degree, it was owing to the influx and competition of the cheaply raised population of the surrounding counties.

It is a just remark of Adam Smith, that the attempts of the legislature to raise the pay of curates had always been ineffectual, on account of the cheap and abundant supply of them, occasioned by the bounties given to young persons educated for the church at the universities. And it is equally true that no human efforts can keep up the price of day-labour so as to enable a man to support on his earnings a family of a moderate size, so long as those who have more than two children are considered as having a valid claim to parish assistance.

If this system were to become universal, and I own it appears to me that the poor-laws naturally lead to it, there is no reason whatever why parish assistance should not by degrees begin earlier and earlier; and I do not hesitate to assert that, if the government and constitution of the country were in all other respects as perfect as the wildest visionary thinks he could make them; if parliaments were annual, suffrage universal, wars, taxes and pensions unknown, and the civil list fifteen hundred a year, the great body of the community might still be a collection of paupers.

I have been accused of proposing a law to prohibit the poor from marrying. This is not true. So far from proposing such a law, I have distinctly said that, if any person chooses to marry without having a prospect of being able to maintain a family, he ought to have the most perfect liberty so to do; and whenever any prohibitory propositions have been suggested to me as advisable by persons who have drawn wrong inferences from what I have said, I have steadily and uniformly reprobated them. I am indeed most decidedly of opinion that any positive law to limit the age of marriage would be both unjust and immoral; and my greatest objection to a system of equality and the system of the poor-laws (two systems which, however different in their outset, are of a nature calculated to produce the same results) is, that the society in which they are effectively carried into execution, will ultimately be reduced to the miserable alternative of choosing between universal want and the enactment of direct laws against marriage.

What I have really proposed is a very different measure. It is the gradual and very gradual abolition of the poor-laws.[5] And the reason why I have ventured to suggest a proposition of this kind for consideration is my firm conviction, that they have lowered very decidedly the wages of the labouring classes, and made their general condition essentially worse than it would have been if these laws had never existed. Their operation is every where depressing; but it falls peculiarly hard upon the labouring classes in great towns. In country parishes the poor do really receive some compensation for their low wages; their children, beyond a certain number, are really supported by the parish; and though it must be a most grating reflection to a labouring man, that it is scarcely possible for him to marry without becoming the father of paupers; yet if he can reconcile himself to this prospect, the compensation, such as it is, is, no doubt, made to him. But in London and all the great towns of the kingdom, the evil is suffered without the compensation. The population raised by bounties in the country naturally and necessarily flows into the towns, and as naturally and necessarily tends to lower wages in them; while, in, point of fact, those who marry in towns, and have large families, receive no assistance from their parishes, unless they are actually starving; and altogether the assistance which the manufacturing classes obtain for the support of their families, in aid of their lowered wages, is perfectly inconsiderable.

To remedy the effects of this competition from the country, the artificers and manufacturers in towns have been apt to combine, with a view to keep up the price of labour, and to prevent persons from working below a certain rate. But such combinations are not only illegal,[6] but irrational and ineffectual; and if the supply of workmen in any particular branch of trade be such as would naturally lower wages, the keeping them up forcibly must have the effect of throwing so many out of employment, as to make the expense of their support fully equal to the gain acquired by the higher wages, and thus render these higher wages in reference to the whole body perfectly futile.

It may be distinctly stated to be an absolute impossibility that all the different classes of society should be both well paid and fully employed, if the supply of labour on the whole exceed the demand; and as the poor-laws tend in the most marked manner to make the supply of labour exceed the demand for it, their effect must be, either to lower universally all wages, or, if some are kept up artificially, to throw great numbers of workmen out of employment, and thus constantly to increase the poverty and distress of the labouring classes of society.

If these things be so (and I am firmly convinced that they are) it cannot but be a subject of the deepest regret to those who are anxious for the happiness of the great mass of the community, that the writers which are now most extensively read among the common people should have selected for the subject of reprobation exactly that line of conduct which can alone generally improve their condition, and for the subject of approbation that system which must inevitably depress them in poverty and wretchedness.

They are taught that there is no occasion whatever for them to put any sort of restraint upon their inclinations, or exercise any degree of prudence in the affair of marriage; because the parish is bound to provide for all that are born. They are taught that there is as little occasion to cultivate habits of economy, and make use of the means afforded them by saving banks, to lay by their earnings while they are single, in order to furnish a cottage when they marry, and enable them to set out in life with decency and comfort; because, I suppose, the parish is bound to cover their nakedness, and to find them a bed and a chair in a workhouse.

They are taught that any endeavour on the part of the higher classes of society to inculcate the duties of prudence and economy can only arise from a desire to save the money which they pay in poor-rates; although it is absolutely certain that the only mode, consistent with the laws of morality and religion, of giving to the poor the largest share of the property of the rich, without sinking the whole community in misery, is the exercise on the part of the poor of prudence in marriage, and of economy both before and after it.

They are taught that the command of the Creator to increase and multiply is meant to contradict those laws which he has himself appointed for the increase and multiplication of the human race; and that it is equally the duty of a person to marry early, when, from the impossibility of adding to the food of the country in which he lives, the greater part of his offspring must die prematurely, and consequently no multiplication follow from it, as when the children of such marriages can all be well maintained, and there is room and food for a great and rapid increase of population.

They are taught that, in relation to the condition of the labouring classes, there is no other difference between such a country as England, which has been long well peopled, and where the land, which is not yet taken into cultivation, is comparatively barren, and such a country as America, where millions and millions of acres of fine land are yet to be had for a trifle, except what arises from taxation.

And they are taught, O monstrous absurdity! that the only reason why the American labourer earns a dollar a day, and the English labourer earns two shillings, is that the English labourer pays a great part of these two shillings in taxes.

Some of these doctrines are so grossly absurd that I have no doubt they are rejected at once by the common sense of many of the labouring classes. It cannot but strike them that, if their main dependence for the support of their children is to be on the parish, they can only expect parish fare, parish clothing, parish furniture, a parish house, and parish government, and they must know that persons living in this way cannot possibly be in a happy and prosperous state.

It can scarcely escape the notice of the common mechanic, that the scarcer workmen are upon any occasion the greater share do they retain of the value of what they produce for their masters; and it is a most natural inference, that prudence in marriage, which is the only moral means of preventing an excess of workmen above the demand, can be the only mode of giving to the poor permanently a large share of all that is produced in the country.

A common man, who has read his Bible, must be convinced that a command given to a rational being by a merciful God cannot be intended so to be interpreted as to produce only disease and death instead of multiplication; and a plain sound understanding would make him see that, if, in a country in which little or no increase of food is to be obtained, every man were to marry at eighteen or twenty, when he generally feels most inclined to it, the consequence must be increased poverty, increased disease, and increased mortality, and not increased numbers, as long, at least, as it continues to be true (which he will hardly be disposed to doubt) that additional numbers cannot live without additional food.

A moderately shrewd judgment would prompt any labourer acquainted with the nature of land to suspect that there must be some great difference, quite independent of taxation, between a country such as America, which might easily be made to support fifty times as many inhabitants as it contains at present, and a country such as England, which could not, without extraordinary exertions, be made to support two or three times as many. He would, at least, see that there would be a prodigious difference in the power of maintaining an additional number of cattle, between a small farm already well stocked, and a very large one which had not the fiftieth part of what it might be made to maintain; and as he would know that both rich and poor must live upon the produce of the earth as well as all other animals, he would be disposed to conclude that what was so obviously true in one case, could not be false in the other. These considerations might make him think it natural and probable that in those countries where there was a great want of people, the wages of labour would be such as to encourage early marriages and large families, for the best of all possible reasons, because all that are born may be very easily and comfortably supported; but that in those countries which were already nearly full, the wages of labour cannot be such as to give the same encouragement to early marriages, for a reason surely not much worse, because the persons so brought into the world cannot be properly supported.

There are few of our mechanics and labourers who have not heard of the high prices of bread, meat and labour in this country compared with the nations of the continent, and they have generally heard at the same time that these high prices were chiefly occasioned by taxation, which, though it had raised among other things the money wages of labour, had done harm rather than good to the labourer, because it had before raised the price of the bread and beer and other articles in which he spent his earnings. With this amount of information, the meanest understanding would revolt at the idea that the very same cause which had kept the money price of labour in all the nations of Europe much lower than in England, namely, the absence of taxation, had been the means of raising it to more than double in America. He would feel quite convinced that, whatever might be the cause of the high money wages of labour in America, which he might not perhaps readily understand, it must be something very different indeed from the mere absence of taxation, which could only have an effect exactly opposite.

With regard to the improved condition of the lower classes of people in France since the revolution, which has also been much insisted upon; if the circumstances accompanying it were told at the same time, it would afford the strongest presumption against the doctrines which have been lately promulgated. The improved condition of the labouring classes in France since the revolution has been accompanied by a greatly diminished proportion of births, which has had its natural and necessary effect in giving to these classes a greater share of the produce of the country, and has kept up the advantage arising from the sale of the church lands and other national domains, which would otherwise have been lost in a short time. The effect of the revolution in France has been, to make every person depend more upon himself and less upon others. The labouring classes are therefore become more industrious, more saving and more prudent in marriage than formerly; and it is quite certain that without these effects the revolution would have done nothing for them. An improved government has, no doubt, a natural tendency to produce these effects, and thus to improve the condition of the poor. But if an extensive system of parochial relief, and such doctrines as have lately been inculcated, counteract them, and prevent the labouring classes from depending upon their own prudence and industry, then any change for the better in other respects becomes comparatively a matter of very little importance; and, under the best form of government imaginable, there may be thousands on thousands out of employment and half starved.

If it be taught that all who are born have a right to support on the land, whatever be their number, and that there is no occasion to exercise any prudence in the affair of marriage so as to check this number, the temptations, according to all the known principles of human nature, will inevitably be yielded to, and more and more will gradually become dependent on parish assistance. There cannot therefore be a greater inconsistency and contradiction than that those who maintain these doctrines respecting the poor, should still complain of the number of paupers. Such doctrines and a crowd of paupers are unavoidably united; and it is utterly beyond the power of any revolution or change of government to separate them.

NOTES

1. This chapter was written in 1817.
2. The years 1816 and 1817.
3. This has, in a considerable degree, taken place; but it has been owing rather to the latter causes noticed than to the former. It appeared, by the returns of 1821, that the scarce years of 1817 and 1818 had but a slight effect in diminishing the number of marriages and births, compared with the effect of the great proportion of plentiful years in increasing them; so that the population proceeded with great rapidity during the ten years ending with 1820. But this great increase of the population has prevented the labouring classes from being so fully employed as might have been expected from the prosperity of commerce and agriculture during the last two or three years.
4. Written in 1817. It increased again afterwards from another great fall in the price of corn, subsequent to 1818.
5. So gradual as not to affect any individuals at present alive, or who will be born within the next two years.
6. This has since been altered; but the subsequent part of the passage is particularly applicable to the present time—the end of the year 1825. The workmen are beginning to find that, if they could raise their wages above what the state of the demand and the prices of goods will warrant, it is absolutely impossible that all, or nearly all, should be employed. The masters could not employ the same number as before, without inevitable ruin.

8

Of the Agricultural System

As it is the nature of agriculture to produce subsistence for a greater number of families than can be employed in the business of cultivation, it might perhaps be supposed that a nation which strictly pursued an agricultural system would always have more food than was necessary for its inhabitants, and that its population could never be checked from the want of the means of subsistence.

It is indeed obviously true that the increase of such a country is not immediately checked, either by the want of power to produce, or even by the deficiency of the actual produce of the soil compared with the population. Yet if we examine the condition of its labouring classes, we shall find that the real wages of their labour are such as essentially to check and regulate their increase, by checking and regulating their command over the means of subsistence.

A country under certain circumstances of soil and situation, and with a deficient capital, may find it advantageous to purchase foreign commodities with its raw produce rather than manufacture them at home: and in this case it will necessarily grow more raw produce than it consumes. But this state of things is very little connected either with the permanent condition of the labouring classes of the society or the rate of their increase; and in a country where the agricultural system entirely predominates, and the great mass of its industry is directed towards the land, the condition of the people is subject to almost every degree of variation.

Under the agricultural system perhaps are to be found the two extremes in the condition of the poor; instances where they are in the best state, and instances where they are in the worst state of any of which we have accounts.

In a country where there is an abundance of good land, where there are no difficulties in the way of its purchase and distribution, and where there is an easy foreign vent for raw produce, both the profits of stock and the wages of labour will be high. These high profits and high wages, if habits of economy pretty generally prevail, will furnish the means of a rapid accumulation of capital and a great and continued demand for labour, while the rapid increase of population which will ensue will maintain undiminished the demand for produce, and check the fall of profits. If the extent of territory be considerable, and the population comparatively inconsiderable, the land may remain understocked both with capital and people for some length of time, notwithstanding a rapid increase of both; and it is under these circumstances of the agricultural system that labour is able to command the greatest portion of the necessaries of life, and that the condition of the labouring classes of society is the best.

The only drawback to the wealth of the labouring classes under these circumstances is the relatively low value of the raw produce.

If a considerable part of the manufactured commodities used in such a country be purchased by the export of its raw produce, it follows as a necessary consequence that the relative value of its raw produce will be lower, and of its manufactured produce higher, than in the countries with which such a trade is carried on. But where a given portion of raw produce will not command so much of manufactured and foreign commodities as in other countries, the condition of the labourer cannot be exactly measured by the quantity of raw produce which falls to his share. If, for instance, in one country the yearly earnings of a labourer amount in money value to fifteen quarters of wheat and in another to nine, it would be incorrect to infer that their relative condition, and the comforts which they enjoy, were in the same proportion, because the whole of a labourer's earnings are not spent in food; and if that part which is not so spent will, in the country where the value of fifteen quarters is earned, not go near so far in the purchase of clothes and other conveniences as in the countries where the value of nine quarters is earned, it is clear that altogether the situation of the labourer in the latter country may approach nearer to that of the labourer in the former than might at first be supposed.

At the same time it should be recollected that quantity always tends powerfully to counterbalance any deficiency of value; and the labourer who earns the greatest number of quarters may still command the greatest quantity of necessaries and conveniences combined, though not to the extent implied by the proportions of the raw produce.

America affords a practical instance of the agricultural system in a state the most favourable to the condition of the labouring classes. The nature of the country is such as to make it answer to employ a very large proportion of its capital in agriculture; and the consequence has been a very rapid increase of it. This rapid increase both of the quantity and value of capital has kept up a steady and continued demand for labour. The labouring classes have in consequence been peculiarly well paid. They have been able to command an unusual quantity of the necessaries of life, and the progress of population has been unusually rapid.

Yet even here, some little drawback has been felt from the relative cheapness of corn. As America till the late war imported the greatest part of its manufactures from England, and as England imported flour and wheat from America, the value of food in America compared with manufactures must have been decidedly less than in England. Nor would this effect take place merely with relation to the foreign commodities imported into America, but also to those of its home manufactures, in which it has no particular advantage. In agriculture, the abundance of good land would counterbalance the high wages of labour and high profits of stock, and keep the price of corn moderate, notwithstanding the great expense of these two elements of price. But in the production of manufactured commodities they must necessarily tell, without any particular advantage to counterbalance them, and must in general occasion in home goods, as well as foreign, a high price compared with food.

Under these circumstances, the condition of the labouring classes of society cannot in point of conveniences and comforts be so much better than that of the labourers of other countries as the relative quantity of food which they earn might seem to indicate; and this conclusion is sufficiently confirmed by experience. In some very intelligent Travels through a great part of England, written in 1810 and 1811 by Mr. Simond, a French gentleman, who had resided above twenty years in America, the author seems to have been evidently much struck with the air of convenience and comfort in the houses of our peasantry, and the neatness and cleanliness of their dress. In some parts of his tour he saw so many neat cottages, so much good clothing, and so little appearance of poverty and distress, that he could not help wondering where the poor of England and their dwellings were concealed. These observations, coming from an able, accurate and apparently most impartial observer, just landed from America and visiting England for the first time, are curious and instructive; and the facts which they notice, though they may arise in part from the different habits and modes of life prevailing in the two countries, must be occasioned in a considerable degree by the causes above mentioned.

A very striking instance of the disadvantageous effect of a low relative price of food on the condition of the poor may be observed in Ireland. The food of Ireland has increased so rapidly during the last century, and so large a portion of that which forms the principal support of the lower classes of society has been obtained by them, that the increase of population has been more rapid than in almost any known country, except America. The Irish labourer paid in potatoes has earned perhaps the means of subsistence for double the number of persons that could be supported by the earnings of an English labourer paid in wheat; and the increase of population in the two countries during the last century has been nearly in proportion to the relative quantity of the customary food awarded to the labourers in each. But their general condition with respect to conveniences and comforts is very far indeed from being in a similar proportion. The great quantity of food which land will bear when planted with potatoes, and the consequent cheapness of the labour supported by them, tends rather to raise than to lower the rents of land, and as far as rent goes, to keep up the price of the materials of manufactures and all other sorts of raw produce, except potatoes. The indolence and want of skill which usually accompany such a state of things tend further to render all wrought commodities comparatively dear. In home manufactures, therefore, a great relative disadvantage will be suffered, and a still greater both in the raw and manufactured produce of foreign countries. The value of the food which the Irish labourer earns above what he and his family consume will go but a very little way in the purchase of clothing, lodging and other conveniences; and the consequence is that his condition in these respects is extremely miserable, at the same time that his means of subsistence, such as they are, may be comparatively abundant.

In Ireland the money price of labour is not much more than the half of what it is in England. The quantity of food earned by no means makes up for its very low price. A certain portion therefore of the Irish labourer's wages (a fourth or a fifth for instance) will go but a very little way in the purchase of manufactures and foreign produce. In the United States, on the other hand, even the money wages of labour are nearly double those of England. Though the American labourer therefore cannot purchase manufactures and foreign produce with the food that he earns so cheap as the English labourer, yet the greater quantity of this food more than makes up for its lower price. His condition, compared with the labouring classes of England, though it may not be so much superior as their relative means of subsistence might indicate, must still on the whole have decidedly the advantage; and altogether, perhaps, the United States may be produced as an instance of the agricultural system in which the condition of the labouring classes is the best of any that we know.

The instances where, under the agricultural system, the condition of the lower classes of society is very wretched, are more frequent. When the accumulation of capital stops, whatever may be the cause, the population, before it comes to a stand, will always be pressed on as near to the limits of the actual means of subsistence, as the habits of the lower classes of the society will allow; that is, the real wages of labour will sink, till they are only just sufficient to maintain a stationary population. Should this happen, as it frequently does, while land is still in abundance and capital scarce, the profits of stock will naturally be high; but corn will be very cheap, owing to the goodness and plenty of the land, and the stationary demand for it, notwithstanding the high profits of stock; while these high profits, together with the want of skill and proper division of labour, which usually attend a scanty capital, will render all domestic manufactured commodities comparatively very dear. This state of things will naturally be unfavourable to the generation of those habits of prudential restraint which most frequently arise from the custom of enjoying conveniences and comforts, and it is to be expected that the population will not stop till the wages of labour, estimated even in food, are very low. But in a country where the wages of labour estimated in food are low, and that food is relatively of a very low value, both with regard to domestic and foreign manufactures, the condition of the labouring classes of society must be the worst possible.

Poland, and some parts of Russia, Siberia and European Turkey, afford instances of this kind. In Poland the population seems to be almost stationary or very slowly progressive; and as both the population and produce are scanty, compared with the extent of territory, we may infer with certainty that its capital is scanty, and yet slowly progressive. It follows, therefore, that the demand for labour increases very slowly, and that the real wages of labour, or the command of the labouring classes over the necessaries and conveniences of life, are such as to keep the population down to the level of the slowly increasing quantity that is awarded to them. And as from the state of the country the peasantry cannot have been much accustomed to conveniences and comforts, the checks to its population are more likely to be of the positive than of the preventive kind.

Yet here corn is in abundance, and great quantities of it are yearly exported. Hence it appears that it is not either the power of the country to produce food, or even what it actually produces, that limits and regulates the progress of population, but the quantity and value of the food which in the actual state of things is awarded to the labourer, and the rate at which these funds appropriated increase.

In the present case the demand for labour is very small, and though the population is inconsiderable, it is greater than the scanty capital of the country can fully employ; the condition of the labourer therefore is depressed by his being able to command only such a quantity of food as will maintain a stationary or very slowly increasing population. It is further depressed by the low relative value of the food that he earns, which gives to any surplus he may possess a very small power in the purchase of manufactured commodities or foreign produce.

Under these circumstances, we cannot be surprised that all accounts of Poland should represent the condition of the lower classes of society as extremely miserable; and the other parts of Europe which resemble Poland in the state of their land and capital, resemble it in the condition of their people.

In justice, however, to the agricultural system, it should be observed that the premature check to the capital and the demand for labour, which occurs in some of the countries of Europe, while land continues in considerable plenty, is not occasioned by the particular direction of their industry, but by the vices of the government and the structure of the society, which prevent its full and fair developement in that direction.

Poland is continually brought forward as an example of the miserable effects of the agricultural system. But nothing surely can be less fair. The misery of Poland does not arise from its directing its industry chiefly to agriculture, but from the little encouragement given to industry of any kind, owing to the state of property and the servile condition of the people. While the land is cultivated by boors, the produce of whose exertions belongs entirely to their masters, and the whole society consists mainly of these degraded beings and the lords and owners of great tracts of territory, there will evidently be no class of persons possessed of the means either of furnishing an adequate demand at home for the surplus produce of the soil, or of accumulating fresh capital and increasing the demand for labour. In this miserable state of things, the best remedy would unquestionably be the introduction of manufactures and commerce; because the introduction of manufactures and commerce could alone liberate the mass of the people from slavery and give the necessary stimulus to industry and accumulation. But were the people already free and industrious, and landed property easily divisible and alienable, it might still answer to such a country as Poland to purchase its finer manufactures from foreign countries by means of its raw products, and thus to continue essentially agricultural for many years. Under these new circumstances, however, it would present a totally different picture from that which it exhibits at present; and the condition of the people would more resemble that of the inhabitants of the United States of America, than of the inhabitants of the unimproved countries of Europe. Indeed America is perhaps the only modern instance of the fair operation of the agricultural system. In every country of Europe, and in most of its colonies in other parts of the world, formidable obstacles still exist to the employment of capital upon the land, arising from the remains of the feudal system. But these obstacles which have essentially impeded cultivation have been very far indeed from proportionably encouraging other branches of industry. Commerce and manufactures are necessary to agriculture; but agriculture is still more necessary to commerce and manufactures. It must ever be true that the surplus produce of the cultivators, taken in its most enlarged sense, measures and limits the growth of that part of the society which is not employed upon the land. Throughout the whole world the number of manufacturers, of merchants, of proprietors, and of persons engaged in the various civil and military professions, must be exactly proportioned to this surplus produce, and cannot in the nature of things increase beyond it. If the earth had been so niggardly of her produce as to oblige all her inhabitants to labour for it, no manufactures or idle persons could ever have existed. But her first intercourse with man was a voluntary present, not very large indeed, but sufficient as a fund for his subsistence till he could procure a greater. And the power to procure a greater was given to him in that quality of the earth by which it may be made to yield a much larger quantity of food, and of the materials of clothing and lodging, than is necessary to feed, clothe and lodge the persons employed in the cultivation of the soil. This quality is the foundation of that surplus produce which peculiarly distinguishes the industry employed upon the land. In proportion as the labour and ingenuity of man exercised upon the land have increased this surplus produce, leisure has been given to a greater number of persons to employ themselves in all the inventions which embellish civilized life; while the desire to profit by these inventions has continued to stimulate the cultivators to increase their surplus produce. This desire indeed may be considered as almost absolutely necessary to give it its proper value, and to encourage its further extension; but still the order of precedence is, strictly speaking, the surplus produce; because the foods for the subsistence of the manufacturer must be advanced to him before he can complete his work; and no step can be taken in any other sort of industry unless the cultivators obtain from the soil more than they themselves consume.

If in asserting the peculiar productiveness of the labour employed upon the land, we look only to the clear monied rent yielded to a certain number of proprietors, we undoubtedly consider the subject in a very contracted point of view. In the advanced stages of society, this rent forms indeed the most prominent portion of the surplus produce here meant; but it may exist equally in the shape of high wages and profits during the earlier periods of cultivation, when there is little or no rent. The labourer who earns a value equal to fifteen or twenty quarters of corn in the year may have only a family of three or four children, and not consume in kind above five or six quarters; and the owner of the farming stock, which yields high profits, may consume but a very moderate proportion of them in food and raw materials. All the rest, whether in the shape of wages and profits, or of rents, may be considered as a surplus produce from the soil, which affords the means of subsistence and the materials of clothing and lodging to a certain number of people according to its extent, some of whom may live without manual exertions, and others employ themselves in modifying the raw materials obtained from the earth into the forms best suited to the gratification of man.

It will depend of course entirely upon its answering to a country to exchange a part of the surplus produce for foreign commodities, instead of consuming it at home, whether it is to be considered as mainly agricultural or otherwise. And such an exchange of raw produce for manufactures, or peculiar foreign products, may for a period of some extent suit a state, which might resemble Poland in scarcely any other feature but that of exporting corn.

It appears then, that countries in which the industry of the inhabitants is principally directed towards the land, and in which corn continues to be exported, may enjoy great abundance or experience great want, according to the particular circumstances in which they are placed. They will in general not be much exposed to the temporary evils of scarcity arising from the variations of the seasons; but the quantity of food permanently awarded to the labourer may be such as not to allow of an increase of population; and their state, in respect to their being progressive, stationary or declining, will depend upon other causes than that of directing their attention principally to agriculture.

9

Of the Commercial System

A country which excels in commerce and manufactures, may purchase corn from a great variety of others; and it may be supposed, perhaps, that, proceeding upon this system, it may continue to purchase an increasing quantity, and to maintain a rapidly increasing population, till the lands of all the nations with which it trades are fully cultivated. As this is an event necessarily at a great distance, it may appear that the population of such a country will not be checked from the difficulty of procuring subsistence till after the lapse of a great number of ages.

There are, however, causes constantly in operation, which will occasion the pressure of this difficulty, long before the event here contemplated has taken place, and while the means of raising food in the surrounding countries may still be comparatively abundant.

In the first place, advantages which depend exclusively upon capital and skill, and the present possession of particular channels of commerce, cannot in their nature be permanent. We know how difficult it is to confine improvements in machinery to a single spot; we know that it is the constant object, both of individuals and countries, to increase their capital; and we know, from the past history of commercial states, that the channels of trade are not unfrequently taking a different direction. It is unreasonable therefore to expect that any one country, merely by the force of skill and capital, should remain in possession of markets uninterrupted by foreign competition. But, when a powerful foreign competition takes place, the exportable commodities of the country in question must soon fall to prices which will essentially reduce profits; and the fall of profits will diminish both the power and the will to save. Under these circumstances the accumulation of capital will be slow, and the demand for labour proportionably slow, till it comes nearly to a stand; while, perhaps, the new competitors either by raising their own raw materials or by some other advantages, may still be increasing their capitals and population with some degree of rapidity.

But, secondly, even if it were possible for a considerable time to exclude any formidable foreign competition, it is found that domestic competition produces almost unavoidably the same effects. If a machine be invented in a particular country, by the aid of which one man can do the work of ten, the possessors of it will of course at first make very unusual profits; but, as soon as the invention is generally known, so much capital and industry will be brought into this new and profitable employment, as to make its products greatly exceed both the foreign and domestic demand at the old prices. These prices, therefore, will continue to fall, till the stock and labour employed in this direction cease to yield unusual profits. In this case it is evident that, though in an early period of such a manufacture, the product of the industry of one man for a day might have been exchanged for such a portion of food as would support forty or fifty persons; yet, at a subsequent period, the product of the same industry might not purchase the support of ten.

In the cotton trade of this country, which has extended itself so wonderfully during the last twenty-five years, very little effect has hitherto been produced by foreign competition.[1] The very great fall which has taken place in the prices of cotton goods has been almost exclusively owing to domestic competition; and this competition has so glutted both the home and foreign markets, that the present capitals employed in the trade, notwithstanding the very peculiar advantages which they possess from the saving of labour, have ceased to possess any advantage whatever in the general rate of their profits. Although, by means of the admirable machinery used in the spinning of cotton, one boy or girl can now do as much as many grown persons could do formerly; yet neither the wages of the labourer, nor the profits of his master, are higher than in those employments where no machinery is used, and no saving of labour accomplished.

The country has, however, in the meantime, been very greatly benefited. Not only have all its inhabitants been enabled to obtain a superior fabric for clothing, at a less expense of labour and property, which must be considered as a great and permanent advantage; but the high temporary profits of the trade have occasioned a great accumulation of capital, and consequently a great demand for labour; while the extending markets abroad and the new values thrown into the market at home, have created such a demand for the products of every species of industry, agricultural and colonial, as well as commercial and manufacturing, as to prevent a fall of profits.

This country, from the extent of its lands, and its rich colonial possessions, has a large arena for the employment of an increasing capital; and the general rate of its profits are not, as it appears, very easily and rapidly reduced by accumulation. But a country, such as we are considering, engaged principally in manufactures, and unable to direct its industry to the same variety of pursuits, would sooner find its rate of profits diminished by an increase of capital, and no ingenuity in machinery which was not continually progressive could save it, after a certain period, from low profits and low wages, and their natural consequences, a check to population.

Thirdly, a country which is obliged to purchase both the raw materials of its manufactures and the means of subsistence for its population from foreign countries, is almost entirely dependent for the increase of its wealth and population on the increasing wealth and demands of the countries with which it trades.

It has been sometimes said, that a manufacturing country is no more dependent upon the country which supplies it with food and raw materials, than the agricultural country is on that which manufactures for it; but this is really an abuse of terms. A country with great resources in land may find it decidedly for its advantage to employ the main part of its capital in cultivation, and to import its manufactures. In so doing, it will often employ the whole of its industry most productively, and most rapidly increase its stock. But, if the slackness of its neighbours in manufacturing, or any other cause, should either considerably check or altogether prevent the importation of manufactures, a country with food and raw materials provided at home cannot be, long at a loss. For a time it would not certainly be so well supplied; but manufacturers and artisans would soon be found, and would soon acquire tolerable skill;[2] and though the capital and population of the country might not, under the new circumstances in which it was placed, increase so rapidly as before, it would still have the power of increasing in both to a great extent.

On the other hand, if food and raw materials were denied to a nation merely manufacturing, it is obvious that it could not longer exist. But not only does the absolute existence of such a nation, on an extreme supposition, depend upon its foreign commerce, but its progress in wealth must be almost entirely measured by the progress and demand of the countries which deal with it. However skilful, industrious and saving such a nation might be, if its customers, from indolence and want of accumulation, would not or could not take off a yearly increasing value of its commodities, the effects of its skill and machinery would be but of very short duration.

That the cheapness of manufactured commodities, occasioned by skill and machinery in one country, is calculated to encourage an increase of raw produce in others, no person can doubt; but we know at the same time that high profits may continue for a considerable period in an indolent and ill-governed state, without producing an increase of wealth; yet, unless such an increase of wealth and demand were produced in the surrounding countries, the increasing ingenuity and exertions of the manufacturing and commercial state would be lost in continually falling prices. It would not only be obliged, as its skill and capital increased, to give a larger quantity of manufactured produce for the raw produce which it received in return; but might be unable, even with the temptation of reduced prices, to stimulate its customers to such purchases as would allow of an increasing importation of food and raw materials; and without such an increasing importation, it is quite obvious that the population must become stationary.

It would come to the same thing, whether this inability to obtain an increasing quantity of food were occasioned by the advancing money price of corn, or the falling money price of manufactures. In either case the effect would be the same; and it is certain that this effect might take place in either way, from increasing competition and accumulation in the manufacturing nation, and the want of them in the agricultural, long before any essential increase of difficulty had occurred in the production of corn.

Fourthly, a nation which is obliged to purchase from others nearly the whole of its raw materials, and the means of its subsistence, is not only dependent entirely upon the demands of its customers, as they may be variously affected by indolence, industry or caprice, but it is subjected to a necessary and unavoidable diminution of demand in the natural progress of these countries towards that proportion of skill and capital which they may reasonably be expected after a certain time to possess. It is generally an accidental and temporary, not a natural and permanent division of labour, which constitutes one state the manufacturer and the carrier of others. While, in these landed nations, agricultural profits continue very high, it may fully answer to them to pay others as their manufacturers and carriers; but when the profits on land fall, or the tenures on which it can be held are not such as to encourage the investment of an accumulating capital, the owner of this capital will naturally look towards commerce and manufactures for its employment; and, according to the just reasoning of Adam Smith and the Economists, finding at home both the materials of manufactures, the means of subsistence, and the power of carrying on their own trade with foreign countries, they will probably be able to conduct the business of manufacturing and carrying for themselves at a cheaper rate than if they allowed it to continue in the hands of others. As long as the agricultural nations continued to apply their increasing capital principally to the land, this increase of capital would be of the greatest possible advantage to the manufacturing and commercial nation. It would be indeed the main cause and great regulator of its progress in wealth and population. But after they had turned their attention to manufactures and commerce, their further increase of capital would be the signal of decay and destruction to the manufactures and commerce, which they had before supported. And thus, in the natural progress of national improvement, and without the competition of superior skill and capital, a purely commercial state must be undersold and driven out of the markets by those who possess the advantage of land.

In the distribution of wealth during the progress of improvement, the interests of an independent state in relation to others are essentially different from those of a particular province, in relation to the kingdom to which it belongs, a point which has not been sufficiently attended to. If agricultural capital increases, and agricultural profits diminish in Sussex, the overflowing stock will go to London, Manchester, Liverpool, or some other place where it can probably be engaged in manufactures or commerce more advantageously than at home. But if Sussex were an independent kingdom, this could not take place; and the corn which is now sent to London must be withdrawn to support manufacturers and traders living within its confines. If England, therefore, had continued to be separated into the seven kingdoms of the Heptarchy, London could not possibly have been what it is; and that distribution of wealth and population which takes place at present, and which we may fairly presume is the most beneficial to the whole of the realm, would have been essentially changed, if the object had been to accumulate the greatest quantity of wealth and population in particular districts, instead of the whole island. But at all times the interest of each independent state is to accumulate the greatest quantity of wealth within its limits. Consequently, the interest of an independent state, with regard to the countries with which it trades, can rarely be the same as the interest of a province with regard to the empire to which it belongs; and the accumulation of capital which would occasion the withdrawing of the exports of corn in the one case, would leave them perfectly undisturbed in the other.

If, from the operation of one or more of the causes above enumerated, the importation of corn into a manufacturing and commercial country should be essentially checked, and should either actually decrease, or be prevented from increasing, it is quite evident that its population must be checked nearly in the same proportion.

Venice presents a striking instance of a commercial state, at once stopped in its progress to wealth and population by foreign competition. The discovery made by the Portuguese of a passage to India by the Cape of Good Hope completely turned the channel of the Indian trade. The high profits of the Venetians, which had been the foundation of their rapidly increasing wealth, and of their extraordinary preponderance as a naval and commercial power, were not only suddenly reduced; but the trade itself, on which these high profits had been made, was almost annihilated, and their power and wealth were shortly contracted to those more confined limits which suited their natural resources.

In the middle of the 15th century, Bruges in Flanders was the great *entrepôt* of the trade between the north and the south of Europe. Early in the 16th century its commerce began to decline under the competition of Antwerp. Many English and foreign merchants in consequence left the declining city, to settle in that which was rapidly increasing in commerce and wealth. About the middle of the 16th century Antwerp was at the zenith of its power. It contained above a hundred thousand inhabitants, and was universally allowed to be the most illustrious mercantile city, and to carry on the most extensive and richest commerce of any in the north of Europe.

The rising greatness of Amsterdam was favoured by the unfortunate siege and capture of Antwerp by the duke of Parma; and the competition of the extraordinary industry and persevering exertions of the Hollanders not only prevented Antwerp from recovering her commerce, but gave a severe blow to the foreign trade of almost all the other Hanse towns.

The subsequent decline of the trade of Amsterdam itself was caused partly by the low profits arising from home competition and abundance of capital; partly by excessive taxation, which raised the price of the necessaries of life; but more than either, perhaps, by the progress of other nations possessing greater natural advantages, and being able, even with inferior skill, industry and capital, beneficially to carry on much of that trade which had before fallen almost exclusively into the hands of the Dutch.

As early as 1669 and 1670, when Sir William Temple was in Holland, the effects of abundance of capital and domestic competition were such, that most of the foreign trades were losing ones, except the Indian, and that none of them gave a profit of more than two or three per cent.[3] In such a state of things both the power and the will to save must be greatly diminished. The capital must have been either stationary or declining, or at the best very slowly progressive. In fact, Sir William Temple gives it as his opinion that the trade of Holland had for some years passed its meridian, and begun sensibly to decay.[4] Subsequently, when the progress of other nations was still more marked, it appeared from undoubted documents that most of the trades of Holland, as well as its fisheries, had decidedly fallen off, and that no branch of its commerce had retained its former vigour, except the American and African trades, and that of the Rhine and Maese, which are independent of foreign power and competition.

In 1669, the whole population of Holland and West Friezeland was estimated by John de Witt at 2,400,000.[5] In 1778, the population of the seven provinces was estimated only at 2,000,000;[6] and thus, in the course of above a hundred years, the population, instead of increasing, as is usual, had greatly diminished.

In all these cases of commercial states, the progress of wealth and population seems to have been checked by one or more of the causes above mentioned, which must necessarily affect more or less the power of commanding the means of subsistence.

Universally it may be observed, that if, from any cause or causes whatever, the funds for the maintenance of labour in any country cease to be progressive, the effective demand for labour will also cease to be progressive; and wages will be reduced to that sum, which, under the existing prices of provisions, and the existing habits of the people, will just keep up, and no more than keep up, a stationary population. A state so circumstanced is under a moral impossibility of increasing, whatever may be the plenty of corn, or however high may be the profits of stock in other countries.[7] It may indeed at a subsequent period, and under new circumstances, begin to increase again. If by some happy invention in mechanics, the discovery of some new channel of trade, or an unusual increase of agricultural wealth and population in the surrounding countries, its exports, of whatever kind, were to become unusually in demand, it might again import an increasing quantity of corn, and might again increase its population. But as long as it is unable to make yearly additions to its imports of food, it will evidently be unable to furnish the means of support to an increasing population; and it will necessarily experience this inability, when, from the state of its commercial transactions, the funds for the maintenance of its labour become stationary, or begin to decline.

NOTES

1. 1816.
2. This has been fully exemplified in America (1816).
3. Temple's Works, vol. i. p. 60, fol.
4. *Id.* p. 67.
5. Interest of Holland, vol. i. p. 9.
6. Richesse de la Hollande, vol. ii. p. 349.
7. It is a curious fact, that among the causes of the decline of the Dutch trade, Sir William Temple reckons the cheapness of corn, which, he says, "has been for these dozen years, or more, general in these parts of Europe." (Vol. i. p. 69.) This cheapness, he says, impeded the vent of spices and other Indian commodities among the Baltic nations, by diminishing their power of purchasing.

10

Of Systems of Agriculture and Commerce Combined

In a country the most exclusively confined to agriculture, some of its raw materials will always be worked up for domestic use. In the most commercial state, not absolutely confined to the walls of a town, some part of the food of its inhabitants, or of its cattle, will be drawn from the small territory in its neighbourhood. But, in speaking of systems of agriculture and commerce combined, something much further than this kind of combination is intended; and it is meant to refer to countries, where the resources in land, and the capitals employed in commerce and manufactures, are both considerable, and neither preponderating greatly over the other.

A country so circumstanced possesses the advantages of both systems, while at the same time it is free from the peculiar evils which belong to each, taken separately.

The prosperity of manufactures and commerce in any state implies at once that it has freed itself from the worst parts of the feudal system. It shows that the great body of the people are not in a state of servitude; that they have both the power and the will to save; that when capital accumulates it can find the means of secure employment, and consequently that the government is such as to afford the necessary protection to property. Under these circumstances, it is scarcely possible that it should ever experience that premature stagnation in the demand for labour, and the produce of the soil, which at times has marked the history of most of the nations of Europe. In a country in which manufactures and commerce flourish, the produce of the soil will always find a ready market at home; and such a market is peculiarly favourable to the progressive increase of capital. But the progressive increase of capital, and particularly of the quantity and value of the funds for the maintenance of labour, is the great cause of a demand for labour, and of good corn wages, while the high relative price of corn, occasioned by the improved machinery and extended capital employed in manufactures, together with the prosperity of foreign commerce, enables the labourer to exchange any given portion of his earnings in corn for a large proportion both of domestic and foreign conveniences and luxuries. Even when the effective demand for labour begins to slacken, and the corn wages to be reduced, still the high relative value of corn keeps up comparatively the condition of the labouring classes; and though their increase is checked, yet a very considerable body of them may still be well lodged and well clothed, and able to indulge themselves in the conveniences and luxuries of foreign produce. Nor can they ever be reduced to the miserable condition of the people in those countries, where, at the same time that the demand for labour is stationary, the value of corn, compared with manufactures and foreign commodities, is extremely low.

All the peculiar disadvantages therefore of a purely agricultural country are avoided by the growth and prosperity of manufactures and commerce.

In the same manner it will be found that the peculiar disadvantages attending states merely manufacturing and commercial will be avoided by the possession of resources in land.

A country which raises its own food cannot by any sort of foreign competition be reduced at once to a necessarily declining population. If the exports of a merely commercial country be essentially diminished by foreign competition, it may lose, in a very short time, its power of supporting the same number of people; but if the exports of a country which has resources in land be diminished, it will merely lose some of its foreign conveniencies and luxuries; and the great and most important of all trades, the domestic trade carried on between the towns and the country, will remain comparatively undisturbed. It may indeed be checked in the rate of its progress for a time by the want of the same stimulus; but there is no reason for its becoming retrograde; and there is no doubt that the capital thrown out of employment by the loss of foreign trade will not lie idle. It will find some channel in which it can be employed with advantage, though not with the same advantage as before; and will be able to maintain an increasing population, though not increasing at the same rate as under the stimulus of a prosperous foreign trade.

The effects of home competition will in like manner be very different in the two states we are comparing.

In a state merely manufacturing and commercial, home competition and abundance of capital may so reduce the price of manufactured compared with raw produce, that the increased capital employed in manufactures may not procure in exchange an increased quantity of food. In a country where there are resources in land this cannot happen; and though from improvements in machinery and the decreasing fertility of the new land taken into cultivation, a greater quantity of manufactures will be given for raw produce, yet the mass of manufactures can never fall in value, owing to a competition of capital in this species of industry, unaccompanied by a correspondent competition of capital on land.

It should also be observed that in a state, the revenue of which consists solely in profits and wages, the diminution of profits and wages may greatly impair its disposable income. The increase in the amount of capital and in the number of labourers may in many cases not be sufficient to make up for the diminished rate of profits and wages. But where the revenue of the country consists of rents as well as profits and wages, a great part of what is lost in profits and wages is gained in rents, and the disposable income remains comparatively unimpaired.

Another eminent advantage possessed by a nation which is rich in land, as well as in commerce and manufactures, is, that the progress of its wealth and population is in a comparatively slight degree dependent upon the state and progress of other countries. A nation, whose wealth depends exclusively on manufactures and commerce, cannot increase without an increase in the raw products of the countries with which it trades; or taking away a share of what they have been in the habit of actually consuming, which will rarely be parted with; and thus the ignorance and indolence of others may not only be prejudicial, but fatal to its progress.

A country with resources in land can never be exposed to these inconveniences; and if its industry, ingenuity, and economy increase, its wealth and population will increase, whatever may be the situation and conduct of the nations with which it trades. When its manufacturing capital becomes redundant, and manufactured commodities are too cheap, it will have no occasion to wait for the increasing raw products of its neighbours. The transfer of its own redundant capital to its own land will raise fresh products, against which its manufactures may be exchanged, and by the double operation of diminishing comparatively the supply, and increasing the demand, enhance their price. A similar operation, when raw produce is too abundant, will restore the level between the profits of agriculture and manufactures. And upon the same principle the stock of the country will be distributed through its various and distant provinces, according to the advantages presented by each situation for the employment, either of agricultural or manufacturing capital.

A country, in which in this manner agriculture, manufactures, and commerce, and all the different parts of a large territory, act and re-act upon each other in turn, might evidently go on increasing in riches and strength, although surrounded by Bishop Berkely's wall of brass. Such a country would naturally make the most of its foreign commerce, whatever might be the actual state of it; and its increase or decrease would be the addition or removal of a powerful stimulus to its own produce; but still the increase of this produce, to a very considerable extent, would be independent of foreign countries; and though it might be retarded by a failure of foreign commerce, it could not either be stopped or be made retrograde.

A fourth advantage derived from the union of agriculture and manufactures, particularly when they are nearly balanced, is, that the capital and population of such a country can never be forced to make a retrograde movement, merely by the natural progress of other countries to that state of improvement to which they are all constantly tending.

According to all general principles, it will finally answer to most landed nations, both to manufacture for themselves, and to conduct their own commerce. That raw cottons should be shipped in America, carried some thousands of miles to another country, unshipped there, to be manufactured and shipped again for the American market, is a state of things which cannot be permanent. That it may last for some time, there can be no doubt; and I am very far from meaning to insinuate that an advantage, while it lasts, should not be used, merely because it will not continue for ever. But if the advantage be in its nature temporary, it is surely prudent to have this in view, and to use it in such a way, that when it ceases, it may not have been productive, on the whole, of more evil than good.

If a country, owing to temporary advantages of this kind, should have its commerce and manufactures so greatly preponderate as to make it necessary to support a large portion of its people on foreign corn, it is certain that the progressive improvement of foreign countries in manufactures and commerce might, after a time, subject it to a period of poverty and of retrograde movements in capital and population, which might more than counterbalance the temporary benefits before enjoyed; while a nation in which the commercial and manufacturing population continued to be supported by its agriculture, might receive a very considerable stimulus to both, from such temporary advantages, without being exposed to any essential evil on their ceasing.

The countries which thus unite great landed resources with a prosperous state of commerce and manufactures, and in which the commercial part of the population never essentially exceeds the agricultural part, are eminently secure from sudden reverses. Their increasing wealth seems to be out of the reach of all common accidents; and there is no reason to say that they might not go on increasing in riches and population for hundreds, nay almost thousands of years.

We must not, however, imagine that there is no limit to this progress though it is distant, and has certainly not been attained by any large landed nation yet known.

We have already seen that the limit to the population of commercial nations is the period when, from the actual state of foreign markets, they are unable regularly to import an increasing quantity of food. And the limit to the population of a nation which raises the whole of its food on its own territory is, when the land has been so fully occupied and worked, that the employment of another labourer on it will not, on an average, raise an additional quantity of food sufficient to support a family of such a size as will admit of an increase of population.

This is evidently the extreme practical limit to the progress of population, which no nation has ever yet reached, nor, indeed, ever will; since no allowance has been here made either for other necessaries besides food, or for the profits of stock, both of which, however low, must always be something not inconsiderable.

Yet, even this limit is very far short of what the earth is capable of producing, if all were employed upon it who were not employed in the production of other necessaries; that is, if soldiers, sailors, menial servants, and all the artificers of luxuries, were made to labour upon the land. They would not, indeed, produce the support of a family, and ultimately not even of themselves; but, till the earth absolutely refused to yield any more, they would continue to add something to the common stock; and, by increasing the means of subsistence, would afford the means of supporting an increasing population. The whole people of a country might thus be employed during their whole time in the production of mere necessaries, and no leisure be left for other pursuits of any kind. But this state of things could only be effected by the forced direction of the national industry into one channel by public authority. Upon the principal of private property, which it may be fairly presumed will always prevail in society, it could never happen. With a view to the individual interest, either of a landlord or farmer, no labourer can ever be employed on the soil, who does not produce more than the value of his wages; and if these wages be not on an average sufficient to maintain a wife, and rear two children to the age of marriage, it is evident that both the population and produce must come to a stand. Consequently, at the most extreme practical limit of population, the state of the land must be such as to enable the last employed labourers to produce the maintenance of as many, probably, as four persons.

And it is happy for mankind that such are the laws of nature. If the competition for the necessaries of life, in the progress of population, could reduce the whole human race to the necessity of incessant labour for them, man would be continually tending to a state of degradation; and all the improvements which had marked the middle stages of his career would be completely lost at the end of it; but, in reality, and according to the universal principle of private property, at the period when it will cease to answer to employ more labour upon the land, the excess of raw produce, not actually consumed by the cultivators, will, in the shape of rents, profits, and wages, particularly the first, bear nearly as great a proportion to the whole as at any previous period, and, at all events, sufficient to support a large part of the society living, either without manual labour, or employing themselves in modifying the raw materials of the land into the forms best suited to the gratification of man.

When we refer, therefore, to the practical limits of population, it is of great importance to recollect that they must be always very far short of the utmost power of the earth to produce food.

It is also of great importance to recollect that, long before this practical limit is attained in any country, the rate of the increase of population will gradually diminish. When the capital of a country becomes stationary from bad government, indolence, extravagance, or a sudden shock to commerce, it is just possible that the check to population may, in some degree, be sudden, though, in that case, it cannot take place without a considerable convulsion. But when the capital of a country comes to a stop from the continued progress of accumulation and the exhaustion of the cultivable land, both the profits of stock and the wages of labour must have been gradually diminishing for a long period, till they are both ultimately so low as to afford no further encouragement to an increase of stock, and no further means for the support of an increasing population. If we could suppose that the capital employed upon the land was, at all times, as great as could possibly be applied with the same profit, and there were no agricultural improvements to save labour, it is obvious that, as accumulation proceeded, profits and wages would regularly fall, and the diminished rate in the progress of population would be quite regular. But practically this can never happen; and various causes, both natural and artificial, will concur to prevent this regularity, and occasion great variations at different times in the rate at which the population proceeds towards its final limit.

In the first place, land is practically almost always understocked with capital. This arises partly from the usual tenures on which farms are held, which, by discouraging the transfer of capital from commerce and manufactures, leaves it principally to be generated on the land; and partly from the very nature of much of the soil of almost all large countries, which is such that the employment of a small capital upon it may be little productive, while the employment of a large capital in draining, or in changing the character of the soil by a sufficient quantity of natural and artificial manures, may be productive in a high degree; and partly also, from the circumstance that after every fall of profits and wages there will often be room for the employment of a much greater capital upon the land than is at the command of those, who, by being in the actual occupation of farms, can alone so employ it.

Secondly; improvements in agriculture. If new and superior modes of cultivation be invented, by which not only the land is better managed, but is worked with less labour, it is obvious that inferior land may be cultivated at higher profits than could be obtained from richer land before; and an improved system of culture, with the use of better instruments, may, for a long period, more than counterbalance the tendency of an extended cultivation and a great increase of capital to yield smaller proportionate returns.

Thirdly; improvements in manufactures. When by increased skill and the invention of unproved machinery in manufactures one man becomes capable of doing as much as eight or ten could before, it is well known that, from the principle of home competition and the consequent great increase of quantity, the prices of such manufactures will greatly fall; and, as far as they include the necessaries and accustomed conveniences of labourers and farmers, they must tend to diminish that portion of the value of the whole produce which is consumed necessarily on the land, and leave a larger remainder. From this larger remainder may be drawn a higher rate of profits, notwithstanding the increase of capital and extension of cultivation.

Fourthly; the prosperity of foreign commerce. If from a prosperous foreign commerce our labour and domestic commodities rise considerably in price, while foreign commodities are advanced comparatively very little, an event which is very common, it is evident that the farmer or labourer will be able to obtain the tea, sugar, cottons, linens, leather, tallow, timber, etc., which he stands in need of, for a smaller quantity of corn or labour than before; and this increased power of purchasing foreign commodities will have precisely the same effect, in allowing the means of an extended cultivation without a fall of profits, as the improvements in manufactures just referred to.

Fifthly; a temporary increase in the relative price of raw produce from increased demand. Allowing, what is certainly not true, that a rise in the price of raw produce, will, after a certain number of years, occasion a proportionate rise in labour[1] and other commodities; yet, during the time that the price of raw produce takes the lead, it is obvious that the profits of cultivation may increase under an extended agriculture, and a continued accumulation of capital. And these intervals, it should be observed, must be of infinite importance in the progress of the wealth of a landed nation, particularly with reference to the causes of deficient capital upon the land before mentioned. If the land, for the most part, generates the new capital which is employed in extending its cultivation; and if the employment of a considerable capital for a certain period will often put land in such a state, that it can be cultivated afterwards at comparatively little expense; a period of high agricultural profits, though it may last only eight or ten years, may often be the means of giving to a country what is equivalent to a fresh quantity of land.

Though it is unquestionably and necessarily true, therefore, that the tendency of a continually increasing capital and extending cultivation is to occasion a progressive fall both of profits and wages; yet the causes above enumerated are evidently sufficient to account for great and long irregularities in this progress.

We see, in consequence, in all the states of Europe, great variations at different periods in the progress of their capital and population. After slumbering for years in a state almost stationary, some countries have made a sudden start, and have begun increasing at a rate almost approaching to that of new colonies. Russia and parts of Prussia have afforded instances of this kind, and have continued this rate of progress after the accumulation of capital and the extension of cultivation had been proceeding with great rapidity for many years.

From the operation of the same causes we have seen similar variations in our own country. About the middle of last century the interest of money was at 3 per cent; and we may conclude that the profits of stock were nearly in proportion. At that time, as far as can be collected from the births and marriages, the population was increasing but slowly. From 1720 to 1750, a period of 30 years, the increase is calculated to have been only about 900,000 on a population of 5,565,000.[2] Since this period it cannot be doubted that the capital of the country has been prodigiously enlarged, and its cultivation very greatly extended; yet, during the last twenty years, we have seen the interest of money at above 5 per cent, with profits in proportion; and, from 1800 to 1811, an increase of population equal to 1,200,000 on 9,287,000, a rate of increase about two and a half times as great as at the former period.

But, notwithstanding these causes of irregularity in the progress of capital and population, it is quite certain that they cannot reach their necessary practical limit but by a very gradual process. Before the accumulation of capital comes to a stop from necessity, the profits of stock must, for a long time, have been so low as to afford scarcely any encouragement to an excess of saving above expenditure; and before the progress of population is finally stopped, the real wages of labour most have been gradually diminishing, till, under the existing habits of the people, they could only support such families as would just keep up, and no more than keep up, the actual population.

It appears then, that it is the union of the agricultural and commercial systems, and not either of them taken separately, that is calculated to produce the greatest national prosperity; that a country with an extensive and rich territory, the cultivation of which is stimulated by improvements in agriculture, manufactures, and foreign commerce, has such various and abundant resources, that it is extremely difficult to say when they will reach their limits. That there is, however, a limit, which, if the capital and population of a country continue increasing, they must ultimately reach, and cannot pass; and that this limit, upon the principle of private property, must be far short of the utmost power of the earth to produce food.

NOTES

1. A rise, which is occasioned exclusively by the increased quantity of labour which may be required in the progress of society to raise a given quantity of corn on the last land taken into cultivation, must, of course, be peculiar to raw produce, and will not be communicated to those commodities, in the production of which there is no increase of labour.
2. Population Abstracts, Preliminary Observations, table, p. xxv.

11

Of Corn-Laws—Bounties Upon Exportation

It has been observed that some countries, with great resources in land, and an evident power of supporting a greatly increased population from their own soil, have yet been in the habit of importing large quantities of foreign corn, and have become dependent upon other states for a great part of their supplies.

The causes which may lead to this state of things seem to be chiefly the following:

First; any obstacles which the laws, constitution and customs of a country present to the accumulation of capital on the land, which do not apply with equal force to the increasing employment of capital in commerce and manufactures.

In every state in which the feudal system has prevailed, there are laws and customs of this kind, which prevent the free division and alienation of land like other property, and render the preparations for an extension of cultivation often both very difficult and very expensive. Improvements in such countries are chiefly carried on by tenants, a large part of whom have not leases, or at least leases of any length; and though their wealth and respectability have of late years very greatly increased, yet it is not possible to put them on a footing with enterprising owners, and to give them the same independence, and the same encouragement to employ their capitals with spirit, as merchants and manufacturers.

Secondly; a system of direct or indirect taxation, of such a nature as to throw a weight upon the agriculture of a country, which is either unequal, or, from peculiar circumstances, can be better borne by commerce and manufactures.

It is universally allowed that a direct tax on corn grown at home, if not counterbalanced by a corresponding tax on the importation of it, might be such as to destroy at once the cultivation of grain, and make a country import the whole of its consumption; and a partial effect of the same kind would follow, if, by a system of indirect taxation, the general price of labour were raised and yet by means of drawbacks on home and foreign commodities, by an abundance of colonial produce, and by those peculiar articles,[1] the demand for which abroad would not be much affected by the increase of price, the value of the whole of the exports, though not the quantity, might admit of increase.

Thirdly; improved machinery, combined with extensive capital and a very advantageous division of labour.

If in any country, by means of capital and machinery, one man be enabled to do the work of ten, it is quite obvious that before the same advantages are extended to other countries, a rise in the price of labour will but very little interfere with the power of selling those sorts of commodities, in the production of which the capital and machinery are so effectively applied. It is quite true that an advance in the necessary wages of labour, which increases the expense of raising corn, may have the same effect upon many commodities besides corn; and if there were no others, no encouragement would be given to the importation of foreign grain, as there might be no means by which it could be purchased cheaper abroad. But a large class of the exportable commodities of a commercial country are of a different description. They are either articles in a considerable degree peculiar to the country and its dependencies, or such as have been produced by superior capital and machinery, the prices of which are determined rather by domestic than foreign competition. All commodities of this kind will evidently be able to support without essential injury an advance in the price of labour, some permanently, and others for a considerable time. The rise in the price of the commodity so occasioned, or rather the prevention of that fall which would otherwise have taken place, may always indeed have the effect of decreasing in some degree the quantity of the commodity exported; but it by no means follows that it will diminish the whole of its bullion value in the foreign country, which is precisely what determines the bullion value, and generally the quantity of the returns. If cottons in this country were now to fall to half their present price, we should undoubtedly export a greater quantity than we do at present; but I very much doubt whether we should export double the quantity, at least for many years, and yet we must do this to enable us to command as much foreign produce as before. In this case, as in numerous others of the same kind, quantity and value go together to a certain point, though not at an equal pace; but, beyond this point, a further increase of quantity only diminishes the whole value produced, and the amount of the returns that can be obtained for it.

It is obvious then that a country, notwithstanding a high comparative price of labour and of materials, may easily stand a competition with foreigners in those commodities to which it can apply a superior capital and machinery with great effect; although such a price of labour and materials might give an undisputed advantage to foreigners in agriculture and some other sorts of produce, where the same saving of labour cannot take place. Consequently such a country may find it cheaper to purchase a considerable part of its supplies of grain from abroad with its manufactures and peculiar products, than to grow the whole at home.

If, from all or any of these causes, a nation becomes habitually dependent on foreign countries for the support of a considerable portion of its population, it must evidently be subjected, while such dependence lasts, to some of those evils which belong to a nation purely manufacturing and commercial. In one respect, indeed, it will still continue to have a great superiority. It will possess resources in land, which may be resorted to when its manufactures and commerce, either from foreign competition, or any other causes, begin to fail. But, to balance this advantage, it will be subjected, during the time that large importations are necessary, to much greater fluctuations in its supplies of corn, than countries wholly manufacturing and commercial. The demands of Holland and Hamburgh may be known with considerable accuracy by the merchants who supply them. If they increase, they increase gradually; and, not being subject from year to year to any great and sudden variations, it might be safe and practicable to make regular contracts for the average quantity wanted. But it is otherwise with such countries as England and Spain. Their wants are necessarily very variable, from the variableness of the seasons; and if the merchants were to contract with exporting countries for the quantity required in average years, two or three abundant seasons might ruin them. They must necessarily wait to see the state of the crops in each year, in order safely to regulate their proceedings; and though it is certainly true that it is only the deficiency from the average crop, and not the whole deficiency, which may be considered altogether in the light of a new demand in Europe; yet the largeness and previous uncertainty of this whole deficiency, the danger of making contracts for a stated quantity annually, and the greater chance of hostile combinations against large and warlike states, must greatly aggravate the difficulties of procuring a steady supply; and if it be true that unfavourable seasons are not unfrequently general, it is impossible to conceive that they should not occasionally be subject to great variations of price.

It has been sometimes stated that scarcities are partial, not general, and that a deficiency in one country is always compensated by a plentiful supply in others. But this seems to be quite an unfounded supposition. In the evidence brought before the Committee of the House of Commons in 1814, relating to the corn-laws, one of the corn merchants being asked whether it frequently happened that crops in the country bordering upon the Baltic failed, when they failed here, replied, "When crops are unfavourable in one part of Europe, it generally happens that they are more or less so in another."[2] If any person will take the trouble to examine the contemporaneous prices of corn in the different countries of Europe for some length of time, he will be convinced that the answer here given is perfectly just. In the last hundred and fifty years, above twenty will be found in which the rise of prices is common to France and England, although there was seldom much intercourse between them in the trade of corn: and Spain and the Baltic nations, as far as their prices have been collected, appear frequently to have shared in the same general deficiency. Even within the last five years, two have occurred, the years 1811-12, and 1816-1817, in which, with extraordinary high prices in this country, the imports have been comparatively inconsiderable; which can only have arisen from those scarcities having been general over the greatest part of Europe.

Under these circumstances let us suppose that two million quarters of foreign grain were the average quantity annually wanted in this country, and suppose, at the same time, that a million quarters were deficient from a bad season; the whole deficiency to be supplied would then be three millions.

If the scarcity were general in Europe, it may fairly be concluded, that some states would prohibit the export of their corn entirely, and others tax it very highly; and if we could obtain a million or fifteen hundred thousand quarters, it is probably as much as we could reasonably expect. We should then, however, be two millions or fifteen hundred thousand quarters deficient. On the other hand, if we had habitually grown our own consumption, and were deficient a million of quarters from a bad season, it is scarcely probable that, notwithstanding a general scarcity, we should not be able to obtain three or four hundred thousand quarters in consequence of our advanced prices; particularly if the usual prices of our corn and labour were higher than in the rest of Europe. And in this case the sum of our whole deficiency would only be six or seven hundred thousand quarters, instead of fifteen hundred thousand or two millions of quarters. If the present year (1816-17) had found us in a state in which our growth of corn had been habitually far short of our consumption, the distresses of the country would have been dreadfully aggravated.

To provide against accidents of this kind, and to secure a more abundant and, at the time, a more steady supply of grain, a system of corn-laws has been recommended, the object of which is to discourage by duties or prohibitions the importation of foreign corn, and encourage by bounties the exportion of corn of home growth.

A system of this kind was completed in our own country in 1688,[3] the policy of which has been treated of at some length by Adam Smith.

In whatever way the general question may be finally decided, it must be allowed by all those who acknowledge the efficacy of the great principle of supply and demand that the line of argument taken by the author of the *Wealth of Nations* against the system is essentially erroneous.

He first states that, whatever extension of the foreign market can be occasioned by the bounty, must in every particular year be altogether at the expense of the home market, as every bushel of corn which is exported by means of the bounty, and which would not have been exported without the bounty, would have remained in the home market to increase the consumption, and to lower the price of that commodity.[4]

In this observation he evidently misapplies the term market. Because, by selling a commodity lower, it is easy to get rid of a greater quantity of it, in any particular market, than would have gone off otherwise, it cannot justly be said that by this process such a market is proportionally extended. Though the removal of the two taxes mentioned by Adam Smith as paid on account of the bounty would certainly increase the power of the lower classes to purchase, yet in each particular year the consumption must ultimately be limited by the population, and the increase of consumption from the removal of these taxes would by no means be sufficient to give the same encouragement to cultivation as the addition of the foreign demand. If the price of British corn in the home market rise in consequence of the bounty, before the price of production is increased, (and an immediate rise is distinctly acknowledged by Adam Smith), it is an unanswerable proof that the effectual demand for British corn is extended by it; and that the diminution of demand at home, whatever it may be, is more than counterbalanced by the extension of demand abroad.

Adam Smith goes on to say that the two taxes paid by the people on account of the bounty, namely, the one to the government to pay this bounty, and the other paid in the advanced price of the commodity, must either reduce the subsistence of the labouring poor, or occasion an augmentation in their pecuniary wages proportioned to that in the pecuniary price of their subsistence. So far as it operates in the one way it must reduce the ability of the labouring poor to educate and bring up their children, and must so far tend to restrain the population of the country. So far as it operates in the other, it must reduce the ability of the employers of the poor to employ so great a number as they otherwise might do, and must so far tend to restrain the industry of the country.

It will be readily allowed that the tax occasioned by the bounty will have the one or the other of the effects here contemplated; but it cannot be allowed that it will have both. Yet it is observed, that though the tax, which that institution imposes upon the whole body of the people, be very burdensome to those who pay it, it is of very little advantage to those who receive it. This is surely a contradiction. If the price of labour rise in proportion to the price of wheat, as it subsequently asserted, how is the labourer rendered less competent to support a family? If the price of labour do not rise in proportion to the price of wheat, how is it possible to maintain that the landlords and farmers are not able to employ more labourers on their land? Yet in this contradiction the author of the *Wealth of Nations* has had respectable followers; and some of those who have agreed with him in his opinion that corn regulates the prices of labour, and of all other commodities, still insist on the injury done to the labouring classes of society by a rise in the price of corn, and the benefit they would derive from a fall.

The main argument however which Adam Smith adduces against the bounty is, that as the money price of corn regulates that of all other home-made commodities, the advantage to the proprietor from the increase of money price is merely apparent, and not real; since what he gains in his sales he must lose in his purchases.

This position, though true to a certain extent, is by no means true to the extent of preventing the movement of capital to or from the land, which is the precise point in question. The money price of corn in a particular country is undoubtedly by far the most powerful ingredient in regulating the price of labour, and of all other commodities; but it is not enough for Adam Smith's position that it should be the most powerful ingredient; it must be shown that, other causes remaining the same, the price of every article will rise and fall exactly in proportion to the price of corn, and this is very far from being the case. Adam Smith himself excepts all foreign commodities; but when we reflect upon the vast amount of our imports, and the quantity of foreign articles used in our manufactures, this exception alone is of the greatest importance. Wool and raw hides, two most important materials of home growth, do not, according to Adam Smith's own reasonings, (Book I. c. xi. p. 363, et seq.), depend much upon the price of corn and the rent of land; and the prices of flax, tallow, and leather, are of course greatly influenced by the quantity we import. But woollen cloths, cotton and linen goods, leather, soap, candles, tea, sugar, etc., which are comprehended in the above-named articles, form almost the whole of the clothing and luxuries of the industrious classes of society.

It should be further observed that in all countries, the industry of which is greatly assisted by fixed capital, the part of the price of the wrought commodity which pays the profits of such capital will not necessarily rise in consequence of an advance in the price of corn, except as it requires gradual renovation; and the advantage derived from machinery which has been constructed before the advance in the price of labour will naturally last for some years.

In the case also of great and numerous taxes on consumption, a rise or fall in the price of corn, though it would increase or decrease that part of the wages of labour which resolves itself into food, evidently would not increase or decrease that part which is destined for the payment of taxes.

It cannot then be admitted as a general position that the money price of corn in any country is a just measure of the real value of silver in that country. But all these considerations, though of great weight to the owners of land, will not influence the farmers beyond the present leases. At the expiration of a lease, any particular advantage which a farmer had received from a favourable proportion between the price of corn and of labour would be taken from him, and any disadvantage from an unfavourable proportion be made up to him. The sole cause which would determine the proportion of capital employed in agriculture, would be the extent of the effectual demand for corn; and if the bounty had really enlarged this demand, which it certainly would have done, it is impossible to suppose that more capital would not be employed than upon the land.

When Adam Smith says that the nature of things has stamped upon corn a real value, which cannot be altered by merely altering the money price, and that no bounty upon exportation, no monopoly of the home market, can raise that value, nor the freest competition lower it, it is obvious that he changes the question from the profits of the growers of corn, or of the proprietors of the land, to the physical value of corn itself. I certainly do not mean to say that the bounty alters the physical value of corn, and makes a bushel of it support equally well a greater number of labourers than it did before; but I certainly do mean to say that the bounty to the British cultivator does, in the actual state of things, really increase the demand for British corn, and thus encourage him to sow more that he otherwise would do, and enables him in consequence to employ more bushels of corn in the maintenance of a greater number of labourers.

If Adam Smith's theory were true, and what he calls the real price of corn were unchangeable, or not capable of experiencing a relative increase or decrease of value compared with labour and other commodities, agriculture would indeed be in an unfortunate situation. It would be at once excluded from the operation of that principle so beautifully explained in the *Wealth of Nations*, by which capital flows from one employment to another, according to the various and necessarily fluctuating wants of society. But surely we cannot doubt that the real price of corn varies, though it may not vary so much as the real price of other commodities; and that there are periods when all wrought commodities are cheaper, and periods when they are dearer, in proportion to the price of corn; and in the one case capital flows from manufactures to agriculture, and in the other from agriculture to manufactures. To overlook these periods or consider them of slight importance, is not allowable; because in every branch of trade these periods form the grand encouragement to an increase of supply. Undoubtedly the profits of trade in any particular branch of industry can never long remain higher than in others; but how are they lowered except by the influx of capital occasioned by these high profits? It never can be a national object permanently to increase the profits of any particular set of dealers. The national object is the increase of supply; but this object cannot be attained except by previously increasing the profits of these dealers, and thus determining a greater quantity of capital to this particular employment. The shipowners and sailors of Great Britain do not make greater profits now than they did before the Navigation Act; but the object of the nation was not to increase the profits of shipowners and sailors, but the quantity of shipping and seamen; and this could not be done but by a law, which, by increasing the demand for them, raised the profits of the capital before employed in this way, and determined a greater quantity to flow into the same channel. The object of a nation in the establishment of a bounty is, not to increase the profits of the farmers, or the rents of the landlords, but to determine a greater quantity of the national capital to the land, and consequently to increase supply; and though, in the case of an advance in the price of corn from an increased demand, the rise of wages, the rise of rents, and the fall of silver tend, in some degree, to obscure our view of the subject; yet we cannot refuse to acknowledge that the real price of corn varies during periods sufficiently long to affect the determination of capital, or we shall be reduced to the dilemma of owning that no possible degree of demand can encourage the growth of corn.

It must be allowed then that the peculiar argument relating to the nature of corn brought forward by Adam Smith upon this occasion cannot be maintained, and that a bounty upon the exportation of corn must enlarge the demand for it and encourage its production in the same manner, if not in the same degree, as a bounty upon the exportation of any other commodity.

But it has been urged further, that this increased production of corn must necessarily occasion permanent cheapness; and a period of considerable length, during the first 64 years of the last century, while a bounty was in full operation in this country, has been advanced as a proof of it. In this conclusion, however, it may be reasonably suspected, that an effect, in its nature temporary, though it may be of some duration, has been mistaken for one which is permanent.

According to the theory of demand and supply, the bounty might be expected to operate, in the following manner:

It is frequently stated in the *Wealth of Nations* that a great demand is followed by a great supply; a great scarcity by a great plenty; an unusual dearness by an unusual cheapness. A great and indefinite demand is indeed generally found to produce a supply more than proportioned to it. This supply as naturally occasions unusual cheapness; but this cheapness, when it comes, must in its turn check the production of the commodity; and this check, upon the same principle, is apt to continue longer than necessary, and again to occasion a return to high prices.

This appears to be the manner in which a bounty upon the exportation of corn, if granted under circumstances favourable to its efficiency, might be expected to operate, and this seems to have been the manner in which it really did operate in the only instance where it has been fairly tried.

Without meaning to deny the concurrence of other causes, or attempting to estimate the relative efficiency of the bounty, it is impossible not to acknowledge that, when the growing price of corn was, according to Adam Smith, only 28 shillings a quarter, and the corn-markets of England were as low as those of the continent, a premium of five shillings a quarter upon exportation must have occasioned an increase of real price, and given encouragement to the cultivation of grain. But the changes produced in the direction of capital to or from the land will always be slow. Those who have been in the habit of employing their stock in mercantile concerns do not readily turn it into the channel of agriculture; and it is a still more difficult and slower operation to withdraw capital from the soil, to employ it in commerce. For the first 25 years after the establishment of the bounty in this country the price of corn rose 2 or 3 shillings in the quarter; but owing probably to the wars of William and Anne, to bad seasons, and a scarcity of money, capital seems to have accumulated slowly on the land, and no great surplus growth was effected. It was not till after the peace of Utrecht that the capital of the country began in a marked manner to increase; and it is impossible that the bounty should not gradually have directed a larger portion of this accumulation to the land than would otherwise have gone to it. A surplus growth, and a fall of price for thirty or forty years, followed.

It will be said that this period of low prices was too long to be occasioned by a bounty, even according to the theory just laid down. This is perhaps true, and in all probability the period would have been shorter if the bounty alone had operated; but in this case other causes powerfully combined with it.

The fall in the price of British corn was accompanied by a fall of prices on the continent. Whatever were the general causes which produced this effect in foreign countries, it is probable that they were not wholly inoperative in England. At all events nothing could be so powerfully calculated to produce cheapness, and to occasion a slow return to high prices, as a considerable surplus growth, which was unwillingly received, and only at low prices, by other nations. When such a surplus growth had been obtained, some time would necessarily be required to destroy it by cheapness, particularly as the moral stimulus of the bounty would probably continue to act long after the fall of prices had commenced. If to these causes we add that a marked fall in the rate of interest, about the same time, evinced an abundance of capital, and a consequent difficulty of finding a profitable employment for it; and consider further the natural obstacles to the moving of capital from the land; we shall see sufficient reason why even a long period might elapse without any essential alteration in the comparative abundance and cheapness of corn.

Adam Smith attributes this cheapness to a rise in the value of silver. The fall in the price of corn which took place in France and some other countries about the same time might give some countenance to the conjecture. But the accounts we have lately had of the produce of the mines during the period in question does not sufficiently support it; and it is much more probable that it arose from the comparative state of peace in which Europe was placed after the termination of the wars of Louis

XIV, which facilitated the accumulation of capital on the land, and encouraged agricultural improvements.

With regard to this country, indeed, it is observed by Adam Smith himself, that labour[5] and other articles were rising; a fact very unfavourable to the supposition of an increased value of the precious metals. Not only the money price of corn fell, but its value relative to other articles was lowered, and this fall of relative value, together with great exportations, clearly pointed to a relative abundance of corn, in whatever way it might be occasioned, as the main cause of the facts observed, rather than a scarcity of silver. This great fall in the British corn-market, particularly during the ten years from 1740 to 1750, accompanied by a great fall in the continental markets, owing in some degree perhaps to the great exportations of British corn, especially during the years 1748, 1749, and 1750, must necessarily have given some check to its cultivation, while the increase of the real price of labour must at the same time have given a stimulus to the increase of population. The united operation of these two causes is exactly calculated first to diminish, and ultimately to destroy a surplus of corn; and as, after 1764, the wealth and manufacturing population of Great Britain increased more rapidly than those of her neighbours, the returning stimulus to agriculture, considerable as it was, arising almost exclusively from a home demand, was incapable of producing a surplus; and not being confined, as before, to British cultivation, owing to the alteration in the corn-laws, was inadequate even to effect an independent supply. Had the old corn-laws remained in full force, we should still probably have lost our surplus growth, owing to the causes above mentioned, although, from their restrictive clauses, we should certainly have been nearer the growth of an independent supply immediately previous to the scarcity of 1800.

It is not therefore necessary, in order to object to the bounty, to say with Adam Smith that the fall in the price of corn which took place during the first half of the last century must have happened in spite of the bounty, and could not possibly have happened in consequence of it. We may allow, on the contrary, what I think we ought to allow according to all general principles, that the bounty, when granted under favourable circumstances, is really calculated, after going through a period of dearness, to produce the surplus and the cheapness which its advocates promise;[6] but according to the same general principles we must allow that this surplus and cheapness, from their operating at once as a check to produce, and an encouragement to population, cannot be for any great length of time maintained.

The objection then to a bounty on corn, independently of the objections to bounties in general, is, that when imposed under the most favourable circumstances it cannot produce permanent cheapness: and if it be imposed under unfavourable circumstances; that is, if an attempt be made to force exportation by an adequate bounty at a time when the country does not fully grow its own consumption; it is obvious not only that the tax necessary for the purpose must be a very heavy one, but that the effect will be absolutely prejudicial to the population, and the surplus growth will be purchased by a sacrifice very far beyond its worth.

But notwithstanding the strong objections to bounties on general grounds, and their inapplicability in cases which are not unfrequent, it must be acknowledged that, while they are operative, that is, while they produce an exportation which would not otherwise have taken place, they unquestionably encourage an increased growth of corn in the countries in which they are established, or maintain it at a point to which it would not otherwise have attained.

Under peculiar and favourable circumstances a country might maintain a considerable surplus growth for a great length of time, with an inconsiderable increase of the growing price of corn: and perhaps little or no increase of the average price, including years of scarcity.[7] If from any period during the last century, when an average excess of growth for exportation had been obtained by the stimulus of a bounty, the foreign demand for our corn had increased at the same rate as the domestic demand, our surplus growth might have become permanent. After the bounty had ceased to stimulate to fresh exertions, its influence would by no means be lost. For some years it would have given the British grower an absolute advantage over the foreign grower. This advantage would of course gradually diminish: because it is the nature of all effectual demand to be ultimately supplied, and oblige the producers to sell at the lowest price they can afford consistently with the general rate of profits. But, after having experienced a period of decided encouragement, the British grower would find himself in the habit of supplying a larger market than his own upon equal terms with his competitors. And if the foreign and British markets continued to extend themselves equally, he would continue to proportion his supplies to both; because, unless a particular increase of demand were to take place at home, he could never withdraw his foreign supply without lowering the price of his whole crop; and the nation would thus be in possession of a constant store for years of scarcity.

But even supposing that, by a bounty, combined with the most favourable state of prices in other countries, a particular state could maintain permanently an average excess of growth for exportation, it must not of course be imagined that its population would not still be checked by the difficulty of procuring subsistence. It would indeed be less exposed to the particular pressure arising from years of scarcity; but in other respects it would be subject to the same checks as those already described in the preceding chapters; and whether there was an habitual exportation or not, the population would be regulated by the real wages of labour, and would come to a stand when the necessaries which these wages could command were not sufficient, under the actual habits of the people, to encourage an increase of numbers.

NOTES

1. A rise in the price of labour in China would certainly increase the returns which it receives for its teas.
2. Report, p. 93.
3. Though the object here stated may not have been the specific object of the law of 1688, it is certainly the object for which the system has been subsequently recommended.
4. Vol. ii. b. iv. c. 5.
5. It is certainly a very remarkable fact, that although Adam Smith repeatedly states, in the most distinct manner, that labour alone is the true measure of the value of silver and of all other commodities, he

should suppose that silver was rising at the very time when he says the money price of labour was rising. There cannot be a more decided contradiction.

6. As far as the bounty might tend to force the cultivation of poorer land, so far no doubt it would have a tendency to raise the price of corn; but we know from experience that the rise of price naturally occasioned in this way is continually counteracted by improvements in agriculture. As a matter of fact it must be allowed, that, during the period of the last century when corn was falling, more land must have been taken into cultivation.
7. The average price is different from the growing price. Years of scarcity, which must occasionally occur, essentially affect the average price; and the growth of a surplus quantity of corn, which tends to present scarcity, will tend to lower this average, and make it approach nearer to the growing price.

12

Of Corn-Laws—Restrictions Upon Importation

The laws which prohibit the importation of foreign grain, though by no means unobjectionable, are not open to the same objections as bounties, and must be allowed to be adequate to the object they have in view,—the maintenance of an independent supply. A country, with landed resources, which determines never to import corn but when the price indicates an approach towards a scarcity, will necessarily, in average years, supply its own wants. Though we may reasonably therefore object to restrictions upon the importation of foreign corn, on the grounds of their tending to present the most profitable employment of the national capital and industry, to check population, and to discourage the export of our manufactures; yet we cannot deny their tendency to encourage the growth of corn at home, and to procure and maintain an independent supply. A bounty, it has appeared, sufficient to make it answer its purpose in forcing a surplus growth, would, in many cases, require so very heavy a direct tax, and would bear so large a proportion to the whole price of the corn, as to make it in some countries next to impracticable. Restrictions upon importation impose no direct tax upon the people. On the contrary, they might be made, if it were thought advisable, sources of revenue to the government, and they can always, without difficulty, be put in execution, and be made infallibly to answer their express purpose of securing, in average years, a sufficient growth of corn for the actual population.

We have considered, in the preceding chapters, the peculiar disadvantages which attend a system either almost exclusively agricultural or exclusively commercial, and the peculiar advantages which attend a system in which they are united, and flourish together. It has further appeared that, in a country with great landed resources, the commercial population may, from particular causes, so far predominate, as to subject it to some of the evils which belong to a state purely commercial and manufacturing, and to a degree of fluctuation in the price of corn greater than is found to take place in such a state. It is obviously possible, by restrictions upon the importation of foreign corn, to maintain a balance between the agricultural and commercial classes. The question is not a question of the effieciency or inefficiency of the measure proposed, but of its policy or impolicy. The object can certainly be accomplished, but it may be purchased too dear; and to those who do not at once reject all inquiries on points of this kind, as impeaching a principle which they hold sacred, the question, whether a balance between the agricultural and commercial classes of society, which would not take place naturally, ought, under certain circumstances, to be maintained artificially, must appear to be a most important practical question.

One of the objections to the admission of the doctrine that restrictions upon importation are advantageous is, that it cannot possibly be laid down as a general rule that every state ought to raise its own corn. There are some states so circumstanced that the rule is clearly and obviously inapplicable to them.

In the first place, there are many states which have made some figure in history, the territories of which have been perfectly inconsiderable compared with their main town or towns, and utterly incompetent to supply the actual population with food. In such communities, what is called the principal internal trade of a large state, the trade which is carried on between the towns and the country, must necessarily be a foreign trade, and the importation of foreign corn is absolutely necessary to their existence. They may be said to be born without the advantage of land, and, to whatever risks and disadvantages a system merely commercial and manufacturing may be exposed, they have no power of choosing any other. All that they can do is to make the most of their own situation, compared with the situation of their neighbours, and to endeavour by superior industry, skill, and capital, to make up for so important a deficiency. In these efforts, some states of which we have accounts have been wonderfully successful; but the reverses to which they have been subject have been almost as conspicuous as the degree of their prosperity compared with the scantiness of their natural resources.

Secondly, restrictions upon the importation of foreign corn are evidently not applicable to a country which, from its soil and climate, is subject to very great and sudden variations in its home supplies, from the variations of the seasons. A country so circumstanced will unquestionably increase its chance of a steady supply of grain by opening as many markets for importation and exportation as possible, and this will probably be true, even though other countries occasionally prohibit or tax the exports of their grain. The peculiar evil to which such a country is subject can only be mitigated by encouraging the freest possible foreign trade in corn.

Thirdly, restrictions upon importation are not applicable to a country which has a very barren territory, although it may be of some extent. An attempt fully to cultivate and improve such a territory by forcibly directing capital to it would probably, under any circumstances, fail; and the actual produce obtained in this way might be purchased by sacrifices which the capital and industry of the nation could not possibly continue to support. Whatever advantages those countries may enjoy, which possess the means of supporting a considerable population from their own soil, such advantages are not within the reach of a state so circumstanced. It must either consent to be a poor and inconsiderable community, or it must place its chief dependence on other resources than those of land. It resembles in many respects those states which have a very small territory; and its policy, with regard to the importation of corn, must of course be nearly the same.

In all these cases there can be no doubt of the impolicy of attempting to maintain a balance between the agricultural and commercial classes of society which would not take place naturally.

Under other and opposite circumstances, however, this impolicy is by no means so clear.

If a nation possesses a large territory consisting of land of an average quality, it may without difficulty support from its own soil a population fully sufficient to maintain its rank in wealth and power among the countries with which it has relations either of commerce or of war. Territories of a certain extent must ultimately in the main support their own population. As each exporting country approaches towards that complement of wealth and population to which it is naturally tending, it will gradually withdraw the corn which for a time it had spared to its more manufacturing and commercial neighbours, and leave them to subsist on their own resources. The peculiar products of each soil and climate are objects of foreign trade, which can never, under any circumstances, fail. But food is not a peculiar product; and the country which produces it in the greatest abundance may, according to the laws which govern the progress of population, have nothing to spare for others. An extensive foreign trade in corn beyond what arises from the variableness of the seasons in different countries is rather a temporary and incidental trade, depending chiefly upon the different stages of improvement which different countries may have reached, and on other accidental circumstances, than a trade which is in its nature permanent, and the stimulus to which will remain in the progress of society unabated. In the wildness of speculation it has been suggested (of course more in jest than in earnest), that Europe ought to grow its corn in America, and devote itself solely to manufactures and commerce, as the best sort of division of the labour of the globe. But even on the extravagant supposition that the natural course of things might lead to such a division of labour for a time, and that by such means Europe could raise a population greater than its lands could possibly support, the consequences ought justly to be dreaded. It is an unquestionable truth that it must answer to every territorial state, in its natural progress to wealth, to manufacture for itself, unless the countries from which it had purchased its manufactures possess some advantages peculiar to them besides capital and skill. But when upon this principle America began to withdraw its corn from Europe, and the agricultural exertions of Europe were inadequate to make up for the deficiency, it would certainly be felt that the temporary advantages of a greater degree of wealth and population (supposing them to have been really attained) had been very dearly purchased by a long period of retrograde movements and misery.

If then a country be of such a size that it may fairly be expected finally to supply its own population with food; if the population which it can thus support from its own resources in land be such as to enable it to maintain its rank and power among other nations; and further, if there be reason to fear not only the final withdrawing of foreign corn used for a certain time, which might be a distant event, but the immediate effects that attend a great predominance of a manufacturing population, such as increased unhealthiness, increased turbulence, increased fluctuations in the price of corn, and increased variableness in the wages of labour; it may not appear impolitic artificially to maintain a more equal balance between the agricultural and commercial classes by restricting the importation of foreign corn, and making agriculture keep pace with manufactures.

Thirdly, if a country be possessed of such a soil and climate, that the variations in its annual growth of corn are less than in most other countries, this may be an additional reason for admitting the policy of restricting the importation of foreign corn. Countries are very different in the degree of variableness to which their annual supplies are subject; and though it is unquestionably true that if all were nearly equal in this respect, and the trade in corn really free, the steadiness of price in a particular state would increase with an increase in the number of the nations connected with it by the commerce of grain; yet it by no means follows that the same conclusion will hold good when the premises are essentially different; that is, when some of the countries taken into the circle of trade are subject to very great comparative variations in their supplies of grain, and when this defect is aggravated by the acknowledged want of real freedom in the foreign trade of corn.

Suppose, for instance, that the extreme variations above and below the average quantity of corn grown, were in England 1/4 and in France 1/3, a free intercourse between the two countries would probably increase the variabless of the English markets. And if, in addition to England and France, such a country as Bengal could be brought near, and admitted into the circle—a country in which, according to Sir George Colebrook, rice is sometimes sold four times as cheap in one year as in the succeeding without famine or scarcity;[1] and where, notwithstanding the frequency of abundant harvests, deficiencies sometimes occur of such extent as necessarily to destroy a considerable portion of the population; it is quite certain that the supplies both of England and France would become very much more variable than before the accession.

In point of fact, there is reason to believe that the British isles, owing to the nature of their soil and climate, are peculiarly free from great variations in their annual produce of grain. If we compare the prices of corn in England and France from the period of the commencement of the Eton tables to the beginning of the revolutionary war, we shall find that in England the highest price of the quarter of wheat of 8 bushels during the whole of that time was £3. 15s. 6¾d. (in 1648), and the lowest price £1. 2s. 1d. (in 1743), while in France the highest price of the septier was 62 francs 78 centimes (in 1662), and the lowest price 8 francs 89 centimes (in 1718).[2] In the one case the difference is a little above 3¼ times, and in the other very nearly 7 times. In the English tables, during periods of ten or twelve years, only two instances occur of a variation amounting to as much as 3 times; in the French tables, during periods of the same length, one instance occurs of a variation of 4 times or above. These variations may, perhaps, have been aggravated by a want of freedom in the internal trade of corn, but they are strongly confirmed by the calculations of Turgot, which relate solely to variations of produce, without reference to any difficulties or obstructions in its free transport from one part of the country to another.

On land of an average quality he estimates the produce at seven septiers the arpent in years of great abundance; and three septiers the arpent in years of great scarcity; while the medium produce he estimates at five septiers the arpent.[3] These calculations he conceives are not far removed from the truth; and proceeding on these grounds he observes that, in a very abundant year, the produce will be five months above its ordinary consumption, and in a very scarce year as much below. These variations are, I should think, much greater than those which take place in this country, at least if we may judge from prices, particularly as in a given degree of scarcity in the two countries there is little doubt that, from the superior riches of England, and the extensive parish relief which it affords to the poorer classes in times of dearth, its prices would rise more above the usual average than those of France.

If we look to the prices of wheat in Spain during the same period, we shall find, in like manner, much greater variations than in England. In a table of the prices of the fanega of wheat in the market of Seville from 1675 to 1764 inclusive, published in the Appendix to the Bullion Report, the highest price is 48 reals vellon (in 1677), and the lowest price 7 reals vellon (in 1720), a difference of nearly seven times; and in periods of ten or twelve years the difference is, in two or three instances, as much as four times. In another table, from 1788 to 1792 inclusive, relating to the towns of Old Castille, the highest price in 1790 was 109 reals vellon the fanega, and in 1792 the lowest was only 16 reals vellon the fanega. In the market of Medina del Rio Seco, a town of the kingdom of Leon, surrounded by a very fine corn country, the price of the load of four fanegas of wheat was, in May, 1800, 100 reals vellon, and in May, 1804, 600 reals vellon, and these were both what are called low prices, as compared with the highest prices of the year. The difference would be greater if the high prices were compared with the low prices. Thus, in 1799, the low price of the four fanegas was 88 reals vellon, and in 1804 the high price of the four fanegas was 640 reals vellon—a difference of above seven times in so short a period as six years.

In Spain, foreign corn is freely admitted; yet the variation of price, in the towns of Andalusia, a province adjoining the sea, and penetrated by the river Guadalquiver, though not so great as those just mentioned, seem to show that the coasts of the Mediterranean by no means furnish very steady supplies. It is known, indeed, that Spain is the principal competitor of England in the purchase of grain in the Baltic; and as it is quite certain that what may be called the growing or usual price of corn in Spain is much lower than in England, it follows, that the difference between the prices of plentiful and scarce years must be very considerable.

I have not the means of ascertaining the variations in the supplies and prices of the northern nations. They are, however, occasionally great, as it is well known that some of these countries are at times subject to very severe scarcities. But the instances already produced are sufficient to show, that a country which is advantageously circumstanced with regard to the steadiness of its home supplies may rather diminish than increase this steadiness by uniting its interests with a country less favourably circumstanced in this respect; and this steadiness will unquestionably be still further diminished, if the country which is the most variable in its supplies is allowed to inundate the other with its crops when they are abundant, while it reserves to itself the privilege of retaining them in a period of slight scarcity, when its commercial neighbour happens to be in the greatest want.[4]

If a nation be possessed of a territory, not only of sufficient extent to maintain under its actual cultivation a population adequate to a state of the first rank, but of sufficient unexhausted fertility to allow of a very great increase of population, such a circumstance would of course make the measure of restricting the importation of foreign corn more applicable to it.

A country which, though fertile and populous, had been cultivated nearly to the utmost, would have no other means of increasing its population than by the admission of foreign corn. But the British isles show at present no symptoms whatever of this species of exhaustion. The necessary accompaniments of a territory worked to the utmost are very low profits and interest, a very slack demand for labour, low wages, and a stationary population. Some of these symptoms may indeed take place without an exhausted territory; but an exhausted territory cannot take place without all these symptoms. Instead, however, of such symptoms, we have seen in this country, during the twenty years previous to 1814, a high rate of profits and interest, a very great demand for labour, good wages, and an increase of population more rapid, perhaps, than during any period of our previous history. The capitals which were laid out in bringing new land into cultivation, or improving the old, must necessarily have yielded good returns, or, under the actual rate of general profits, they would not have been so employed: and although it is strictly true that, as capital accumulates upon the land, its profits must ultimately diminish; yet owing to the increase of agricultural skill, and other causes noticed in a former chapter, these two events do not by any means always keep pace with each other. Though they must, finally unite and terminate the career of their progress together, they are often, during the course of their progress, separated for a considerable time, and at a considerable distance. In some countries, and some soils, the quantity of capital which can be absorbed before any essential diminution of profits necessarily takes place is so great, that its limit is not easily calculated; and certainly, when we consider what has been actually done in some districts of England and Scotland, and compare it with what remains to be done in other districts, we must allow that no near approach to this limit has yet been made. On account of the high money price of labour, and of the materials of agricultural capital, occasioned partly by direct and indirect taxation, and partly, or perhaps chiefly by the great prosperity of our foreign commerce,[5] new lands cannot be brought into cultivation, nor great improvements made on the old, without a high money price of grain; but these lands, when they have been so brought into cultivation, or improved, have by no means turned out unproductive. The quantity and value of their produce have borne a full and fair proportion to the quantity of capital and labour employed upon them; and they were cultivated with great advantage both to individuals and the state, as long as the same, or nearly the same, relations between the value of produce and the cost of production, which prompted this cultivation, continued to exist.

In such a state of the soil, the British empire might unquestionably be able not only to support from its own agricultural resources its present population, but double, and in time, perhaps, even treble the number; and consequently a restriction upon the importation of foreign corn, which might be thought greatly objectionable in a country which had reached nearly the end of its resources, might appear in a very different light in a country capable of supporting from its own lands a very great increase of population.

But it will be said, that although a country may be allowed to be capable of maintaining from its own soil not only a great, but an increasing population, yet, if it be acknowledged that, by opening its ports for the free admission of foreign corn, it may be made to support a greater and more rapidly increasing population, it is unjustifiable to go out of our way to check this tendency, and to prevent that degree of wealth and population which would naturally take place.

This is unquestionably a powerful argument; and granting fully the premises, it cannot be answered upon the principles of political economy solely. I should say, however, that if it could be clearly ascertained that the addition of wealth and population so acquired would subject the society to a greater degree of uncertainty in its supplies corn, greater fluctuations in the wages of labour, greater unhealthiness and immorality owing to a larger proportion of the population being employed in manufactories, and a greater chance of long and depressing retrograde movements occasioned by the natural progress of those countries from which corn had been imported; I should have no hesitation in considering such wealth and population as much too dearly purchased. The happiness of a society is, after all, the legitimate end even of its wealth, power, and population. It is certainly true that with a view to the structure of society most favourable to this happiness, and an adequate stimulus to the production of wealth from the soil, a very considerable admixture of commercial and manufacturing population with the agricultural is absolutely necessary; but there is no argument so frequently and obviously fallacious as that which infers that what is good to a certain extent is good to any extent; and though it will be most readily admitted that, in a large landed nation, the evils which belong to the manufacturing and commercial system are much more than counterbalanced by its advantages, as long as it is supported by agriculture; yet, in reference to the effect of the excess which is not so supported, it may fairly be doubted whether the evils do not decidedly predominate.

It is observed by Adam Smith, that the "capital which is acquired to any country by commerce and manufactures is all a very uncertain and precarious possession, till some part of it has been secured and realized in the cultivation and improvement of its lands."[6]

It is remarked in another place, that the monopoly of the colony trade, by raising the rate of mercantile profit, discourages the improvement of the soil, and retards the natural increase of that great original source of revenue—the rent of land.[7]

Now it is certain that, at no period, have the manufactures, commerce and colony trade of the country been in a state to absorb so much capital as during the twenty years ending with 1814. From the year 1764 to the peace of Amiens, it is generally allowed that the commerce and manufactures of the country increased faster than its agriculture, and that it became gradually more and more dependent on foreign corn for its support. Since the peace of Amiens the state of its colonial monopoly and its manufactures has been such as to demand an unusual quantity of capital; and if the peculiar circumstances of the subsequent war, the high freights and insurance, and the decrees of Buonaparte, had not rendered the importation of foreign corn extremely difficult and expensive, we should at this moment, according to all general principles, have been in the habit of supporting a much larger portion of our population upon it, than at any former period of our history. The cultivation of the country would be in a very different state from what it is at present. Very few or none of those great improvements would have taken place which may be said to have purchased fresh land for the state that no fall of price can destroy. And the peace, or accidents of different kinds, might have curtailed essentially both our colonial and manufacturing advantages, and destroyed or driven away our capital before it had spread itself on the soil, and become national property.

As it is, the practical restrictions thrown in the way of importing foreign corn during the war have forced our steam-engines and our colonial monopoly to cultivate our lands; and those very causes which, according to Adam Smith, tend to draw capital from agriculture, and would certainly have so drawn it if we could have continued to purchase foreign corn at the market prices of France and Holland, have been the means of giving such a spur to our agriculture, that it has not only kept pace with a very rapid increase of commerce and manufactures, but has recovered the distance at which it had for many years been left behind, and now marches with them abreast.

But restrictions upon the importation of foreign corn in a country which has great landed resources, not only tend to spread every commercial and manufacturing advantage possessed, whether permanent or temporary, on the soil, and thus, in the language of Adam Smith, secure and realize it; but also tend to prevent those great oscillations in the progress of agriculture and commerce, which are seldom unattended with evil.

It is to be recollected, and it is a point of great importance to keep constantly in our minds, that the distress which has been experienced among almost all classes of society from the sudden fall of prices, except as far as it has been aggravated by the state of the currency, has been occasioned by natural, not artificial causes.

There is a tendency to an alternation in the rate of the progress of agriculture and manufactures in the same manner as there is a tendency to an alternation in the rate of the progress of food and population. In periods of peace and uninterrupted trade, these alternations, though not favourable to the happiness and quiet of society, may take place without producing material evil; but the intervention of war is always liable to give them a force and rapidity that must unavoidably produce a convulsion in the state of property.

The war that succeeded to the peace of Amiens found us dependent upon foreign countries for a very considerable portion of our supplies of corn; and we now grow our own consumption, notwithstanding an unusual increase of population in the interval.

This great and sudden change in the state of our agriculture could only have been effected by very high prices occasioned by an inadequate home supply and the great expense and difficulty of importing foreign corn. But the rapidity with which this change has been effected must necessarily create a glut in the market as soon as the home growth of corn became fully equal or a little in excess above the home consumption; and, aided only by a small foreign importation, must inevitably occasion a very sudden fall of prices. If the ports had continued open for the free importation of foreign corn, there can be little doubt that the price of corn in 1815 would have been still considerably lower. This low price of corn, even if by means of lowered rents our present state of cultivation could be in a great degree preserved, must give such a check to future improvement, that if the ports were to continue open, we should certainly not grow a sufficiency at home to keep pace with our increasing population; and at the end of ten or twelve years we might be found by a new war in the same state that we were at the commencement of the present. We should then have the same career of high prices to pass through, the same excessive stimulus to agriculture[8] followed by the same sudden and depressing check to it, and the same enormous loans borrowed with the price of wheat at 90 or 100 shillings a quarter, and the monied incomes of the landholders and industrious classes of society nearly in proportion, to be paid when wheat is at 50 or 60 shillings a quarter, and the incomes of the landlords and industrious classes of society greatly reduced—a state of things which cannot take place without an excessive aggravation of the difficulty of paying taxes, and particularly that invariable monied amount which pays the interest of the national debt.

On the other hand a country which so restricts the importations of foreign corn as on an average to grow its own supplies, and to import merely in periods of scarcity, is not only certain of spreading every invention in manufactures and every peculiar advantage it may possess from its colonies or general commerce on the land, and thus of fixing them to the spot and rescuing them from accidents; but is necessarily exempt from those violent and distressing convulsions of property which almost unavoidably arise from the coincidence of a general war and an insufficient home supply of corn.

If the late war had found us independent of foreigners for our average consumption, not even our paper currency could have made the prices of our corn approach to the prices which were at one time experienced.[9] And if we had continued, during the course of the contest, independent of foreign supplies, except in an occasional scarcity, it is impossible that the growth of our own consumption, or a little above it, should have produced at the end of the war so universal a feeling of distress.

The chief practical objection to which restrictions on the importation of corn are exposed is a glut from an abundant harvest, which cannot be relieved by exportation. And in the consideration of that part of the question which relates to the fluctuations of prices this objection ought to have its full and fair weight. But the fluctuation of prices arising from this cause has sometimes been very greatly exaggerated. A glut which might essentially distress the farmers of a poor country, might be comparatively little felt by the farmers of a rich one; and it is difficult to conceive that a nation with an ample capital, and not under the influence of a great shock to commercial confidence, as this country was in 1815, would find much difficulty in reserving the surplus of one year to supply the wants of the next or some future year. It may fairly indeed be doubted whether, in such a country as our own, the fall of price arising from this cause would be so great as that which would be occasioned by the sudden pouring in of the supplies from an abundant crop in Europe, particularly from those states which do not regularly export corn. If our ports were always open, the existing laws of France would still prevent such a supply as would equalize prices; and French corn would only come in to us in considerable quantities in years of great abundance, when we were the least likely to want it, and when it was most likely to occasion a glut.[10]

But if the fall of price occasioned in these two ways would not be essentially different, as it is quite certain that the rise of price in years of general scarcity would be less in those countries which habitually grow their own supplies; it must be allowed that the range of variation will be the least under such a system of restrictions as, without preventing importation when prices are high, will secure in ordinary years a growth equal to the consumption.[11]

One objection however to systems of restriction must always remain. They are essentially unsocial. I certainly think that, in reference to the interests of a particular state, a restriction upon the importation of foreign corn may sometimes be advantageous; but I feel still more certain that in reference to the interests of Europe in general the most perfect freedom of trade in corn, as well as in every other commodity, would be the most advantageous. Such a perfect freedom, however, could hardly fail to be followed by a more free and equal distribution of capital, which, though it would greatly advance the riches and happiness of Europe, would unquestionably render some parts of it poorer and less populous than they are at present; and there is little reason to expect that individual states will ever consent to sacrifice the wealth within their own confines to the wealth of the world.

It is further to be observed, that, independently of more direct regulations, taxation alone produces a system of discouragements and encouragements which essentially interferes with the natural relations of commodities to each other; and as there is no hope of abolishing taxation, it may sometimes be only by a further interference that these natural relations can be restored.

A perfect freedom of trade therefore is a vision which it is to be feared can never be realized. But still it should be our object to make as near approaches to it as we can. It should always be considered as the great general rule. And when any deviations from it are proposed, those who propose them are bound clearly to make out the exception.

NOTES

1. Husbandry of Bengal, p. 108. Note. He observes in the text of the same page that the price of corn fluctuates much more than in Europe.
2. Garnier's edition of the *Wealth of Nations*, vol. ii. table, p. 188.
3. Œuvres de Turgot, tom. vi. p. 143. Edit. 1808.

4. These two circumstances essentially change the premises on which the question of a free importation, as applicable to a particular state, must rest.

5. No restrictions upon the importation of grain, however absurdly severe, could permanently maintain our corn and labour at a much higher price than in the rest of Europe, if such restrictions were essentially to interfere with the prosperity of our foreign commerce. When the money price of labour is high in any country, or, what is the same thing, when the value of money is low, nothing can prevent it from going out to find its level, but some comparative advantages, either natural or acquired, which enable such country to maintain the abundance of its exports, notwithstanding the high money price of its labour.

6. Vol. ii. b. iii c. 4. p. 137.

7. Vol. ii. b. iv. c. 8. p. 495.

8. According to the evidence before the House of Lords (Reports, p. 49), the freight and insurance alone on a quarter of corn were greater by 48 shillings in 1811 than in 1814. Without any artificial interference, then, it appears that war alone may occasion unavoidably a prodigious increase of price.

9. According to Mr. Tooke (*High and Low Prices*, p. 215), if the last war had found us with a growth beyond our consumption, we should have witnessed a totally different set of phenomena connected with prices. It will be found upon examination, that the prices of our corn led the way to the excess and diminution of our paper currency, rather than followed, although the prices of corn could never have been either so high or so low if this excess and diminution had not taken place.

10. Almost all the corn merchants who gave their evidence before the committees of the two houses in 1814 seemed fully aware of the low prices likely to be occasioned by an abundant crop in Europe, if our ports were open to receive it.

11. In the sixth number of the *Westminster Review*, in which prodigious stress is laid upon the necessary effect of the corn laws in occasioning great fluctuation, in the prices of corn, a table, said to be from the very highest mercantile authority, is given of the average prices of wheat at Rotterdam for each of the ten years ending with 1824. The purpose for which the table is produced, is to show the average price of wheat in Holland during these ten years; but it incidentally shows that, even in Holland, which in many respects must be peculiarly favourable to steady prices, a free trade in corn can by no means secure them.

In the year 1817, the price per last of 86 Winchester bushels was 574 guilders; and in 1824, it was only 147 guilders; a difference of nearly four times. During the same period of ten years the greatest variation in the average price of each year in England, was between 94s. 9d., which was the price in 1817, and 43s. 9d. which was the price in 1822, (Appendix to Mr. Tooke's work on High and Low Prices. Table xii. p. 31.)—a difference short of 2 1/5!!

It is repeated over and over again, apparently without the slightest reference to facts, that the freedom of the trade in corn would infallibly secure us from the possibility of a scarcity. The writer of the article *Corn Laws* in the supplement to the *Encyclopaedia Britannica* goes so far as to say, "it is constantly found that when the crops of one country fail, plenty reigns in some other quarter.... There is always abundance of food in the world. To enjoy a constant plenty, we have only to lay aside our prohibitions and restrictions, and cease to counteract the benevolent wisdom of Providence." The same kind of language is repeated in the Review above adverted to: "If there be a bad harvest," it is said, "in one country, there is a good one in another, and the surplus produce of the latter supplies the deficiency of the former, etc., etc." Now there are the best reasons for believing that these statements are decidedly contradicted by the most enlarged experience. In the first place, if they were true, and if the general plenty alluded to were only prevented by the want of a free trade in corn, we should necessarily see a great rise of prices in one country, contemporaneous with a great fall in others; but a slight glance at the prices of corn in the countries of the commercial world for the last one or two centuries will be sufficient to convince any impartial person that, on the contrary, there is a very remarkable sympathy of prices at the same periods, which is absolutely inconsistent the truth of the above statements. Secondly, all travellers who have paid any attention to the seasons, agree in stating that the same sort of weather often prevails in different countries at the same time. The peculiar and excessive heats of the very last summer not only prevailed generally over the greatest part of Europe, but extended even to America. Mr. Tooke, *On High and Low Prices*, (p. 247. 2nd Edit.) quotes a passage from Mr. Lowe's work on the Present State of England, in which he observes, that "The public, particularly the untravelled part of the public, are hardly of the similarity of temperature prevailing throughout what may be called the corn-country of Europe, we mean Great Britain, Ireland, the North of France, the Netherlands, Denmark, the northwest of Germany, and in some measure Poland and the northeast of Germany." He then goes on to state instances of scarcity in different countries of Europe at the same time. And in the justness of these remarks, on the prevalence of a general similarity of seasons in Europe within certain latitudes, Mr. Tooke says he perfectly concurs. Many of the corn-merchants examined before the Committees of the two Houses, both in 1814 and 1821, expressed similar opinions; and I do not recollect a single instance of the opinion, that good and bad harvests generally balance each other in different countries, being stated by any person who had been in a situation to observe the facts. Such statements, therefore, must be considered as mere assertions quite unsupported by the least shadow of proof.

I am very far however from meaning to say that the circumstance of different countries having often an abundance or deficiency of corn at the same time, though it must prevent the possibility of steady prices, is a decisive reason against the abolition or alteration of the corn-laws. The most powerful of all the arguments against restrictions is their unsocial tendency, and the acknowledged injury which they must do to the interests of the commercial world in general. The weight of this argument is increased rather than diminished by the numbers which may suffer from scarcity at the same time. And at a period when our ministers are the most laudably setting an example of a more liberal system of commercial policy, it would be greatly desirable that foreign nations should not have so marked an exception as our present corn-laws to cast in our teeth. A duty on importation not too high, and a bounty nearly such as was recommended by Mr. Ricardo, would probably be best suited to our present situation, and best secure steady prices. A duty on foreign corn would resemble the duties laid by other countries on our manufactures as objects of taxation, and would not in the same manner impeach the principles of free trade.

But whatever system we may adopt, it is essential to a sound determination, and highly useful in preventing disappointments, that all the arguments both for and against corn-laws should be thoroughly and impartially considered; and it is because on a calm, and, as far as I can judge, an impartial review of the arguments of this chapter, they still appear to me of weight sufficient to deserve such consideration, and not as a kind of protest against the abolition or change of the corn-laws, that I republish them in another edition.

13

Of Increasing Wealth, as It Affects the Condition of the Poor

The professed object of Adam Smith's *Inquiry* is *the Nature and Causes of the Wealth of Nations*. There is another, however, still more interesting, which he occasionally mixes with it—the causes which affect the happiness and comfort of the lower orders of society, which in every nation form the most numerous class. These two subjects are, no doubt, nearly connected; but the nature and extent of this connexion, and the mode in which increasing wealth operates on the condition of the poor, have not been stated with sufficient correctness and precision.

Adam Smith, in his chapter on the wages of labour, considers every increase in the stock or revenue of the society as an increase in the funds for the maintenance of labour; and having before laid down the position that the demand for those who live by wages can only increase in proportion to the increase of the funds for the payment of wages, the conclusion naturally follows, that every increase of wealth tends to increase the demand for labour and to improve the condition of the lower classes of society.[1]

Upon a nearer examination, however, it will be found that the funds for the maintenance of labour do not necessarily increase with the increase of wealth, and very rarely increase in proportion to it; and that the condition of the lower classes of society does not depend exclusively upon the increase of the funds for the maintenance of labour, or the power of supporting a greater number of labourers.

Adam Smith defines the wealth of a state to be the annual produce of its land and labour. This definition evidently includes manufactured produce as well as the produce of the land. Now, upon the supposition that a nation, from peculiar situation and circumstances, was unable to procure an additional quantity of food, it is obvious that the produce of its labour would not necessarily come to a stand, although the produce of its land or its power of importing corn were incapable of further increase. If the materials of manufactures could be obtained either at home or from abroad, improved skill and machinery might work them up to a greatly increased amount with the same number of hands, and even the number of hands might be considerably increased by an increased taste for manufactures, compared with war and menial service, and by the employment consequently of a greater proportion of the whole population in manufacturing and commercial labour.

That such a case does not frequently occur will be most readily allowed. It is not only however possible, but forms the specific limit to the increase of population in the natural progress of cultivation, with which limit, the limit to the further progress of wealth is obviously not contemporary. But though cases of this kind do not often occur, because these limits are seldom reached; yet approximations to them are constantly taking place, and in the usual progress of improvement the increase of wealth and capital is rarely accompanied with a proportionately increased power of supporting an additional number of labourers.

Some ancient nations, which, according to the accounts we have received of them, possessed but an inconsiderable quantity of manufacturing and commercial capital, appear to have cultivated their lands highly by means of an agrarian division of property, and were unquestionably very populous. In such countries, though full of people already, there would evidently be room for a very great increase of capital and riches; but, allowing all the weight that is in any degree probable to the increased production or importation of food occasioned by the stimulus of additional capital, there would evidently not be room for a proportionate increase of the means of subsistence.

If we compare the early state of our most flourishing European kingdoms with their present state, we shall find this conclusion confirmed almost universally by experience.

Adam Smith, in treating of the different progress of opulence in different nations, says, that England, since the time of Elizabeth, has been continually advancing in commerce and manufactures. He then adds, "The cultivation and improvement of the country has no doubt been gradually advancing. But it seems to have followed slowly and at a distance the more rapid progress of commerce and manufactures. The greater part of the country must probably have been cultivated before the reign of Elizabeth, and a very great part of it still remains uncultivated, and the cultivation of the far greater part is much inferior to what it might be."[2] The same observation is applicable to most of the other countries of Europe. The best land would naturally be the first occupied. This land, even with that sort of indolent cultivation and great waste of labour which particularly marked the feudal times, would be capable of supporting a considerable population; and on the increase of capital, the increasing taste for conveniences and luxuries, combined with the decreasing power of production in the new land to be taken into cultivation, would naturally and necessarily direct the greatest part of this new capital to commerce and manufactures, and occasion a more rapid increase of wealth than of population.

The population of England accordingly in the reign of Elizabeth appears to have been nearly five millions, which would not be very far short of the half of what it is at present (1811); but when we consider the very great proportion which the products of commercial and manufacturing industry now bear to the quantity of food raised for human consumption, it is probably a very low estimate to say that the mass of wealth or the stock and revenue of the country must, independently of any change in the value of the circulating medium, have increased above four times. Few of the other countries in Europe have increased to the same extent in commercial and manufacturing wealth as England; but as far as they have proceeded in this career, all appearances clearly indicate that the progress of their general wealth has been greater than the progress of their means of supporting an additional population.

That every increase of the stock or revenue of a nation cannot be considered as an increase of the real funds for the maintenance of labour will appear in a striking light in the case of China.

Adam Smith observes, that China has probably long been as rich as the nature of her laws and institutions will admit; but intimates that, with other laws and institutions, and if foreign commerce were held in honour, she might still be much richer.

If trade and foreign commerce were held in great honour in China, it is evident that, from the great number of her labourers and the cheapness of her labour, she might work up manufactures for foreign sale to a great amount. It is equally evident that, from the great bulk of provisions and the prodigious extent of her inland territory, she could not in return import such a quantity as would be any sensible addition to her means of subsistence. Her immense amount of manufactures, therefore, she would either consume at home, or exchange for luxuries collected from all parts of the world. At present the country appears to be over-peopled compared with what its stock can employ, and no labour is spared in the production of food. An immense capital could not be employed in China in preparing manufactures for foreign trade, without altering this state of things, and taking off some labourers from agriculture, which might have a tendency to diminish the produce of the country. Allowing, however, that this would be made up, and, indeed, more than made up, by the beneficial effects of improved skill and economy of labour in the cultivation of the poorest lands, yet, as the quantity of subsistence could be but little increased, the demand for manufactures which would raise the price of labour, would necessarily be followed by a proportionate rise in the price of provisions, and the labourer would be able to command but little more food than before. The country would, however, obviously be advancing in wealth; the exchangeable value of the annual produce of its land and labour would be annually augmented; yet the real funds for the maintenance of labour would be nearly stationary. The argument perhaps appears clearer when applied to China, because it is generally allowed that its wealth has been long stationary, and its soil cultivated nearly to the utmost.[3]

In all those cases, it is not on account of any undue preference given to commerce and manufactures, compared with agriculture, that the effect just described takes place, but merely because the powers of the earth in the production of food have narrower limits than the skill and tastes of mankind in giving value to raw materials, and consequently in the approach towards the limits of subsistence there is naturally more room, and consequently more encouragement, for the increase of the one species of wealth than of the other.

It must be allowed then, that the funds for the maintenance of labour do not necessarily increase with the increase of wealth, and very rarely increase in proportion to it.

But the condition of the lower classes of society certainly does not depend exclusively upon the increase of the funds for the maintenance of labour, or the means of supporting more labourers. That these means form always a very powerful ingredient in the condition of the labouring classes, and the main ingredient in the increase of population, is unquestionable. But, in the first place, the comforts of the lower classes of society do not depend solely upon food, nor even upon strict necessaries; and they cannot be considered as in a good state unless they have the command of some conveniences and even luxuries. Secondly, the tendency in population fully to keep pace with the means of subsistence must in general prevent the increase of these means from having a great and permanent effect in improving the condition of the poor. And, thirdly, the cause which has the most lasting effect in improving the situation of the lower classes of society depends chiefly upon the conduct and prudence of the individuals themselves, and is, therefore, not immediately and necessarily connected with an increase in the means of subsistence.

With a view, therefore, to the other causes which affect the condition of the labouring classes, as well as the increase of the means of subsistence, it may be desirable to trace more particularly the mode in which increasing wealth operates, and to state both the disadvantages as well as the advantages with which it is accompanied.

In the natural and regular progress of a country to a state of great wealth and population, there are two disadvantages to which the lower classes of society seem necessarily to be subjected.

The first is, a diminished power of supporting children under the existing habits of the society with respect to the necessaries of life. And the second, the employment of a larger proportion of the population in occupations less favourable to health, and more exposed to fluctuations of demand and unsteadiness of wages.

A diminished power of supporting children is an absolutely unavoidable consequence of the progress of a country towards the utmost limits of its population. If we allow that the power of a given quantity of territory to produce food has some limit, we must allow that as this limit is approached, and the increase of population becomes slower and slower, the power of supporting children will be less and less, till finally, when the increase of produce stops, it becomes only sufficient to maintain, on an average, families of such a size as will not allow of a further addition of numbers. This state of things is generally accompanied by a fall in the corn price of labour; but should this effect be prevented by the prevalence of prudential habits among the lower classes of society, still the result just described must take place; and though, from the powerful operation of the preventive check to increase, the wages of labour estimated even in corn might not be low, yet it is obvious that, in this case, the power of supporting children would rather be nominal than real; and the moment this power began to be exercised to its apparent extent, it would cease to exist.

The second disadvantage to which the lower classes of society are subjected in the progressive increase of wealth is, that a larger portion of them is engaged in unhealthy occupations, and in employments in which the wages of labour are exposed to much greater fluctuations than in agriculture, and the simpler kinds of domestic trade.

On the state of the poor employed in manufactories with respect to health, and the fluctuations of wages, I will beg leave to quote a passage from Dr. Aikin's Description of the Country round Manchester:

"The invention and improvements of machines to shorten labour have had a surprising influence to extend our trade, and also to call in hands from all parts, particularly children for the cotton-mills. It is the wise plan of Providence, that in this life there shall be no good without its attendant inconvenience. There are many which are too obvious in these cotton-mills, and similar factories, which counteract that increase of population usually consequent on the improved facility of labour. In these, children of a very tender age are employed, many of them collected from the workhouses in London and Westminster, and transported in crowds as apprentices to masters resident many hundred miles distant, where they serve unknown, unprotected and forgotten by those to whose care nature or the laws had consigned them. These children are usually too long confined to work in close rooms, often during the whole night. The air they breathe from the oil, etc. employed in the machinery, and other circumstances, is injurious; little attention is paid to their cleanliness; and frequent changes from a warm and dense to a cold and thin atmosphere are pre-disposing causes to sickness and debility, and particularly to the epidemic fever which is so generally to be met with in these factories. It is also much to be questioned if society does not receive detriment from the manner in which children are thus employed during their early years. They are not generally strong to labour, or capable of pursuing any other branch of business when the term of their apprenticeship expires. The females are wholly uninstructed in sewing, knitting, and other domestic affairs requisite to make them notable and frugal wives and mothers. This is a very great misfortune to them and to the public, as is sadly proved by a comparison of the families of labourers in husbandry and those of manufacturers in general. In the former we meet with neatness, cleanliness, and comfort; in the latter with filth, rags, and poverty, although their wages may be nearly double to those of the husbandman. It must be added, that the want of early religious instruction and example, and the numerous and indiscriminate association in these buildings, are very unfavourable to their future conduct in life."[4]

In the same work it appears that the register for the collegiate church of Manchester, from Christmas, 1793, to Christmas 1794, showed a decrease of 168 marriages, 538 christenings, and 250 burials. In the parish of Rochdale, in the neighbourhood, a still more melancholy reduction in proportion to the number of people took place. In 1792 the births were 746, the burials 646, and the marriages 339. In 1794 the births were 373, the burials 671, and the marriages 199. The cause of this sudden check to population was the failure of demand and of commercial credit which occurred at the commencement of the war, and such a check could not have taken place in so sudden a manner without the most severe distress, occasioned by the sudden reduction of wages.

In addition to the fluctuations arising from the changes from peace to war and from war to peace, it is well known how subject particular manufactures are to fail from the caprices of taste. The weavers of Spitalfields were plunged into the most severe distress by the fashion of muslins instead of silks; and great numbers of workmen in Sheffield and Birmingham were for a time thrown out of employment owing to the adoption of shoe strings and covered buttons, instead of buckles and metal buttons. Our manufactures, taken in the mass, have increased with prodigious rapidity, but in particular places they have failed; and the parishes where this has happened are invariably loaded with a crowd of poor in the most distressed and miserable condition.

In the evidence brought before the House of Lords during the inquiries which preceded the Corn-Bill of 1815, various accounts are produced from different manufactories, intended to show that the high price of corn has rather the effect of lowering than of raising the price of manufacturing labour.[5] Adam Smith has clearly and correctly stated that the money price of labour depends upon the money price of provisions, and the state of the demand and the supply of labour. And he shows how much he thinks it is occasionally affected by the latter cause, by explaining in what manner it may vary in an opposite direction from the price of provisions during the pressure of a scarcity. The accounts brought before the House of Lords are a striking illustration of this part of his proposition; but they certainly do not prove the incorrectness of the other part of it, as it is quite obvious that, whatever may take place for a few years, the supply of manufacturing labour cannot possibly be continued in the market unless the natural or necessary price, that is, the price necessary to continue it in the market, be paid, and this of course is not done unless the money price be so proportioned to the price of provisions that labourers are enabled to bring up families of such a size as will supply the number of hands required.

But though these accounts do not in any degree invalidate the usual doctrines respecting labour, or the statements of Adam Smith, they show very clearly the great fluctuations to which the condition of the manufacturing labourer is subjected.

In looking over these accounts it will be found that in some cases the price of weaving has fallen a third, or nearly one-half, at the same time that the price of wheat has risen a third, or nearly one-half; and yet these proportions do not always express the full amount of the fluctuations, as it sometimes happens that when the price is low, the state of the demand will not allow of the usual number of hours of working; and when the price is high, it will admit of extra hours.

That from the same causes there are sometimes variations of a similar kind in the price of task-work in agriculture will be readily admitted; but, in the first place, they do not appear to be nearly so considerable; and secondly, the great mass of agricultural labourers is employed by the day, and a sudden and general fall in the money price of agricultural day-labour is an event of extremely rare occurrence.[6]

It must be allowed then, that in the natural and usual progress of wealth, the means of marrying early and supporting a family are diminished, and a greater proportion of the population is engaged in employments less favourable to health and morals, and more subject to fluctuations in the price of labour, than the population employed in agriculture.

These are no doubt considerable disadvantages, and they would be sufficient to render the progress of riches decidedly unfavourable to the condition of the poor, if they were not counteracted by advantages which nearly, if not fully, counterbalance them.

And, first, it is obvious that the profits of stock are that source of revenue from which the middle classes are chiefly maintained; and the increase of capital, which is both the cause and effect of increasing riches, may be said to be the efficient cause of the emancipation of the great body of society from a dependence on the landlords. In a country of limited extent, consisting of fertile land divided into large properties, as long as the capital remains inconsiderable, the structure of society is most unfavourable to liberty and good government. This was exactly the state of Europe in the feudal times. The landlords could in no other way spend their incomes than by maintaining a great number of idle followers; and it was by the growth of capital in all the employments to which it is directed, that the pernicious power of the landlords was destroyed, and their dependent followers were turned into merchants, manufacturers, tradesmen, farmers, and independent labourers;—a change of prodigious advantage to the great body of society, including the labouring classes.

Secondly; in the natural progress of cultivation and wealth, the production of an additional quantity of corn will require more labour, while, at the same time, from the accumulation and better distribution of capital, the continual improvements made in machinery, and the facilities opened to foreign commerce, manufactures and foreign commodities will be produced or purchased with less labour; and consequently a given quantity of corn will command a much greater quantity of manufactures and foreign commodities than while the country was poor. Although, therefore, the labourer may earn less corn than before, the superior value which every portion which he does not consume in kind will have in the purchase of conveniences, may more than counterbalance this diminution. He will not indeed have the same power of maintaining a large family; but with a small family he may be better lodged and clothed, and better able to command the decencies and comforts of life.

Thirdly; it seems to be proved by experience, that the labouring classes of society seldom acquire a decided taste for conveniences and comforts till they become plentiful compared with food, which they never do till food has become in some degree scarce. If the labourer can obtain the bill support of himself and family by two or three days' labour; and if, to furnish himself with conveniences and comforts, he must work three or four days more, he will generally think the sacrifice too great compared with the objects to be obtained, which are not strictly necessary to him, and will therefore often prefer the luxury of idleness to the luxury of improved lodging and clothing. This is said by Humboldt to be particularly the case in some parts of South America, and to a certain extent prevails in Ireland, India, and all countries where food is plentiful compared with capital and manufactured commodities. On the other hand, if the main part of the labourer's time be occupied in procuring food, habits of industry are necessarily generated, and the remaining time, which is but inconsiderable compared with the commodities it will purchase, is seldom grudged. It is under these circumstances, particularly when combined with a good government, that the labouring classes of society are most likely to acquire a decided taste for the conveniences and comforts of life; and this taste may be such as even to prevent, after a certain period, a further fall in the corn price of labour. But if the corn price of labour continues tolerably high while the relative value of commodities compared with corn falls very considerably, the labourer is placed in a most favourable situation. Owing to his decided taste for conveniences and comforts, the good corn wages of labour will not generally lead to early marriages; yet in individual cases, where large families occur, there will be the means of supporting them independently, by the sacrifice of the accustomed conveniences and comforts; and thus the poorest of the lower classes will rarely be stinted in food, while the great mass of them will not only have sufficient means of subsistence, but be able to command no inconsiderable quantity of those conveniences and comforts, which, at the same time that they gratify a natural or acquired want, tend unquestionably to improve the mind and elevate the character.

On an attentive review, then, of the effects of increasing wealth on the condition of the poor, it appears that, although such an increase does not imply a proportionate increase of the funds for the maintenance of labour, yet it brings with it advantages to the lower classes of society which may fully counterbalance the disadvantages with which it is attended; and, strictly speaking, the good or bad condition of the poor is not necessarily connected with any particular stage in the progress of society to its full complement of wealth. A rapid increase of wealth indeed, whether it consists principally in additions to the means of subsistence or to the stock of conveniences and comforts, will always, *caeteris paribus*, have a favourable effect on the poor; but the influence even of this cause is greatly modified and altered by other circumstances, and nothing but the union of individual prudence with the skill and industry which produce wealth can permanently secure to the lower classes of society that share of it which it is, on every account, so desirable that they should possess.

NOTES

1. Vol i. book i. c. 8.
2. Vol. ii. book iv. c. 4. p. 133.
3. How far this latter opinion is to be depended upon it is not very easy to say. Improved skill and a saving of labour would certainly enable the Chinese to cultivate some lands with advantage which they cannot cultivate now, but the more general use of horses, instead of men, might prevent this extended cultivation from giving any encouragement to an increase of people.
4. P. 219. Dr. Aikin says that endeavours have been made to remedy these evils, which in some factories have been attended with success. And it is very satisfactory to be able to add, that, since this account was written, the situation of the children employed in the cotton-mills has been further very essentially improved, partly by the interference of the legislature, and partly by the humane and liberal exertions of individuals.
5. Reports, p. 51.
6. Almost the only instance on record in this country is that which has lately taken place (1815 and 1816), occasioned by an unparalleled fall in the exchangeable value of the raw produce, which has necessarily disabled the holders of it from employing the same quantity of labour at the same price.

14

General Observations

It has been observed, that many countries at the period of their greatest degree of populousness have lived in the greatest plenty, and have been able to export corn; but at other periods, when their population was very low, have lived in continual poverty and want, and have been obliged to import corn. Egypt, Palestine, Rome, Sicily and Spain are cited as particular exemplifications of this fact; and it has been inferred that an increase of population in any state, not cultivated to the utmost, will tend rather to augment than diminish the relative plenty of the whole society: and that, as Lord Kaimes observes, a country cannot easily become too populous for agriculture; because agriculture has the signal property of producing food in proportion to the number of consumers.[1]

The general facts, from which these inferences are drawn, there is no reason to doubt; but the inferences by no means follow from the premises. It is the nature of agriculture, (as it has before been observed), particularly when well conducted, to produce support for a considerable number above that which it employs; and consequently if these members of the society, as Sir James Steuart calls them, the free hands, do not increase so as to reach the limit of the number which can be supported by the surplus produce, the whole population of the country may continue for ages increasing with the improving state of agriculture, and yet always be able to export corn. But this increase, after a certain period, will be very different from the natural and unrestricted increase of population; it will merely follow the slow augmentation of produce from the gradual improvement of agriculture; and population will still be checked by the difficulty of procuring subsistence. The precise measure of the population in a country thus circumstanced will not indeed be the quantity of food, because part of it is exported, but the quantity of employment. The state of this employment however will necessarily regulate the wages of labour, on which the power of the lower classes of people to procure food depends; and according as the employment of the country is increasing, whether slowly or rapidly, these wages will be such, as either to check or encourage early marriages; such, as to enable a labourer to support only two or three, or as many as five or six children.

In stating that in this, and all the other cases and systems which have been considered, the progress of population will be mainly regulated and limited by the real wages of labour, it is necessary to remark that, practically, the current wages of day-labour estimated in the necessaries of life do not always correctly represent the quantity of these necessaries which it is in the power of the lower classes to consume; and that sometimes the error is in excess and sometimes in defect.

In a state of things when the prices of corn and of all sorts of commodities are rising, the money wages of labour do not always rise in proportion; but this apparent disadvantage to the labouring classes is sometimes more than counterbalanced by the plenty of employment, the quantity of task-work that can be obtained, and the opportunity given to women and children to add considerably to the earnings of the family. In this case, the power of the labouring classes to command the necessaries of life is much greater than is implied by the current rate of their wages, and will of course have a proportionably greater effect on the population.

On the other hand, when prices are generally falling, it often happens that the current rate of wages does not fall in proportion; but this apparent advantage is in the same manner often more than counterbalanced by the scarcity of work, and the impossibility of finding employment for all the members of a labourer's family who are able and willing to be industrious. In this case, the powers of the labouring classes to command the necessaries of life will evidently be less than is implied by the current rate of their wages.

In the same manner parish allowances distributed to families, the habitual practice of task-work, and the frequent employment of women and children, will affect population like a rise in the real wages of labour. And, on the other hand, the paying of every sort of labour by the day, the absence of employment for women and children, and the practice among labourers of not working more than three or four days in the week, either from inveterate indolence, or any other cause, will affect population like a low price of labour.

In all these cases the real earnings of the labouring classes throughout the year, estimated in food, are different from the apparent wages; but it will evidently be the average earnings of the families of the labouring classes throughout the year on which the encouragement to marriage, and the power of supporting children, will depend, and not merely the wages of day-labour estimated in food.

An attention to this very essential point will explain the reason why, in many instances, the progress of population does not appear to be regulated by what are usually called the real wages of labour; and why this progress may occasionally be greater, when the price of a day's labour will purchase rather less than the medium quantity of corn, than when it will purchase rather more.

In our own country, for instance, about the middle of the last century, the price of corn was very low; and, for twenty years together, from 1735 to 1755 a day's labour would, on an average, purchase a peck of wheat. During this period, population increased at a moderate rate; but not by any means with the same rapidity as from 1790 to 1811, when the average wages of day-labour would not in general purchase so much as a peck of wheat. In the latter case, however, there was a more rapid accumulation of capital, and a greater demand for labour; and though the continued rise of provisions still kept them rather ahead of wages, yet the fuller employment for every body that would work, the greater quantity of task-work done, the higher relative value of corn compared with manufactures, the increased use of potatoes, and the greater sums distributed in parish allowances, unquestionably gave to the lower classes of society the power of commanding a greater quantity of food, and will account for the more rapid increase of population in the latter period, in perfect consistency with the general principle.

On similar grounds, if, in some warm climates and rich soils, where corn is cheap, the quantity of food earned by a day's labour be such as to promise a more rapid progress in population than is really known to take place, the fact will be fully accounted for, if it be found that inveterate habits of indolence fostered by a vicious government, and a slack demand for labour, prevent any thing like constant employment.[2] It would of course require high corn wages of day-labour even to keep up the supply of a stationary population, where the days of working would only amount to half of the year.

In the case also of the prevalence of prudential habits, and a decided taste for the conveniences and comforts of life, as, according to the supposition, these habits and tastes do not operate as an encouragement to early marriages, and are not in fact spent almost entirely in the purchase of corn, it is quite consistent with the general principles laid down, that the population should not proceed at the same rate as is usual, *caeteris paribus*, in other countries, where the corn wages of labour are equally high.

The quantity of employment in any country will not of course vary from year to year, in the same manner as the quantity of produce must necessarily do, from the variation of the seasons; and consequently the check from want of employment will be much more steady in its operation, and much more favourable to the lower classes of people, than the check from the immediate want of food. The first will be the preventive check; the second the positive check. When the demand for labour is either stationary, or increasing very slowly, people not seeing any employment open by which they can support a family, or the wages of common labour being inadequate to this purpose, will of course be deterred from marrying. But if a demand for labour continue increasing with some rapidity, although the supply of food be uncertain, on account of variable seasons and a dependence on other countries, the population will evidently go on, till it is positively checked by famine or the diseases arising from severe want.

Scarcity and extreme poverty, therefore, may or may not accompany an increasing population, according to circumstances:

but they must necessarily accompany a permanently declining population; because there never has been, nor probably ever will be, any other cause than want of food, which makes the population of a country permanently decline. In the numerous instances of depopulation which occur in history, the causes may always be traced to the want of industry or the ill direction of that industry, arising from violence, bad government, ignorance, etc., which first occasion a want of food, and of course depopulation follows. When Rome adopted the custom of importing all her corn, and laying all Italy into pasture, she soon declined in population. The causes of the depopulation of Egypt and Turkey have already been adverted to; and in the case of Spain, it was certainly not the numerical loss of people occasioned by the expulsion of the Moors, but the industry and capital thus expelled, which permanently injured her population. When a country has been depopulated by violent causes, if a bad government with its usual concomitant insecurity of property ensue, (which has generally been the case in all those countries which are now less peopled than formerly), neither the food nor the population can recover itself; and the inhabitants will probably live in severe want. But when an accidental depopulation takes place in a country which was before populous and industrious, and in the habit of exporting corn, if the remaining inhabitants be left at liberty to exert, and do exert, their industry in the same direction as before, it is a strange idea to entertain, that they would then be unable to supply themselves with corn in the same plenty; particularly as the diminished numbers would of course cultivate principally the more fertile parts of their territory, and not be obliged, as in their more populous state, to apply to ungrateful soils. Countries in this situation would evidently have the same chance of recovering their former number, as they had originally of reaching this number; and indeed if absolute populousness were necessary to relative plenty, as some agriculturists have supposed,[3] it would be impossible for new colonies to increase with the same rapidity as old states.

The prejudices on the subject of population bear a very striking resemblance to the old prejudices about specie; and we know how slowly and with what difficulty these last have yielded to juster conceptions. Politicians, observing that states which were powerful and prosperous were, almost invariably populous, have mistaken an effect for a cause, and have concluded, that their population was the cause of their prosperity, instead of their prosperity being the cause of their population; as the old political economists concluded that the abundance of specie was the cause of national wealth, instead of being the effect of it. The annual produce of the land and labour, in both these instances, became in consequence a secondary consideration; and its increase, it was conceived, would naturally follow the increase of specie in the one case, or of population in the other. The folly of endeavouring by forcible means to increase the quantity of specie in any country, and the absolute impossibility of accumulating it beyond a certain level by any human laws that can be devised, are now fully established, and have been completely exemplified in the instances of Spain and Portugal. But the illusion still remains respecting population; and under this impression almost every political treatise has abounded in proposals to encourage population, with little or no comparative reference to the means of its support. Yet surely the folly of endeavouring to increase the quantity of specie in any country, without an increase of the commodities which it is to circulate, is not greater than that of endeavouring to increase the number of people, without an increase of the food which is to maintain them; and it will be found that the level, above which no human laws can raise the population of a country, is a limit more fixed and impassable than the limit to the accumulation of specie. However improbable in fact, it is possible to conceive that means might be invented of retaining a quantity of specie in a state, greatly beyond what was demanded by the produce of its land and labour, and the relative state of other countries. But when by great encouragements population has been raised to such a height, that this produce is meted out to each individual in the smallest portions that can support life, no stretch of ingenuity can even conceive the possibility of going farther.

It has appeared, I think, clearly, in the review of different societies given in the former part of this work, that those countries, the inhabitants of which were sunk in the most barbarous ignorance, or oppressed by the most cruel tyranny, however low they might be in actual population, were very populous in proportion to their means of subsistence; and upon the slightest failure of the seasons generally suffered the severities of want. Ignorance and despotism seem to have no tendency to destroy the passion which prompts to increase; but they effectually destroy the checks to it from reason and foresight. The improvident barbarian who thinks only of his present wants, or the miserable peasant who, from his political situation, feels little security of reaping what he has sown, will seldom be deterred from gratifying his passions by the prospect of inconveniences, which cannot be expected to press on him under three or four years. But though this want of foresight, which is fostered by ignorance and despotism, tends thus rather to encourage the procreation of children, it is absolutely fatal to the industry which is to support them. Industry cannot exist without foresight and security. The indolence of the savage is well known; and the poor Egyptian or Abyssinian farmer without capital, who rents land which is let out yearly to the highest bidder, and who is constantly subject to the demands of his tyrannical masters, to the casual plunder of an enemy, and not unfrequently to the violation of his miserable contract, can have no heart to be industrious, and, if he had, could not exercise that industry with success. Even poverty itself, which appears to be the great spur to industry, when it has once passed certain limits, almost ceases to operate. The indigence which is hopeless destroys all vigorous exertion, and confines the efforts to what is sufficient for bare existence. It is the hope of bettering our condition, and the fear of want, rather than want itself, that is the best stimulus to industry; and its most constant and best directed efforts will almost invariably be found among a class of people above the class of the wretchedly poor.

The effect of ignorance and oppression will therefore always be to destroy the springs of industry, and consequently to diminish the annual produce of the land and labour in any country; and this diminution will inevitably be followed by a decrease of the population, in spite of the birth of any number of children whatever annually. The desire of immediate gratification, and the removal of the restraints to it from prudence, may perhaps, in such countries, prompt universally to early marriages; but when these habits have once reduced the people to the lowest possible state of poverty, they can evidently have no further effect upon the population. Their only effect must be on the degree of mortality; and there is no doubt, that, if we could obtain accurate bills of mortality in those southern countries, where very few women remain unmarried, and all marry young, the proportion of the annual deaths would be 1 in 17, 18, or 20, instead of 1 in 34, 36, or 40, as in European states where the preventive check operates.

That an increase of population, when it follows in its natural order, is both a great positive good in itself, and absolutely necessary to a further increase in the annual produce of the land and labour of any country, I should be the last to deny. The only question is, what is the order of its progress? In this point Sir James Steuart, who has in general explained this subject so well, appears to me to have fallen into an error. He determines, that multiplication is the efficient cause of agriculture, and not agriculture of multiplication.[4] But though it may be allowed, that the increase of people, beyond what could easily subsist on the natural fruits of the earth, first prompted man to till the ground; and that the view of maintaining a family, or of obtaining some valuable consideration in exchange for the products of agriculture, still operates as the principal stimulus to cultivation; yet it is clear that these products, in their actual state, must be beyond the lowest wants of the existing population, before any permanent increase can possibly be supported. We know, that a multiplication of births has in numberless instances taken place, which has produced no effect upon agriculture, and has merely been followed by an increase of diseases; but perhaps there is no instance, where a permanent increase of agriculture has not effected a permanent increase of population somewhere or other. Consequently, agriculture may with more propriety be termed the efficient cause of population, than population of agriculture;[5] though they certainly re-act upon each other, and are mutually necessary to each other's support. This indeed seems to be the hinge on which the subject turns; and all the prejudices respecting population have, perhaps, arisen from a mistake about the order of precedence.

The author of *L'Ami des Hommes*, in a chapter on the effects of a decay of agriculture upon population, acknowledges that he had fallen into a fundamental error in considering population as the source of revenue; and that he was afterwards fully convinced that revenue was the source of population.[6] From a want of attention to this most important distinction, statesmen, in pursuit of the desirable object of population, have been led to encourage early marriages, to reward the fathers of families, and to disgrace celibacy; but this, as the same author justly observes, is to dress and water a piece of land without sowing it, and yet to expect a crop.

What is here said of the order of precedence with respect to agriculture and population, does not invalidate what was said in an earlier part of this work on the tendency to an oscillation or alternation in the increase of population and food in the natural course of their progress. In this progress nothing is more usual than for the population to increase at certain periods faster than food; indeed it is a part of the general principle that it should do so; and when the money wages of labour are prevented from falling by the employment of the increasing population in manufactures, the rise in the price of corn which the increased competition for it occasions is practically the most natural and frequent stimulus to agriculture. But then it must be recollected that the greater relative increase of population absolutely implies a previous increase of food at some time or other greater than the lowest wants of the people. Without this, the population could not possibly have gone forward.[7]

Universally, when the population of a country is for a longer or shorter time stationary, owing to the low corn wages of labour, a case which is not unfrequent, it is obvious that nothing but a previous increase of food, or at least an increase of the portion awarded to the labourer, can enable the population again to proceed forwards.

And, in the same manner, with a view to any essential improvement in the condition of the labourer, which is to give him a greater command over the means of comfortable subsistence, it is absolutely necessary that, setting out from the lowest point, the increase of food must precede and be greater than the increase of population.

Strictly speaking then, as man cannot live without food, there can be no doubt that in the order of precedence food must take the lead; although when, from the state of cultivation and other causes, the average quantity of food awarded to the labourer is considerably more than sufficient to maintain a stationary population, it is quite natural that the diminution of this quantity, from the tendency of population to increase, should be one of the most powerful and constant stimulants to agriculture.

It is worthy also of remark that on this account a stimulus to the increase of agriculture is much more easy when, from the prevalence of prudential restraint, or any other cause, the labourer is well paid; as in this case a rise in the price of corn, occasioned either by the increase of population or a foreign demand, will increase for a time the profits of the farmer, and often enable him to make permanent improvements; whereas, when the labourer is paid so scantily that his wages will not allow even of any temporary diminution without a diminution of population, the increase of cultivation and population must from the first be accompanied with a fall of profits. The prevalence of the preventive check to population and the good average wages of the labourer will rather promote than prevent that occasional increase and decrease of them, which as a stimulus seems to be favourable to the increase both of food and population.

Among the other prejudices which have prevailed on the subject of populations it has been generally thought that, while there is either waste among the rich, or land remaining uncultivated in any country, the complaints for want of food cannot be justly founded; or at least that the pressure of distress upon the poor is to be attributed to the ill conduct of the higher classes of society and the bad management of the land. The real effect however of these two circumstances is merely to narrow the limit of the actual population; but they have little or no influence on what may be called the average pressure of distress on the poorer members of society. If our ancestors had been so frugal and industrious, and had transmitted such habits to their posterity, that nothing superfluous was now consumed by the higher classes, no horses were used for pleasure, and no land was left uncultivated, a striking difference would appear in the state of the actual population; but probably none whatever in the state of the lower classes of people, with respect to the price of labour, and the facility of supporting a family. The waste among the rich, and the horses kept for pleasure, have indeed a little the effect of the consumption of grain in distilleries, noticed before with regard to China. On the supposition, that the food consumed in this manner may be withdrawn on the occasion of a scarcity, and be applied to the relief of the poor, they operate certainly, as far as they go, like granaries, which are only opened at the time that they are most wanted, and must therefore tend rather to benefit than to injure the lower classes of society.

With regard to uncultivated land, it is evident that its effect upon the poor is neither to injure nor to benefit them. The sudden cultivation of it will indeed tend to improve their condition for a time, and the neglect of lands before cultivated will certainly make their situation worse for a certain period; but when no changes of this kind are going forward, the effect of uncultivated land on the lower classes operates merely like the possession of a smaller territory. It may indeed be a point of some importance to the poor, whether a country be in the habit of exporting or importing corn; but this point is not necessarily connected with the complete or incomplete cultivation of the whole territory, but depends upon the proportion of the surplus produce to those who are supported by it; and in fact this proportion is generally the greatest, in countries which have not yet completed the cultivation of all their territory. If every inch of land in this country were well cultivated, there would be no reason to expect, merely from this circumstance, that we should be able to export corn. Our power in this respect would depend entirely on the proportion of the surplus produce to the commercial population: and this of course would in its turn depend on the direction of capital to agriculture or commerce.

It is not probable that any country with a large territory should ever be completely cultivated: and I am inclined to think that we often draw very inconsiderate conclusions against the industry and government of states from the appearance of uncultivated lands in them. It seems to be the clear and express duty of every government to remove all obstacles and give every facility to the inclosure and cultivation of land; but when this has been done, the rest must be left to the operation of individual interest; and upon this principle it cannot be expected that any new land should be brought into cultivation, the manure and the labour necessary for which might be employed to greater advantage on the improvement of land already in cultivation; and this is a case which will very frequently occur. In countries possessed of a large territory, there will always be a great quantity of land of a middling quality, which requires constant dressing to prevent it from growing worse, but which would admit of very great improvement, if a greater quantity of manure and labour could be employed upon it. The great obstacle to the melioration of land is the difficulty, the expense, and sometimes the impossibility, of procuring a sufficient quantity of dressing. As this instrument of improvement, therefore, is in practice limited, whatever it may be in theory, the question will always be, how it may be most profitably employed? And in any instance, where a certain quantity of dressing and labour, employed to bring new land into cultivation, would have yielded a permanently greater produce, if employed upon old land, both the individual and the nation are losers. Upon this principle, it is not uncommon for farmers in some situations never to dress their poorest land, but to get from it merely a scanty crop every three or four years, and to employ the whole of their manure, which they practically feel is limited, on those parts of their farms where it will produce a greater proportional effect.

The case will be different, of course, in a small territory with a great population, supported on funds not derived from their own soil. In this case there will be a little or no choice of land, and a comparative superabundance of manure; and under such circumstances the poorest soils may be brought under cultivation. But for this purpose, it is not mere population that is wanted, but a population which can obtain the produce of other countries, while it is gradually improving its own; otherwise it would be immediately reduced in proportion to the limited produce of this small and barren territory; and the melioration of the land might perhaps never take place; or, if it did, it would take place very slowly indeed, and the population would always be exactly measured by this tardy rate, and could not possibly increase beyond it.

This subject is illustrated in the cultivation of the Campine in Brabant, which, according to the Abbé Mann,[8] consisted originally of the most barren and arid sand. Many attempts were made by private individuals to bring it under cultivation, but without success; which proves, that, as a farming project, and considered as a sole dependence, the cultivation of it would not answer. Some religious houses, however, at last settled there; and being supported by other funds, and improving the land merely as a secondary object, they by degrees, in the course of some centuries, brought nearly the whole under cultivation, letting it out to farmers as soon as it was sufficiently improved.

There is no spot, however barren, which might not be made rich this way, or by the concentrated population of a manufacturing town; but this is no proof whatever that, with respect to population and food, population has the precedence; because this concentrated population could not possibly exist without the preceding existence of an adequate quantity of food in the surplus produce of some other district.

In a country like Brabant or Holland, where territory is the principal want, and not manure, such a district as the Campine is described to be may perhaps be cultivated with advantage. But in countries possessed of a large territory, and with a considerable quantity of land of a middling quality, the attempt to cultivate such a spot would be a palpable misdirection and waste both of individual and national resources.

The French have already found their error in bringing under cultivation too great a quantity of poor land. They are now sensible, that they have employed in this way a portion of labour and dressing, which would have produced a permanently better effect, if it had been applied to the further improvement of better land. Even in China, which is so fully cultivated and so fully peopled, barren heaths have been noticed in some districts, which proves that, distressed as the people appear to be for subsistence, it does not answer to them to employ any of their manure on such spots. These remarks will be still further confirmed, if we recollect that, in the cultivation of a large surface of bad land, there must necessarily be a great waste of seed corn.

We should not therefore be too ready to make inferences against the internal economy of a country from the appearance of uncultivated heaths, without other evidence. But the fact is, that, as no country has ever reached, or probably ever will reach, its highest possible acme of produce, it appears always as if the want of industry, or the ill direction of that industry, was the actual limit to a further increase of produce and population, and not the absolute refusal of nature to yield any more: but a man who is locked up in a room may be fairly said to be confined by the walls of it, though he may never touch them; and with regard to the principle of population, it is never the question whether a country will produce any more, but whether it may be made to produce a sufficiency to keep pace with a nearly unchecked increase of people. In China, the question is not, whether a certain additional quantity of rice might be raised by improved culture; but whether such an addition could be expected during the next twenty-five years, as would be sufficient to support an additional three hundred millions of people. And in this country, it is not the question whether, by cultivating all our commons, we could raise considerably more corn than at present; but whether we could raise sufficient for a population of twenty millions in the next twenty-five years, and forty millions in the next fifty years.[9]

The allowing of the produce of the earth to be absolutely unlimited, scarcely removes the weight of a hair from the argument, which depends entirely upon the differently increasing ratios of population and food: and all that the most enlightened governments and the most persevering and best guided efforts of industry can do is to make the necessary checks to population operate more equably, and in a direction to produce the least evil; but to remove them is a task absolutely hopeless.

NOTES

1. *Sketches of the History of Man*, b. i. sketch i. pp. 106, 107. 8vo. 1788.
2. This observation is exemplified in the slow progress of population in some parts of the Spanish dominions in America, compared with its progress in the United States.
3. Among others, I allude more particularly to Mr. Anderson, who, in a *Calm Investigation into the Circumstances which have led to the present Scarcity of Grain in Britain* (published in 1801), has laboured with extraordinary earnestness, and I believe with the best intentions, to impress this curious truth on the minds of his countrymen. The particular position which he attempts to prove is, that an increase of population in any state, whose fields have not been made to attain their highest possible degree of productiveness (a thing that probably has never yet been seen on this globe), will necessarily have its means of subsistence rather augmented than diminished by that augmentation of its population; and the reverse. The proposition is, to be sure, expressed rather obscurely; but from the context his meaning evidently is, that every increase of population tends to increase relative plenty, and *vice versâ*. He concludes his proofs by observing that, if the facts which he has thus brought forward and connected do not serve to remove the fears of those, who doubt the possibility of this country producing abundance to sustain its increasing population, (were it to augment in a ratio greatly more progressive than it has yet done), he should doubt whether they could be convinced of it, were one even to rise from the dead to tell them so. I agree with Mr. A. entirely, respecting the importance of directing a greater part of the national industry to agriculture; but from the circumstance of its being possible for a country, with a certain direction of its industry, always to grow corn sufficient for its own supplies, although it may be very populous, he has been led into the strange error of supposing, that an agricultural country could support an unchecked population.
4. *Polit. Econ.* vol. i. b. i. c. xviii. p. 114.
5. Sir James Steuart explains himself afterwards by saying, that he means principally the multiplication of those persons, who have some valuable consideration to give for the products of agriculture: but this is evidently not mere increase of population, and such an explanation seems to admit the incorrectness of the general proposition.
6. Tom. viii. p. 84, 12mo. 9 vols. 1762.
7. According to the principle of population, the human race has a tendency to increase faster than food. It has therefore a constant tendency to people a country fully up to the limits of subsistence, but by the laws of nature it can never go beyond them, meaning, of course, by these limits, the lowest quantity of food which will maintain a stationary population. Population, therefore, can never, strictly speaking, precede food.

8. Memoir on the Agriculture of the Netherlands, published in vol. i. of Communications to the Board of Agriculture, p. 225.

9. It may be thought that the effects here referred to as resulting from greatly increased resources, could not take place in a country where there were towns and manufactories; and that they are not consistent with what was said in a former part of this work, namely, that the ultimate check to population (the want of food) is never the immediate check, except in cases of actual famine.

   If the expressions are unguardedly strong, they will certainly allow of considerable mitigation, without any sensible diminution in the practical force and application of the argument. But I am inclined to think that, though they are unquestionably strong, they are not very far from the truth. The great cause which fills towns and manufactories is an insufficiency of employment, and consequently the means of support in the country; and if each labourer, in the parish where he was born, could command food, clothing, and lodging for ten children, the population of the towns would soon bear but a small proportion to the population of the country. And if to this consideration we add that, in the case supposed, the proportion of births and marriages in towns would be greatly increased, and all the mortality arising from poverty almost entirely removed, I should by no means be surprised (after a short interval for the change of habits) at an increase of population, even in China, equal to that which is referred to in the text.

   With regard to this country, as it is positively known that the rate of increase has changed from that which would double the population in 120 years, or more, to that which would double it in 55 years, under a great increase of towns and manufactures, I feel very little doubt that, if the resources of the country were so augmented and distributed, as that every man could marry at 18 or 20, with the certainty of being able to support the largest family, the population of the British isles would go on increasing at a rate which would double the population in 25 years. It appears, from our registers, that England is a healthier country than America. At the time that America was increasing with extraordinary rapidity, in some of the towns the deaths exceeded the births. In the English towns, with their present improvements, I do not think this would ever be the case, if all the lower classes could marry as soon as they pleased, and there was little or no premature mortality from the consequences of poverty.

   But whether the habits and customs of an old state could be so changed by an abundance of food, as to make it increase nearly like a new colony, is a question of mere curiosity. The argument only requires that a change from scanty to abundant means of supporting a family should occasion, in old states, a marked increase of population; and this, it is conceived, cannot possibly be denied.

BOOK IV

OF OUR FUTURE PROSPECTS RESPECTING THE REMOVAL OR MITIGATION OF THE EVILS ARISING FROM THE PRINCIPLE OF POPULATION

1

Of Moral Restraint and Our Obligation to Practise this Virtue

As it appears that, in the actual state of every society which has come within our review, the natural progress of population has been constantly and powerfully checked; and as it seems evident that no improved form of government, no plans of emigration, no benevolent institutions, and no degree or direction of national industry, can prevent the continued action of a great check to population in some form or other; it follows that we must submit to it as an inevitable law of nature; and the only inquiry that remains is, how it may take place with the least possible prejudice to the virtue and happiness of human society.

All the immediate checks to population, which have been observed to prevail in the same and different countries, seem to be resolvable into moral restraint, vice and misery; and if our choice be confined to these three, we cannot long hesitate in our decision respecting which it would be most eligible to encourage.

In the first edition of this essay I observed, that as from the laws of nature it appeared, that some check to population must exist, it was better that this check should arise from a foresight of the difficulties attending a family and the fear of dependent poverty, than from the actual presence of want and sickness. This idea will admit of being pursued farther; and I am inclined to think that, from the prevailing opinions respecting population, which undoubtedly originated in barbarous ages, and have been continued and circulated by that part of every community which may be supposed to be interested in their support, we have been prevented from attending to the clear dictates of reason and nature on this subject.

Natural and moral evil seem to be the instruments employed by the Deity in admonishing us to avoid any mode of conduct which is not suited to our being, and will consequently injure our happiness. If we are intemperate in eating and drinking, our health is disordered; if we indulge the transports of anger, we seldom fail to commit acts of which we afterwards repent; if we multiply too fast, we die miserably of poverty and contagious diseases. The laws of nature in all these cases are similar and uniform. They indicate to us that we have followed these impulses too far, so as to trench upon some other law, which equally demands attention. The uneasiness we feel from repletion, the injuries that we inflict on ourselves or others in anger, and the inconveniencies we suffer on the approach of poverty, are all admonitions to us to regulate these impulses better; and if we heed not this admonition, we justly incur the penalty of our disobedience, and our sufferings operate as a warning to others.

From the inattention of mankind hitherto to the consequences of increasing too fast, it must be presumed, that these consequences are not so immediately and powerfully connected with the conduct which leads to them, as in the other instances: but the delayed knowledge of particular effects does not alter their nature, or our obligation to regulate our conduct accordingly, as soon as we are satisfied of what this conduct ought to be. In many other instances it has not been till after long and painful experience, that the conduct most favourable to the happiness of man has been forced upon his attention. The kind of food, and the mode of preparing it, best suited to the purposes of nutrition and the gratification of the palate; the treatment and remedies of different disorders; the bad effects on the human frame of low and marshy situations; the invention of the most convenient and comfortable clothing; the construction of good houses; and all the advantages and extended enjoyments, which distinguish civilized life, were not pointed out to the attention of man at once; but were the slow and late result of experience, and of the admonitions received by repeated failures.

Diseases have been generally considered as the inevitable inflictions of Providence; but, perhaps, a great part of them may more justly be considered as indications that we have offended against some of the laws of nature. The plague at Constantinople, and in other towns of the East, is a constant admonition of this kind to the inhabitants. The human constitution cannot support such a state of filth and torpor; and as dirt, squalid poverty, and indolence are, in the highest degree, unfavourable to happiness and virtue, it seems a benevolent dispensation, that such a state should, by the laws of nature, produce disease and death, as a beacon to others to avoid splitting on the same rock.

The prevalence of the plague in London till the year 1666 operated in a proper manner on the conduct of our ancestors; and the removal of nuisances, the construction of drains, the widening of the streets, and the giving more room and air to the houses, had the effect of eradicating completely this dreadful disorder, and of adding greatly to the health and happiness of the inhabitants.

In the history of every epidemic it has almost invariably been observed that the lower classes of people, whose food was poor and insufficient, and who lived crowded together in small and dirty houses, were the principal victims. In what other manner can Nature point out to us that, if we increase too fast for the means of subsistence, so as to render it necessary for a considerable part of the society to live in this miserable manner, we have offended against one of her laws? This law she has declared exactly in the same manner as she declares that intemperance in eating and drinking will be followed by ill health; and that, however grateful it may be to us at the moment to indulge this propensity to excess, such indulgence will ultimately produce unhappiness. It is as much a law of nature that repletion is bad for the human frame, as that eating and drinking, unattended with this consequence, are good for it.

An implicit obedience to the impulses of our natural passions would lead us into the wildest and most fatal extravagances; and yet we have the strongest reasons for believing that all these passions are so necessary to our being, that they could not be generally weakened or diminished, without injuring our happiness. The most powerful and universal of all our desires is the desire of food, and of those things, such as clothing, houses, etc., which are immediately necessary to relieve us from the pains of hunger and cold. It is acknowledged by all, that these desires put in motion the greatest part of that activity, from which the multiplied improvements and advantages of civilized life are derived; and that the pursuit of these objects, and the gratification of these desires, form the principal happiness of the larger half of mankind, civilized or uncivilized, and are indispensably necessary to the more refined enjoyments of the other half. We are all conscious of the inestimable benefits that we derive from these desires, when directed in a certain manner; but we are equally conscious of the evils resulting from them, when not directed in this manner; so much so, that society has taken upon itself to punish most severely what it considers as an irregular gratification of them. And yet the desires in both cases are equally natural, and, abstractedly considered, equally virtuous. The act of the hungry man who satisfies his appetite by taking a loaf from the shelf of another, is in no respect to be distinguished from the act of him who does the same thing with a loaf of his own, but by its consequences. From the consideration of these consequences, we feel the most perfect conviction, that, if people were not prevented from gratifying their natural desires with the loaves in the possession of others, the number of loaves would universally diminish. This experience is the foundation of the laws relating to property, and of the distinctions of virtue and vice, in the gratification of desires otherwise perfectly the same.

If the pleasure arising from the gratification of these propensities were universally diminished in vividness, violations of property would become less frequent; but this advantage would be greatly overbalanced by the narrowing of the sources of enjoyment. The diminution in the quantity of all those productions, which contribute to human gratification, would be much greater in proportion than the diminution of thefts; and the loss of general happiness on the one side would be beyond comparison greater than the gain of happiness on the other. When we contemplate the constant and severe toils of the greatest part of mankind, it is impossible not to be forcibly impressed with the reflection, that the sources of human happiness would be most cruelly diminished, if the prospect of a good meal, a warm house, and a comfortable fireside in the evening, were not incitements sufficiently vivid, to give interest and cheerfulness to the labours and privations of the day.

After the desire of food, the most powerful and general of our desires is the passion between the sexes, taken in an enlarged sense. Of the happiness spread over human life by this passion very few are unconscious. Virtuous love, exalted by friendship, seems to be that sort of mixture of sensual and intellectual enjoyment, particularly suited to the nature of man, and most powerfully calculated to awaken the sympathies of the soul, and produce the most exquisite gratifications. Perhaps there is scarcely a man, who has once experienced the genuine delight of virtuous love, however great his intellectual pleasures may have been, who does not look back to that period as the sunny spot in his whole life, where his imagination loves most to bask, which he recollects and contemplates with the fondest regret, and which he would wish to live over again.

It has been said by Mr. Godwin, in order to show the evident inferiority of the pleasures of sense, "Strip the commerce of the sexes of all its attendant circumstances, and it would be generally despised." He might as well say to a man who admires trees, strip them of their spreading branches and lovely foliage, and what beauty can you see in a bare pole? But it was the tree with the branches and foliage, and not without them, that excited admiration. It is "the symmetry of person, the vivacity, the voluptuous softness of temper, the affectionate kindness of feeling, the imagination, and the wit"[1] of a woman, which excites the passion of love, and not the mere distinction of her being a female.

It is a very great mistake to suppose that the passion between the sexes only operates and influences human conduct, when the immediate gratification of it is in contemplation. The formation and steady pursuit of some particular plan of life has been justly considered as one of the most permanent sources of happiness; but I am inclined to believe, that there are not many of these plans formed, which are not connected in a considerable degree with the prospect of the gratification of this passion, and with the support of children arising from it. The evening meal, the warm house, and the comfortable fireside, would lose half their interest, if we were to exclude the idea of some object of affection, with whom they were to be shared.

We have also great reason to believe that the passion between the sexes has the most powerful tendency to soften and meliorate the human character, and keep it more alive to all the kindlier emotions of benevolence and pity. Observations on savage life have generally tended to prove that nations, in which this passion appeared to be less vivid, were distinguished by a ferocious and malignant spirit, and particularly by tyranny and cruelty to the sex. If, indeed, this bond of conjugal affection were considerably weakened, it seems probable, either that the man would make use of his superior physical strength, and turn his wife into a slave, as among the generality of savages; or, at best, that every little inequality of temper, which must necessarily occur between two persons, would produce a total alienation of affection; and this could hardly take place, without a diminution of parental fondness and care, which would have the most fatal effect on the happiness of society.

It may be further remarked, and observations on the human character in different countries warrant us in the conclusion, that the passion is stronger, and its general effects in producing gentleness, kindness, and suavity of manners, much more powerful, where obstacles are thrown in the way of very early and universal gratification. In some of the southern countries, where every impulse may be almost immediately indulged, the passion sinks into mere animal desire, is soon weakened and almost extinguished by excess, and its influence on the character is extremely confined. But, in European countries, where, though the women are not secluded, yet manners have imposed considerable restraints on this gratification, the passion not only rises in force, but in the universality and beneficial tendency of its effects; and has often the greatest influence in the formation and improvement of the character, where it is the least gratified.

Considering then the passion between the sexes in all its bearings and relations, and including the endearing engagement of parent and child resulting from it, few will be disposed to deny that it is one of the principal ingredients of human happiness. Yet experience teaches us that much evil flows from the irregular gratification of it; and though the evil be of little weight in the scale, when compared with the good, yet its absolute quantity cannot be inconsiderable, on account of the strength and universality of the passion. It is evident, however, from the general conduct of all governments in their distribution of punishments, that the evil resulting from this cause is not so great and so immediately dangerous to society, as the irregular gratification of the desire of property; but placing this evil in the most formidable point of view, we should evidently purchase a diminution of it at a very high price, by the extinction or diminution of the passion which causes it; a change, which would probably convert human life either into a cold and cheerless blank, or a scene of savage and merciless ferocity.

A careful attention to the remote as well as immediate effect of all the human passions, and all the general laws of nature, leads us strongly to the conclusion, that, under the present constitution of things, few or none of them will admit of being greatly diminished, without narrowing the sources of good, more powerfully than the sources of evil. And the reason seems to be obvious. They are, in fact, the materials of all our pleasures, as well as of all our pains; of all our happiness, as well as of all our misery; of all our virtues, as well as of all our vices. It must therefore be regulation and direction that are wanted, not diminution or extinction.

It is justly observed by Paley, that "Human passions are either necessary to human welfare, or capable of being made, and in a great majority of instances are in fact made, conducive to its happiness. These passions are strong and general; and perhaps would not answer their purpose, unless they were so. But strength and generality, when it is expedient that particular circumstances should be respected, become, if left to themselves, excess and misdirection. From which excess and misdirection the vices of mankind (the causes no doubt of much misery) appear to spring. This account, while it shews us the principle of vice, shows us at the same time the province of reason and self-government."[2]

Our virtue, therefore, as reasonable beings, evidently consists in educing from the general materials, which the Creator has placed under our guidance, the greatest sum of human happiness; and as natural impulses are abstractedly considered good, and only to be distinguished by their consequences, a strict attention to these consequences, and the regulation of our conduct conformably to them, must be considered as our principal duty.

The fecundity of the human species is, in some respects, a distinct consideration from the passion between the sexes, as it evidently depends more upon the power of women in bearing children, than upon the strength and weakness of this passion. It is a law however exactly similar in its great features to all the other laws of nature. It is strong and general, and apparently would not admit of any very considerable diminution, without being inadequate to its object; the evils arising from it are incidental to those necessary qualities of strength and generality; and these evils are capable of being very greatly mitigated and rendered comparatively light by human energy and virtue. We cannot but conceive that it is an object of the Creator, that the earth should be replenished; and it appears to me clear, that this could not be effected without a tendency in population to increase faster than food; and as, with the present law of increase, the peopling of the earth does not proceed very rapidly, we have undoubtedly some reason to believe, that this law is not too powerful for its apparent object. The desire of the means of subsistence would be comparatively confined in its effects, and would fail of producing that general activity so necessary to the improvement of the human faculties, were it not for the strong and universal effort of population to increase with greater rapidity than its supplies. If these two tendencies were exactly balanced, I do not see what motive there would be sufficiently strong to overcome the acknowledged indolence of man, and make him proceed in the cultivation of the soil. The population of any large territory, however fertile, would be as likely to stop at five hundred, or five thousand, as at five millions, or fifty millions. Such a balance therefore would clearly defeat one great purpose of creation; and if the question be merely a question of degree, a question of a little more or a little less strength, we may fairly distrust our competence to judge of the precise quantity necessary to answer the object with the smallest sum of incidental evil. In the present state of things we appear to have under our guidance a great power, capable of peopling a desert region in a small number of years; and yet, under other circumstances, capable of being confined by human energy and virtue to any limits however narrow, at the expense of a small comparative quantity of evil. The analogy of all the other laws of nature would be completely violated, if in this instance alone there were no provision for accidental failures, no resources against the vices of mankind, or the partial mischiefs resulting from other general laws. To effect the apparent object without any attendant evil, it is evident that a perpetual change in the law of increase would be necessary, varying with the varying circumstances of each country. But instead of this, it is not only more consonant to the analogy of the other parts of nature, but we have reason to think that it is more conducive to the formation and improvement of the human mind, that the law should be uniform, and the evils incidental to it, under certain circumstances, left to be mitigated or removed by man himself. His duties in this case vary with his situation; he is thus kept more alive to the consequences of his actions; and his faculties have evidently greater play and opportunity of improvement, than if the evil were removed by a perpetual change of the law according to circumstances.

Even if from passions too easily subdued, or the facility of illicit intercourse, a state of celibacy were a matter of indifference, and not a state of some privation, the end of nature in the peopling of the earth would be apparently liable to be defeated. It is of the very utmost importance to the happiness of mankind, that population should not increase too fast; but it does not appear, that the object to be accomplished would admit of any considerable diminution in the desire of marriage. It is clearly the duty of each individual not to marry till he has a prospect of supporting his children; but it is at the same time to be wished that he should retain undiminished his desire of marriage, in order that he may exert himself to realize this prospect, and be stimulated to make provision for the support of greater numbers.

It is evidently therefore regulation and direction which are required with regard to the principle of population, not diminution or alteration. And if moral restraint be the only virtuous mode of avoiding the incidental evils arising from this principle, our obligation to practise it will evidently rest exactly upon the same foundation as our obligation to practise any of the other virtues.

Whatever indulgence we may be disposed to allow to occasional failures in the discharge of a duty of acknowledged difficulty, yet of the strict line of duty we cannot doubt. Our obligation not to marry till we have a fair prospect of being able to support our children will appear to deserve the attention of the moralist, if it can be proved that an attention to this obligation is of most powerful effect in the prevention of misery; and that, if it were the general custom to follow the first impulse of nature, and marry at the age of puberty, the universal prevalence of every known virtue in the greatest conceivable degree, would fail of rescuing society from the most wretched and desperate state of want, and all the diseases and famines which usually accompany it.

NOTES

1. *Political Justice* vol. i. b. i. c. v. p. 72. 8vo.
2. *Natural Theology*, c. xxvi. p. 547.

2

Of the Effects which would Result to Society from the Prevalence of Moral Restraint

One of the principal reasons which have prevented an assent to the doctrine of the constant tendency of population to increase beyond the means of subsistence, is a great unwillingness to believe that the Deity would by the laws of nature bring beings into existence, which by the laws of nature could not be supported in that existence. But if, in addition to that general activity and direction of our industry put in motion by these laws, we further consider that the incidental evils arising from them are constantly directing our attention to the proper check to population, moral restraint; and if it appear that, by a strict obedience to the duties pointed out to us by the light of nature and reason, and confirmed and sanctioned by revelation, these evils may be avoided, the objection will, I trust, be removed, and all apparent imputation on the goodness of the Deity be done away.

The heathen moralists never represented happiness as attainable on earth, but through the medium of virtue; and among their virtues prudence ranked in the first class, and by some was even considered as including every other. The Christian religion places our present as well as future happiness in the exercise of those virtues which tend to fit us for a state of superior enjoyment; and the subjection of the passions to the guidance of reason, which, if not the whole, is a principal branch of prudence, is in consequence most particularly inculcated.

If, for the sake of illustration, we might be permitted to draw a picture of society, in which each individual endeavoured to attain happiness by the strict fulfilment of those duties, which the most enlightened of the ancient philosophers deduced from the laws of nature, and which have been directly taught, and received such powerful sanctions in the moral code of Christianity, it would present a very different scene from that which we now contemplate. Every act, which was prompted by the desire of immediate gratification, but which threatened an ultimate overbalance of pain, would be considered as a breach of duty; and consequently no man, whose earnings were only sufficient to maintain two children, would put himself in a situation in which he might have to maintain four or five, however he might be prompted to it by the passion of love. This prudential restraint, if it were generally adopted, by narrowing the supply of labour in the market, would, in the natural course of things, soon raise its price. The period of delayed gratification would be passed in saving the earnings which were above the wants of a single man, and in acquiring habits of sobriety, industry and economy, which would enable him in a few years to enter into the matrimonial contract without fear of its consequences. The operation of the preventive check in this way, by constantly keeping the population within the limits of the food, though constantly following its increase, would give a real value to the rise of wages and the sums saved by labourers before marriage, very different from those forced advances in the price of labour or arbitrary parochial donations, which, in proportion to their magnitude and extensiveness, must of necessity be followed by a proportional advance in the price of provisions. As the wages of labour would thus be sufficient to maintain with decency a large family, and as every married couple would set out with a sum for contingencies, all abject poverty would be removed from society; or would at least be confined to a very few, who had fallen into misfortunes, against which no prudence or foresight could provide.

The interval between the age of puberty and the period at which each individual might venture on marriage must, according to the supposition, be passed in strict chastity; because the law of chastity cannot be violated without producing evil. The effect of any thing like a promiscuous intercourse, which prevents the birth of children, is evidently to weaken the best affections of the heart, and in a very marked manner to degrade the female character. And any other intercourse would, without improper arts, loving as many children into the society as marriage, with a much greater probability of their becoming a burden to it.

These considerations shew that the virtue of chastity is not, as some have supposed, a forced produce of artificial society; but that it has the most real and solid foundation in nature and reason; being apparently the only virtuous means of avoiding the vice and misery which result so often from the principle of population.

In such a society as we have been supposing, it might be necessary for some of both sexes to pass many of the early years of life in the single state; and if this were general, there would certainly be room for a much greater number to marry afterwards, so that fewer, upon the whole, would be condemned to pass their lives in celibacy. If the custom of not marrying early prevailed generally, and if violations of chastity were equally dishonourable in both sexes, a more familiar and friendly intercourse between them might take place without danger. Two young people might converse together intimately without its being immediately supposed that they either intended marriage or intrigue; and a much better opportunity would thus be given to both sexes of finding out kindred dispositions, and of forming those strong and lasting attachments, without which the married state is generally more productive of misery than of happiness. The earlier years of life would not be spent without love, though without the full gratification of it. The passion, instead of being extinguished, as it now too frequently is, by early sensuality, would only be repressed for a time, that it might afterwards burn with a brighter, purer, and steadier flame; and the happiness of the married state, instead of only affording the means of immediate indulgence, would be looked forward to as the prize of industry and virtue, and the reward of a genuine and constant attachment.[1]

The passion of love is a powerful stimulus in the formation of character, and often prompts to the most noble and generous exertions; but this is only when the affections are centred in one object, and generally when full gratification is delayed by difficulties.[2] The heart is perhaps never so much disposed to virtuous conduct, and certainly at no time is the virtue of chastity so little difficult to men, as when under the influence of such a passion. Late marriages taking place in this way would be very different from those of the same name at present, where the union is too frequently prompted solely by interested views, and the parties meet, not unfrequently, with exhausted constitutions, and generally with exhausted affections. The late marriages at present are indeed principally confined to the men; of whom there are few, however advanced in life, who, if they determine to marry, do not fix their choice on a young wife. A young woman without fortune, when she has passed her twenty-fifth year, begins to fear, and with reason, that she may lead a life of celibacy; and with a heart capable of forming a strong attachment, feels, as each year creeps on, her hopes of finding an object on which to rest her affections gradually diminishing, and the uneasiness of her situation aggravated by the silly and unjust prejudices of the world. If the general age of marriage among women were later, the period of youth and hope would be prolonged, and fewer would be ultimately disappointed.

That a change of this kind would be a most decided advantage to the more virtuous half of society, we cannot for a moment doubt. However impatiently the privation might be borne by the men, it would be supported by the women readily and cheerfully; and if they could look forward with just confidence to marriage at twenty-seven or twenty-eight, I fully believe, that, if the matter were left to their free choice, they would clearly prefer waiting till this period, to the being involved in all the cares of a large family at twenty-five. The most eligible age of marriage however could not be fixed; but must depend entirely on circumstances and situation. There is no period of human life, at which nature more strongly prompts to a union of the sexes, than from seventeen or eighteen to twenty. In every society above that state of depression, which almost excludes reason and foresight, these early tendencies must necessarily be restrained; and if, in the actual state of things, such a restraint on the impulses of nature be found unavoidable, at what time can we be consistently released from it, but at that period, whatever it may be, when, in the existing circumstances of the society, a fair prospect presents itself of maintaining a family?

The difficulty of moral restraint will perhaps be objected to this doctrine. To him who does not acknowledge the authority of the Christian religion, I have only to say that, after the most careful investigation, this virtue appears to be absolutely necessary, in order to avoid certain evils which would otherwise result from the general laws of nature. According to his own principles, it is his duty to pursue the greatest good consistent with these laws; and not to fail in this important end, and produce an overbalance of misery by a partial obedience to some of the dictates of nature, while he neglects others. The path of virtue, though it be the only path which leads to permanent happiness, has always been represented by the heathen moralists as of difficult ascent.

To the Christian I would say that the Scriptures most clearly and precisely point it out to us as our duty, to restrain our passions within the bounds of reason; and it is a palpable disobedience of this law to indulge our desires in such a manner as reason tells us will unavoidably end in misery. The Christian cannot consider the difficulty of moral restraint as any argument against its being his duty; since, in almost every page of the sacred writings, man is described as encompassed on all aides by temptations which it is extremely difficult to resist; and though no duties are enjoined, which do not contribute to his happiness on earth as well as in a future state, yet an undeviating obedience is never represented as an easy task.

There is in general so strong a tendency to love in early youth, that it is extremely difficult at this period to distinguish a genuine from a transient passion. If the earlier years of life were passed by both sexes in moral restraint, from the greater facility that this would give to the meeting of kindred dispositions, it might even admit of a doubt, whether more happy marriages would not take place, and consequently more pleasure from the passion of love, than in a state such as that of America, the circumstances of which allow of a very early union of the sexes. But if we compare the intercourse of the sexes in such a society as I have been supposing, with that which now exists in Europe, taken under all its circumstances, it may safely be asserted, that, independently of the load of misery which would be removed, the sum of pleasurable sensations from the passion of love would be increased in a very great degree.

If we could suppose such a system general, the accession of happiness to society in its internal economy would scarcely be greater than in its external relations. It might fairly be expected that war, that great pest of the human race, would, under such circumstances, soon cease to extend its ravages so widely and so frequently as it does at present.

One of its first causes and most powerful impulses was undoubtedly an insufficiency of room and food; and greatly as the circumstances of mankind have changed since it first began, the same cause still continues to operate and to produce, though in a smaller degree, the same effects. The ambition of princes would want instruments of destruction, if the distresses of the lower classes of people did not drive them under their standards. A recruiting serjeant always prays for a bad harvest and a want of employment, or, in other words, a redundant population.

In the earlier ages of the world, when war was the great business of mankind, and the drains of population from this cause were, beyond comparison, greater than in modern times, the legislators and statesmen of each country, adverting principally to the means of offence and defence, encouraged an increase of people in every possible way, fixed a stigma on barrenness and celibacy, and honoured marriage. The popular religions followed these prevailing opinions. In many countries the prolific power of nature was the object of solemn worship. In the religion of Mahomet, which was established by the sword, and the promulgation of which in consequence could not be unaccompanied by an extraordinary destruction of its followers, the procreation of children to glorify the Creator was laid down as one of the principal duties of man; and he, who had the most numerous offspring, was considered as having best answered the end of his creation. The prevalence of such moral sentiments had naturally a great effect in encouraging marriage; and the rapid procreation, which followed, was partly the effect and partly the cause of incessant war. The vacancies occasioned by former desolations made room for the rearing of fresh supplies; and the overflowing rapidity, with which these supplies followed, constantly furnished fresh incitements and fresh instruments for renewed hostilities. Under the influence of such moral sentiments, it is difficult to conceive how the fury of incessant war should ever abate.

It is a pleasing confirmation of the truth and divinity of the Christian religion, and of its being adapted to a more improved state of human society, that it places our duties respecting marriage and the procreation of children in a different light from that in which they were before beheld.

Without entering minutely into the subject, which would evidently lead too far, I think it will be admitted, that, if we apply the spirit of St. Paul's declarations respecting marriage to the present state of society and the known constitution of our nature, the natural inference seems to be, that, when marriage does not interfere with higher duties, it is right; when it does, it is wrong. According to the genuine principles of moral science, "The method of coming at the will of God from the light of nature is, to inquire into the tendency of the action to promote or diminish the general happiness."[3] There are perhaps few actions that tend so directly to diminish the general happiness, as to marry without the means of supporting children. He who commits this act, therefore, clearly offends against the will of God; and having become a burden on the society in which he lives, and plunged himself and family into a situation, in which virtuous habits are preserved with more difficulty than in any other, he appears to have violated his duty to his neighbours and to himself, and thus to have listened to the voice of passion in opposition to his higher obligations.

In a society, such as I have supposed, all the members of which endeavour to attain happiness by obedience to the moral code derived from the light of nature, and enforced by strong sanctions in revealed religion, it is evident that no such marriages could take place; and the prevention of a redundant population, in this way, would remove one of the principal encouragements to offensive war; and at the same time tend powerfully to eradicate those two fatal political disorders, internal tyranny and internal tumult, which mutually produce each other.

Indisposed to a war of offence, in a war of defence, such a society would be strong as a rock of adamant. Where every family possessed the necessaries of live in plenty, and a decent portion of its comforts and conveniences, there could not exist that hope of change, or at best that melancholy and disheartening indifference to it, which sometimes prompts the lower classes of people to say, "Let what will come, we cannot be worse off than we are now." Every heart and hand will be united to repel an invader, when each individual felt the value of the solid advantages which he enjoyed, and a prospect of change presented only a prospect of being deprived of them.

As it appears therefore, that it is in the power of each individual to avoid all the evil consequences to himself and society resulting from the principle of population, by the practice of a virtue clearly dictated to him by the light of nature, and expressly enjoined in revealed religion; and as we have reason to think, that the exercise of this virtue to a certain degree would tend rather to increase than diminish individual happiness; we can have no reason to impeach the justice of the Deity, because his general laws make this virtue necessary, and punish our offences against it by the evils attendant upon vice, and the pains that accompany the various forms of premature death. A really virtuous society, such as I have supposed, would avoid these evils. It is the apparent object of the Creator to deter us from vice by the pains which accompany it, and to lead us to virtue by the happiness that it produces. This object appears to our conceptions to be worthy of a benevolent Creator. The laws of nature respecting population tend to promote this object. No imputation, therefore, on the benevolence of the Deity, can be founded on these laws, which is not equally applicable to any of the evils necessarily incidental to all imperfect state of existence.

NOTES

1. Dr. Currie, in his interesting observations on the character and condition of the Scotch peasantry, prefixed to his Life of Burns,

remarks, with a just knowledge of human nature, that, "in appreciating the happiness and virtue of a community, there is perhaps no single criterion on which so much dependence may be placed as the state of the intercourse between the sexes. Where this displays ardour of attachment, accompanied by purity of conduct, the character and the influence of women rise, our imperfect nature mounts in the scale of moral excellence; and from the source of this single affection, a stream of felicity descends, which branches into a thousand rivulets that enrich and adorn the field of life. Where the attachment between the sexes sinks into an appetite, the heritage of our species is comparatively poor, and man approaches to the condition of the brutes that perish." Vol. i. p. 18.

2. Dr. Currie observes, that the Scottish peasant in the course "of his passion often exerts a spirit of adventure, of which a Spanish cavalier need not be ashamed." Burns' *Works*, vol. i. p. 16. It is not to be doubted that this kind of romantic passion, which, Dr. C. says, characterizes the attachment of the humblest people of Scotland, and which has been greatly fostered by the elevation of mind given to them by a superior education, has had a most powerful and most beneficial influence on the national character.

3. Paley's *Moral Philosophy*, vol. i. b. ii, c. iv. p. 65.

3

Of the Only Effectual Mode of Improving the Condition of the Poor

He who publishes a moral code, or system of duties, however firmly he may be convinced of the strong obligation on each individual strictly to conform to it, has never the folly to imagine that it will be universally or even generally practised. But this is no valid objection against the publication of the code. If it were, the same objection would always have applied; we should be totally without general rules; and to the vices of mankind arising from temptation would be added a much longer list, than we have at present, of vices from ignorance.

Judging merely from the light of nature, if we feel convinced of the misery arising from a redundant population on the one hand, and of the evils and unhappiness, particularly to the female sex, arising from promiscuous intercourse, on the other, I do not see how it is possible for any person who acknowledges the principle of utility, as the great criterion of moral rules, to escape the conclusion, that moral restraint, or the abstaining from marriage till we are in a condition to support a family, with a perfectly moral conduct during that period, is the strict line of duty; and when revelation is taken into the question, this duty undoubtedly receives very powerful confirmation. At the same time I believe that few of my readers can be less sanguine than I am in their expectations of any sudden and great change in the general conduct of men on this subject: and the chief reason why in the last chapter I allowed myself to suppose the universal prevalence of this virtue was, that I might endeavour to remove any imputation on the goodness of the Deity, by showing, that the evils arising from the principle of population were exactly of the same nature as the generality of other evils which excite fewer complaints; that they were increased by human ignorance and indolence, and diminished by human knowledge and virtue; and on the supposition that each individual strictly fulfilled his duty, would be almost totally removed; and this without any general diminution of those sources of pleasure, arising from the regulated indulgence of the passions, which have been justly considered as the principal ingredients of human happiness.

If it will answer any purpose of illustration, I see no harm in drawing the picture of a society, in which each individual is supposed strictly to fulfil his duties; nor does a writer appear to be justly liable to the imputation of being visionary, unless he make such universal or general obedience necessary to the practical utility of his system, and to that degree of moderate and partial improvement, which is all that can rationally be expected from the most complete knowledge of our duties.

But in this respect there is an essential difference between that improved state of society, which I have supposed in the last chapter, and most of the other speculations on this subject. The improvement there supposed, if we ever should make approaches towards it, is to be effected in the way in which we have been in the habit of seeing all the greatest improvements effected, by a direct application to the interest and happiness of each individual. It is not required of us to act from motives to which we are unaccustomed; to pursue a general good, which we may not distinctly comprehend, or the effect of which may be weakened by distance and diffusion. The happiness of the whole is to be the result of the happiness of individuals, and to begin first with them. No cooperation is required. Every step tells. He who performs his duty faithfully will reap the full fruits of it, whatever may be the number of others who fail. This duty is intelligible to the humblest capacity. It is merely, that he is not to bring beings into the world, for whom he cannot find the means of support. When once this subject is cleared from the obscurity thrown over it by parochial laws and private benevolence, every man must feel the strongest conviction of such an obligation. If he cannot support his children, they must starve; and if he marry in the face of a fair probability that he shall not be able to support his children, he is guilty of all the evils, which he thus brings upon himself, his wife and his offspring. It is clearly his interest, and will tend greatly to promote his happiness, to defer marrying, till by industry and economy he is in a capacity to support the children that he may reasonably expect from his marriage; and as he cannot in the mean time gratify his passions without violating an express command of God, and running a great risk of injuring himself; or some of his fellow-creatures, considerations of his own interest and happiness will dictate to him the strong obligation to a moral conduct while he remains unmarried.

However powerful may be the impulses of passion, they are generally in some degree modified by reason. And it does not seem entirely visionary to suppose that, if the true and permanent cause of poverty were clearly explained and forcibly brought home to each man's bosom, it would have some, and perhaps not an inconsiderable influence on his conduct; at least the experiment has never yet been fairly tried. Almost every thing, that has been hitherto done for the poor, has tended, as if with solicitous care, to throw a veil of obscurity over this subject, and to hide from them the true cause of their poverty. When the wages of labour are hardly sufficient to maintain two children, a man marries, and has five or six; he of course finds himself miserably distressed. He accuses the insufficiency of the price of labour to maintain a family. He accuses his parish for their tardy and sparing fulfilment of their obligation to assist him. He accuses the avarice of the rich, who suffer him to want what they can so well spare. He accuses the partial and unjust institutions of society, which have awarded him an inadequate share of the produce of the earth. He accuses perhaps the dispensations of Providence, which have assigned to him a place in society so beset with unavoidable distress and dependence. In searching for objects of accusation, he never adverts to the quarter from which his misfortunes originate. The last person that he would think of accusing is himself, on whom in fact the principal blame lies, except so far as he has been deceived by the higher classes of society. He may perhaps wish that he had not married, because he now feels the inconveniences of it; but it never enters into his head that he can have done any thing wrong. He has always been told, that to raise up subjects for his king and country is a very meritorious act. He has done this, and yet is suffering for it; and it cannot but strike him as most extremely unjust and cruel in his king and country, to allow him thus to suffer, in return for giving them what they are continually declaring that they particularly want.

Till these erroneous ideas have been corrected, and the language of nature and reason has been generally heard on the subject of population, instead of the language of error and prejudice, it cannot be said, that any fair experiment has been made with the understandings of the common people; and we cannot justly accuse them of improvidence and want of industry, till they act as they do now, after it has been brought home to their comprehensions, that they are themselves the cause of their own poverty; that the means of redress are in their own hands, and in the hands of no other persons whatever; that the society in which they live and the government which presides over it, are without any direct power in this respect; and that however ardently they may desire to relieve them, and whatever attempts they may make to do so, they are really and truly unable to execute what they benevolently wish but unjustly promise; that, when the wages of labour will not maintain a family, it is an incontrovertible sign that their king and country do not want more subjects, or at least that they cannot support them; that, if they marry in this case, so far from fulfilling a duty to society, they are throwing an useless burden on it, at the same time that they are plunging themselves into distress; and that they are acting directly contrary to the will of God, and bringing down upon themselves various diseases, which might all, or the greater part, have been avoided, if they had attended to the repeated admonitions which he gives by the general laws of nature to every being capable of reason.

Paley, in his *Moral Philosophy*, observes, that in "countries in which subsistence is become scarce, it behoves the state to watch over the public morals with increased solicitude; for nothing but the instinct of nature, under the restraint of chastity, will induce men to undertake the labour, or consent to the sacrifice of personal liberty and indulgence, which the support of a family in such circumstances requires."[1] That it is always the duty of a state to use every exertion likely to be effectual in discouraging vice and promoting virtue, and that no temporary circumstances ought to cause any relaxation in these exertions, is certainly true. The means therefore proposed are always good; but the particular end in view in this case appears to be absolutely criminal. We wish to force people into marriage, when from the acknowledged scarcity of subsistence they will have little chance of being able to support their children. We might as well force people into the water who are unable to swim. In both cases we rashly tempt Providence. Nor have we more reason to believe that a miracle will be worked to save us from the misery and mortality resulting from our conduct in the one case than in the other.

The object of those who really wish to better the condition of the lower classes of society, must be to raise the relative proportion between the price of labour and the price of provisions, so as to enable the labourer to command a larger share of the necessaries and comforts of life. We have hitherto principally attempted to attain this end by encouraging the married poor, and consequently increasing the number of labourers, and overstocking the market with a commodity which we still say that we wish to be dear. It would seem to have required no great spirit of divination to foretell the certain failure of such a plan of proceeding. There is nothing however like experience. It has been tried in many different countries, and for many hundred years, and the success has always been answerable to the nature of the scheme. It is really time now to try something else.

When it was found that oxygen, or pure vital air, would not cure consumptions as was expected, but rather aggravated their symptoms, trial was made of an air of the most opposite kind. I wish we had acted with the same philosophical spirit in our attempts to cure the disease of poverty; and having found that the pouring in of fresh supplies of labour only tended to aggravate the symptoms, had tried what would be the effect of withholding a little these supplies.

In all old and fully-peopled states it is from this method, and this alone, that we can rationally expect any essential and permanent melioration in the condition of the labouring classes of the people.

In an endeavour to raise the proportion of the quantity of provisions to the number of consumers in any country, our attention would naturally be first directed to the increasing of the absolute quantity of provisions; but finding that, as fast as we did this, the number of consumers more than kept pace with it, and that with all our exertions we were still as far as ever behind, we should be convinced, that our efforts directed only in this way would never succeed. It would appear to be setting the tortoise to catch the hare. Finding, therefore, that from the laws of nature we could not proportion the food to the population, our next attempt should naturally be, to proportion the population to the food. If we can persuade the hare to go to sleep, the tortoise may have some chance of overtaking her.

We are not however to relax our efforts in increasing the quantity of provisions, but to combine another effort with it; that of keeping the population, when once it has been overtaken, at such a distance behind, as to effect the relative proportion which we desire; and thus unite the two grind *desiderata*, a great actual population, and a state of society, in which abject poverty and dependence are comparatively but little known; two objects which are far from being incompatible.

If we be really serious in what appears to be the object of such general research, the mode of essentially and permanently bettering the condition of the poor, we must explain to them the true nature of their situation, and show them, that the withholding of the supplies of labour is the only possible way of really raising its price, and that they themselves, being the possessors of this commodity, have alone the power to do this.

I cannot but consider this mode of diminishing poverty as so perfectly clear in theory, and so invariably confirmed by the analogy of every other commodity which is brought to market, that nothing but its being shown to be calculated to produce greater evils than it proposes to remedy, can justify us in not making the attempt to put it into execution.

NOTE

1. Vol. ii. c. xi. p. 352.

4

Objections to this Mode Considered

One objection which perhaps will be made to this plan is, that from which alone it derives its value—a market rather understocked with labour. This must undoubtedly take place in a certain degree; but by no means in such a degree as to affect the wealth and prosperity of the country. But putting this subject of a market understocked with labour in the must unfavourable point of vices, if the rich will not submit to a slight inconvenience necessarily attendant on the attainment of what they profess to desire, they cannot really be in earnest in their professions. Their benevolence to the poor must be either childish play or hypocrisy; it must be, either to amuse themselves or to pacify the minds of the common people with a mere show of attention to their wants. To wish to better the condition of the poor by enabling them to command a greater quantity of the necessaries and comforts of life, and then to complain of high wages, is the act of a silly boy who gives away his cake and then cries for it. A market overstocked with labour, and an ample remuneration to each labourer, are objects perfectly incompatible with each other. In the annals of the world they never existed together; and to couple them even in imagination betrays a gross ignorance of the simplest principles of political economy.

A second objection that may be made to this plan is the diminution of population that it would cause. It is to be considered, however, that this diminution is merely relative; and when once this relative diminution has been effected, by keeping the population stationary, while the supply of food has increased, it might then start afresh, and continue increasing for ages, with the increase of food, maintaining always nearly the same relative proportion to it. I can easily conceive that this country, with a proper direction of the national industry, might, in the course of some centuries, contain two or three times its present population, and yet every man in the kingdom be much better fed and clothed than he is at present. While the springs of industry continue in vigour, and a sufficient part of that industry is directed to agriculture, we need be under no apprehensions of a deficient population; and nothing perhaps would tend so strongly to excite a spirit of industry and economy among the poor, as a thorough knowledge that their happiness must always depend principally upon themselves; and that, if they obey their passions in opposition to their reason, or be not industrious and frugal while they are single, to save a sum for the common contingencies of the married state, they must expect to suffer the natural evils which Providence has prepared for those who disobey its repeated admonitions.

A third objection which may be started to this plan, and the only one which appears to me to have any kind of plausibility, is that, by endeavouring to urge the duty of moral restraint on the poor, we may increase the quantity of vice relating to the sex.

I should be extremely sorry to say any thing which could either directly or remotely be construed unfavourably to the cause of virtue; but I certainly cannot think that the vices which relate to the sex are the only vices which are to be considered in a moral question; or that they are even the greatest and most degrading to the human character. They can rarely or never be committed without producing unhappiness somewhere or other, and therefore ought always to be strongly reprobated: but there are other vices, the effects of which are still more pernicious; and there are other situations which lead more certainly to moral offences than the refraining from marriage. Powerful as may be the temptations to a breach of chastity, I am inclined to think that they are impotent, in comparison of the temptations arising from continued distress. A large class of women, and many men, I have no doubt, pass a considerable part of their lives consistently with the laws of chastity; but I believe there will be found very few who pass through the ordeal of squalid and hopeless poverty, or even of long-continued embarrassed circumstances, without a great moral degradation of character.

In the higher and middle classes of society, it is a melancholy and distressing sight to observe, not unfrequently, a man of a noble and ingenuous disposition, once feelingly alive to a sense of honour and integrity, gradually sinking under the pressure of circumstances, making his excuses at first with a blush of conscious shame, afraid of seeing the faces of his friends from whom he may have borrowed money, reduced to the meanest tricks and subterfuges to delay or avoid the payment of his just debts; till ultimately grown familiar with falsehood and at enmity with the world he loses all the grace and dignity of man.

To the general prevalence of indigence, and the extraordinary encouragements which we afford in this country to a total want of foresight and prudence among the common people,[1] is to be attributed a considerable part of those continual depredations on property, and other more atrocious crimes which drive us to the painful resource of such a number of executions.[2] According to Mr. Colquhoun, above twenty thousand miserable individuals of various classes rise up every morning without knowing how or by what means they are to be supported during the passing day, or where, in many instances, they are to lodge on the succeeding night.[3] It is by these unhappy persons that the principal depredations on the public are committed: and supposing but few of them to be married, and driven to these acts from the necessity of supporting their children; yet still it is probably true, that the too great frequency of marriage amongst the poorest classes of society is one of the principal causes of the temptations to these crimes. A considerable part of these unhappy wretches will probably be found to be the offspring of such marriages, educated in workhouses where every vice is propagated, or bred up at home in filth and rags, with an utter ignorance of every moral obligation.[4] A still greater part perhaps consists of persons, who, being unable for some time to get employment owing to the full supply of labour, have been urged to these extremities by their temporary wants; and, having thus lost their characters, are rejected even when their labour may be wanted, by the well-founded caution of civil society.[5]

When indigence does not produce overt acts of vice, it palsies every virtue. Under the continued temptations to a breach of chastity, occasional failures may take place, and the moral sensibility in other respects not be very strikingly impaired; but the continued temptations which beset hopeless poverty, and the strong sense of injustice that generally accompanies it from an ignorance of its true cause, tend so powerfully to sour the disposition, to harden the heart, and deaden the moral sense, that, generally speaking, virtue takes her flight clear away from the tainted spot, and does not often return.

Even with respect to the vices which relate to the sex, marriage has been found to be by no means a complete remedy. Among the higher classes, our Doctors' Commons, and the lives that many married men are known to lead, sufficiently prove this; and the same kind of vice, though not so much heard of among the lower classes of people, is probably in all our great towns not much less frequent.

Add to this, that abject poverty, particularly when joined with idleness, is a state the most unfavourable to chastity that can well be conceived. The passion is as strong, or nearly so, as in other situations; and every restraint on it from personal respect, or a sense of morality, is generally removed. There is a degree of squalid poverty, in which, if a girl was brought up, I should say, that her being really modest at twenty was an absolute miracle. Those persons must have extraordinary minds indeed, and such as are not usually formed under similar circumstances, who can continue to respect themselves when no other person whatever respects them. If the children thus brought up were even to marry at twenty, it is probable, that they would have passed some years in vicious habits before that period.

If after all, however, these arguments should appear insufficient; if we reprobate the idea of endeavouring to encourage the virtue of moral restraint among the poor, from a fear of producing vice; and if we think, that to facilitate marriage by all possible means is a point of the first consequence to the morality and happiness of the people; let us act consistently, and before we proceed, endeavour to make ourselves acquainted with the mode by which alone we can effect our object.

NOTES

1. Mr. Colquhoun, speaking of the poor-laws, observes, that "In spite of all the ingenious arguments which have been used in favour of a system, admitted to be wisely conceived in its origin, the effects it has produced incontestably prove that, with respect to the mass of the poor, there is something radically wrong in the execution. If it were not so, it is impossible that there could exist in the metropolis such an inconceivable portion of human misery, amidst examples of munificence and benevolence unparalleled in any age or country," *Police of Metropolis*, c. xiii. p. 359.

   In the effects of the poor-laws I fully agree with Mr. Colquhoun; but I cannot agree with him in admitting that the system was well conceived in its origin. I attribute still more evil to the original ill conception, than to the subsequent ill execution.

2. Mr. Colquhoun observes, that "Indigence in the present state of society may be considered as a principal cause of the increase of crimes." *Police of Metropolis*, c. xiii. p. 352.

3. *Police of Metropolis*, c. xi. p. 313.

4. *Id.* c. xi. xii. pp. 355, 370.

5. *Id.* c. xiii. p. 353, et seq. In so large a town as London, which must necessarily encourage a prodigious influx of strangers from the country, there must be always a great many persons out of work; and it is probable, that some public institution for the relief of the casual poor, upon a plan similar to that proposed by Mr. Colquhoun (c. xiii. p. 371) would, under very judicious management, produce more good than evil. But for this purpose it would be absolutely necessary that, if work were provided by the institution, the sum that a man could earn by it should be less than the worst paid common labour; otherwise the claimants would rapidly increase, and the funds would soon be inadequate to their object. In the institution at Hamburgh, which appears to have been the most successful of any yet established, the nature of the work was such, that, though paid above the usual price, a person could not easily earn by it more than eighteen pence a week. It was the determined principle of the managers of the institution, to reduce the support which they gave lower than what any industrious man or woman in such circumstances could earn. (*Account of the Management of the Poor in Hamburgh*, by C. Voght, p. 18.) And it is to this principle that they attribute their success. It should be observed however, that neither the institution at Hamburgh, not that planned by Count Rumford in Bavaria, has subsisted long enough for us to be able to pronounce on their permanent good effects. It will not admit of a doubt, that institutions for the relief of the poor, on their first establishment, remove a great quantity of

distress. The only question is, whether, as succeeding generations arise, the increasing funds necessary for their support, and the increasing numbers that become dependent, are not greater evils than that which was to be remedied; and whether the country will not ultimately be left with as much mendicity as before, besides all the poverty and dependence accumulated in the public institutions. This seems to be nearly the case in England at present. It may be doubted whether we should have more beggars if we laid no poor-laws.

5

Of the Consequences of Pursuing the Opposite Mode

It is an evident truth that, whatever may be the rate of increase in the means of subsistence, the increase of population must be limited by it, at least after the food has once been divided into the smallest shares that will support life. All the children born, beyond what would be required to keep up the population to this level, must necessarily perish, unless room be made for them by the deaths of grown persons. It has appeared indeed clearly in the course of this work, that in all old states the marriages and births depend principally upon the deaths, and that there is no encouragement to early unions so powerful as a great mortality. To act consistently therefore, we should facilitate, instead of foolishly and vainly endeavouring to impede, the operations of nature in producing this mortality; and if we dread the too frequent visitation of the horrid form of famine, we should sedulously encourage the other forms of destruction, which we compel nature to use. Instead of recommending cleanliness to the poor, we should encourage contrary habits. In our towns we should make the streets narrower, crowd more people into the houses, and court the return of the plague. In the country, we should build our villages near stagnant pools, and particularly encourage settlements in all marshy and unwholesome situations.[1] But above all, we should reprobate specific remedies for ravaging diseases; and those benevolent, but much mistaken men, who have thought they were doing a service to mankind by projecting schemes for the total extirpation of particular disorders. If by these and similar means the annual mortality were increased from 1 in 36 or 40, to 1 in 18 or 20, we might probably every one of us marry at the age of puberty, and yet few be absolutely starved.

If, however, we all marry at this age, and yet still continue our exertions to impede the operations of nature, we may rest assured that all our efforts will be vain. Nature will not, nor cannot, be defeated in her purposes. The necessary mortality must come, in some form or other; and the extirpation of one disease will only be the signal for the birth of another perhaps more fatal. We cannot lower the waters of misery by pressing them down in different places, which must necessarily make them rise somewhere else; the only way in which we can hope to effect our purpose, is by drawing them off. To this course nature is constantly directing our attention by the chastisements which await a contrary conduct. These chastisements are more or less severe, in proportion to the degree in which her admonitions produce their intended effect. In this country at present these admonitions are by no means entirely neglected. The preventive check to population prevails to a considerable degree, and her chastisements are in consequence moderate: but if we were all to marry at the age of puberty, they would be severe indeed. Political evils would probably be added to physical. A people goaded by constant distress, and visited by frequent returns of famine, could not be kept down but by a cruel despotism. We should approach to the state of the people in Egypt or Abyssinia; and I would ask, whether in that case it is probable, that we should be more virtuous?

Physicians have long remarked the great changes which take place in diseases; and that, while some appear to yield to the efforts of human care and skill, others seem to become in proportion more malignant and fatal. Dr. William Heberden published, not long since, some valuable observations on this subject deduced from the London bills of mortality. In his preface, speaking of these bills, he says, "the gradual changes they exhibit in particular diseases correspond to the alterations, which in time are known to take place in the channels through which the great stream of mortality is constantly flowing."[2] In the body of his work, afterwards, speaking of some particular diseases, he observes with that candour which always distinguishes true science; "It is not easy to give a satisfactory reason for all the changes which may be observed to take place in the history of diseases. Nor is it any disgrace to physicians, if their causes are often so gradual in their operation, or so subtle, as to elude investigation."[3]

I hope I shall not be accused of presumption, in venturing to suggest that, under certain circumstances, such changes must take place; and perhaps without any alteration in those proximate causes, which are usually looked to on these occasions. If this should appear to be true, it will not seem extraordinary that the most skilful and scientific physicians, whose business it is principally to investigate proximate causes, should sometimes search for these causes in vain.

In the country which keeps its population at a certain standard, if the average number of marriages and births be given, it is evident that the average number of deaths will also be given; and, to use Dr. Heberden's metaphor, the channels, through which the great stream of mortality is constantly flowing, will always convey off a given quantity. Now if we stop up any of these channels, it is perfectly clear, that the stream of mortality must run with greater force through some of the other channels; that is, if we eradicate some diseases, others will become proportionally more fatal. In this case the only distinguishable cause is the damming up a necessary outlet of mortality.[4] Nature, in the attainment of her great purposes, seems always to seize upon the weakest part. If this part be made strong by human skill, she seizes upon the next weakest part, and so on in succession; not like a capricious deity, with an intention to sport with our sufferings, and constantly to defeat our labours; but, like a kind, though sometimes severe instructor, with the intention of teaching us to make all parts strong, and to chase vice and misery from the earth. In avoiding one fault we are too apt to run into some other; but we always find Nature faithful to her great object, at every false step we commit, ready to admonish us of our errors, by the infliction of some physical or moral evil. If the prevalence of the preventive check to population in a sufficient degree were to remove many of those diseases, which now afflict us, yet be accompanied by a considerable increase of the vice of promiscuous intercourse, it is probable that the disorders and unhappiness, the physical and moral evils arising from this vice, would increase in strength and degree; and, admonishing us severely of our error, would point to the only line of conduct approved by nature, reason and religion, abstinence from marriage till we can support our children, and chastity till that period arrives.

In the case just stated, in which the population and the number of marriages are supposed to be fixed, the necessity of a change in the mortality of some diseases, from the diminution or extinction of others, is capable of mathematical demonstration. The only obscurity which can possibly involve this subject, arises from taking into consideration the effect that might be produced by a diminution of mortality in increasing the population, or in decreasing the number of marriages. That the removal of any of the particular causes of mortality can have no further effect upon population than the means of subsistence will allow, and that it has no certain and necessary influence on these means of subsistence, are facts of which the reader must be already convinced. Of its operation in tending to prevent marriage, by diminishing the demand for fresh supplies of children, I have no doubt; and there is reason to think, that it had this effect in no inconsiderable degree on the extinction of the plague, which had so long and so dreadfully ravaged this country. Dr. Heberden draws a striking picture of the favourable change observed in the health of the people of England since this period; and justly attributes it to the improvements which have gradually taken place, not only in London but in all great towns; and in the manner of living throughout the kingdom, particularly with respect to cleanliness and ventilation.[5] But these causes would not have produced the effect observed, if they had not been accompanied by an increase of the preventive check; and probably the spirit of cleanliness, and better mode of living, which then began to prevail, by spreading more generally a decent and useful pride, principally contributed to this increase. The diminution in the number of marriages, however, was not sufficient to make up for the great decrease of mortality, from the extinction of the plague, and the striking reduction of the deaths in the dysentery.[6] While these and some other disorders became almost evanescent, consumption, palsy, apoplexy, gout, lunacy, and the small-pox, became more mortal.[7] The widening of these drains was necessary to carry off the population which still remained redundant, notwithstanding the increased operation of the preventive check, and the part which was annually disposed of and enabled to subsist by the increase of agriculture.

Dr. Haygarth, in the Sketch of his benevolent plan for the extermination of the casual small-pox, draws a frightful picture of the mortality which has been occasioned by this distemper, attributes to it the slow progress of population, and makes some curious calculations on the favourable effects which would be produced in this respect by its extermination.[8] His conclusions, however, I fear, would not follow from his premises. I am far from doubting that millions and millions of human beings have been destroyed by the small-pox. But were its devastations, as Dr. Haygarth supposes, many thousand degrees greater than the plague,[9] I should still doubt whether the average population of the earth had been diminished by them. The small-pox is certainly one of the channels, and a very broad one, which nature has opened for the last thousand years, to keep down the population to the level of the means of subsistence; but had this been closed, others would have become wider, or new ones would have been formed. In ancient times the mortality from war and the plague was incomparably greater than in modern. On the gradual diminution of this stream of mortality, the generation and almost universal prevalence of the small-pox is a great and striking instance of one of those changes in the channels of mortality, which ought to awaken our attention and animate us to patient and persevering investigation. For my own part I feel not the slightest doubt, that, if the introduction of the cow-pox should extirpate the small-pox, and yet the number of marriages continue the same, we shall find a very perceptible difference in the increased mortality of some other diseases. Nothing could prevent this effect but a sudden start in our agriculture; and if this should take place, it will not be so much owing to the number of children saved from death by the cow-pox inoculation, as to the alarms occasioned among the people of property by the late scarcities,[10] and to the increased gains of farmers, which have been so absurdly reprobated. I am strongly however inclined to believe that the number of marriages will not, in this case, remain the same; but that the gradual light, which may be expected to be thrown on this interesting topic of human inquiry, will teach us how to make the extinction of a mortal disorder a real blessing to us, a real improvement in the general health and happiness of the society.

If, on contemplating the increase of vice which might contingently follow an attempt to inculcate the duty of moral restraint, and the increase of misery that must necessarily follow the attempts to encourage marriage and population, we come to the conclusion, not to interfere in any respect, but to leave every man to his own free choice, and responsible only to God for the evil which he does in either way; this is all I contend for; I would on no account do more; but I contend, that at present we are very far from doing this.

Among the lower classes of society, where the point is of the greatest importance, the poor-laws afford a direct, constant and systematical encouragement to marriage, by removing from each individual that heavy responsibility, which he would incur by the laws of nature, for bringing beings into the world which he could not support. Our private benevolence has the same direction as the poor-laws, and almost invariably tends to encourage marriage, and to equalize as much as possible the circumstances of married and single men.

Among the higher classes of people, the superior distinctions which married women receive, and the marked inattentions to which single women of advanced age are exposed, enable many men, who are agreeable neither in mind nor person, and are besides in the wane of life, to choose a partner among the young and fair, instead of being confined, as nature seems to dictate, to persons of nearly their own age and accomplishments. It is scarcely to be doubted, that the fear of being an old maid, and of that silly and unjust ridicule, which folly sometimes attaches to this came, drives many women into the marriage union with men whom they dislike, or at best to whom they are perfectly indifferent. Such marriages must to every delicate mind appear little better than legal propositions; and they often burden the earth with unnecessary children, without compensating for it by an accession of happiness and virtue to the parties themselves.

Throughout all the ranks of society the prevailing opinions respecting the duty and obligation of marriage cannot but have a very powerful influence. The man who thinks that, in going out of the world without leaving representatives behind him, he shall have failed in an important duty to society, will be disposed to force rather than to repress his inclinations on this subject; and when his reason represents to him the difficulties attending a family, he will endeavour not to attend to these suggestions, will still determine to venture, and will hope that, in the discharge of what he conceives to be his duty, he shall not be deserted by Providence.

In a civilized country, such as England, where a taste for the decencies and comforts of life prevails among a very large class of people, it is not possible that the encouragements to marriage from positive institutions and prevailing opinions should entirely obscure the light of nature and reason on this subject; but still they contribute to make it comparatively weak and indistinct. And till this obscurity is removed, and the poor are undeceived with respect to the principal cause of their poverty, and taught to know, that their happiness or misery must depend chiefly upon themselves, it cannot be said that, with regard to the great question of marriage, we leave every man to his own free and fair choice.

NOTES

1. Necker, speaking of the proportion of the births in France, makes use of a new and instructive expression on this subject, though he hardly seems to be sufficiently aware of it himself. He says, "Le nombre des naissances est à celui des habitans de un à vingt-trois et vingt-quatre dans les lieux *contrariés par la nature, ou par des circonstances morales*: *ce même rapport*, dans la plus grande partie de la France, est de un à 25, 25½, et 26." *Administ. des Finances*, tom. i. c. ix. p. 254. 12mo. It appears, therefore, that we have nothing more to do, than to settle people in marshy situations, and oppress them by a bad government, in order to attain what politicians have hitherto considered as so desirable—a great proportion of marriages and a great proportion of births.

2. *Observations on the Increase and Decrease of Different Diseases*. Preface, p. 5. 4to. 1801.
3. *Id*. p. 43, 4to. 1801.
4. The way in which it operates is probably by increasing poverty, in consequence of a supply of labour too rapid for the demand.
5. *Observations on Increase and Decrease of Diseases*, p. 35.
6. *Id*. p. 34.
7. *Id*. p. 35, et seq.
8. Vol. i. part ii. sect. v, and vi.
9. *Id*. s. viii. p. 164.
10. The scarce harvests of 1799 and 1800. The start here alluded to, certainly took place from 1801 to 1814, and provision was really made for the diminished mortality.

6

Effects of the Knowledge of the Principal Cause of Poverty on Civil Liberty

It may appear, perhaps, that a doctrine, which attributes the greatest part of the sufferings of the lower classes of society exclusively to themselves, is unfavourable to the cause of liberty, as affording a tempting opportunity to governments of oppressing their subjects at pleasure, and laying the whole blame on the laws of nature and the imprudence of the poor. We are not, however, to trust to first appearances; and I am strongly disposed to believe that those who will be at the pains to consider this subject deeply will be convinced, that nothing would so powerfully contribute to the advancement of rational freedom, as a thorough knowledge generally circulated of the principal cause of poverty; and that the ignorance of this cause, and the natural consequences of this ignorance, form, at present, one of the chief obstacles to its progress.

The pressure of distress on the lower classes of people, together with the habit of attributing this distress to their rulers, appears to me to be the rock of defence, the castle, the guardian spirit of despotism. It affords to the tyrant the fatal and unanswerable plea of necessity. It is the reason why every free government tends constantly to destruction; and that its appointed guardians become daily less jealous of the encroachments of power. It is the reason why so many noble efforts in the cause of freedom have failed; and why almost every revolution, after long and painful sacrifices, has terminated in a military despotism. While any dissatisfied man of talents has power to persuade the lower classes of people that all their poverty and distress arise solely from the iniquity of the government, though, perhaps, the greatest part of what they suffer is unconnected with this cause, it is evident that the seeds of fresh discontents and fresh revolutions are continually sowing. When an established government has been destroyed, finding that their poverty is not removed, their resentment naturally falls upon the successors to power; and when these have been immolated without producing the desired effect, other sacrifices are called for, and so on without end. Are we to be surprised that, under such circumstances, the majority of well-disposed people, finding that a government with proper restrictions is unable to support itself against the revolutionary spirit, and weary and exhausted with perpetual change to which they can see no end, should give up the struggle in despair, and throw themselves into the arms of the first power which can afford them protection against the horrors of anarchy?

A mob, which is generally the growth of a redundant population goaded by resentment for real sufferings, but totally ignorant of the quarter from which they originate, is of all monsters the most fatal to freedom. It fosters a prevailing tyranny, and engenders one where it was not; and though, in its dreadful fits of resentment, it appears occasionally to devour its unsightly offspring; yet no sooner is the horrid deed committed, than, however unwilling it may be to propagate such a breed, it immediately groans with a new birth.

Of the tendency of mobs to produce tyranny we may not, perhaps, be long without an example in this country. As a friend to freedom, and naturally an enemy to large standing armies, it is with extreme reluctance that I am compelled to acknowledge that, had it not been for the great organized force in the country, the distresses of the people during the late scarcities,[1] encouraged by the extreme ignorance and folly of many among the higher classes, might have driven them to commit the most dreadful outrages, and ultimately to involve the country in all the horrors of famine. Should such periods often recur, (a recurrence which we have too much reason to apprehend from the present state of the country), the prospect which opens to our view is melancholy in the extreme. The English constitution will be seen hastening with rapid strides to the Euthanasia foretold by Hume, unless its progress be interrupted by some popular commotion; and this alternative presents a picture still more appalling to the imagination. If political discontents were blended with the cries of hunger, and a revolution were to take place by the instrumentality of a mob clamouring for want of food, the consequences would be unceasing change and unceasing carnage, the bloody career of which nothing but the establishment of some complete despotism could arrest.

We can scarcely believe that the appointed guardians of British liberty should quietly have acquiesced in those gradual encroachments of power which have taken place of late years, but from the apprehension of these still more dreadful evils. Great as has been the influence of corruption, I cannot yet think so meanly of the country gentlemen of England, as to believe that they would thus have given up a part of their birthright of liberty, if they had not been actuated by a real and genuine fear that it was then in greater danger from the people than from the crown. They appeared to surrender themselves to government, on condition of being protected from the mob; but they never would have made this melancholy and disheartening surrender, if such a mob had not existed either in reality or in imagination. That the fears on this subject were artfully exaggerated and increased beyond the limits of just apprehension, is undeniable; but I think it is also undeniable that the frequent declamations which were heard against the unjust institutions of society, and the delusive arguments on equality which were circulated among the lower classes, gave us just reason to suppose that, if the *vox populi* had been allowed to speak, it would have appeared to be the voice of error and absurdity, instead of the *vox Dei*.

To say that our conduct is not to be regulated by circumstances, is to betray an ignorance of the most solid and incontrovertible principles of morality. Though the admission of this principle may sometimes afford a cloak to changes of opinion that do not result from the purest motives; yet the admission of a contrary principle would be productive of infinitely worse consequences. The phrase of "existing circumstances" has, I believe, not unfrequently created a smile in the English House of Commons; but the smile should have been reserved for the application of the phrase, and not have been excited by the phrase itself. A very frequent repetition of it has indeed, of itself, rather a suspicious air; and its application should always be watched with the most jealous and anxious attention; but no man ought to be judged *in limine* for saying, that existing circumstances had obliged him to alter his opinions and conduct. The country gentlemen were, perhaps, too easily convinced that existing circumstances called upon them to give up some of the most valuable privileges of Englishmen; but as far as they were really convinced of this obligation, they acted consistently with the clearest rule of morality.

The degree of power to be given to the civil government, and the measure of our submission to it, must be determined by general expediency; and in judging of this expediency every circumstance is to be taken into consideration; particularly the state of public opinion, and the degree of ignorance and delusion prevailing among the common people. The patriot who might be called upon by the love of his country to join with heart and hand in a rising of the people for some specific attainable object of reform, if he knew that they were enlightened respecting their own situation, and would stop short when they had attained their demand, would be called upon by the same motive to submit to very great oppression rather than give the slightest countenance to a popular tumult, the members of which, at least the greater number of them, were persuaded that the destruction of the Parliament, the Lord Mayor, and the monopolizers, would make bread cheap, and that a revolution would enable them all to support their families. In this case it is more the ignorance and delusion of the lower classes of the people that occasions the oppression, than the actual disposition of the government to tyranny.

That there is, however, in all power a constant tendency to encroach is an incontrovertible truth, and cannot be too strongly inculcated. The checks, which are necessary to secure the liberty of the subject, will always in some degree embarrass and delay the operations of the executive government. The members of this government feeling these inconveniences, while they are exerting themselves, as they conceive, in the service of their country, and conscious, perhaps, of no ill intention towards the people, will naturally be disposed, on every occasion, to demand the suspension or abolition of these checks; but if once the convenience of ministers be put in competition with the liberties of the people, and we get into a habit of relying on fair assurances and personal character, instead of examining, with the most scrupulous and jealous care, the merits of each particular case, there is an end of British freedom. If we once admit the principle, that the government must know better with regard to the quantity of power which it wants, than we can possibly do with our limited means of information, and that, therefore, it is our duty to surrender up our private judgments, we may just as well at the same time surrender up the whole of our constitution. Government is a quarter in which liberty is not, nor cannot be, very faithfully preserved. If we are wanting to ourselves, and inattentive to our great interests in this respect, it is the height of folly and unreasonableness to expect that government will attend to them for us. Should the British constitution ultimately lapse into a despotism, as has been prophesied, I shall think that the country gentlemen of England will have much more to answer for than the ministers.

To do the country gentlemen justice, however, I should readily acknowledge that in the partial desertion of their posts as guardians of British freedom, which has already taken place, they have been actuated more by fear than corruption. And the principal reason of this fear was, I conceive, the ignorance and delusions of the common people, and the prospective horrors which were contemplated, if in such a state of mind they should by any revolutionary movement obtain an ascendant.

The circulation of Paine's *Rights of Man*, it is supposed, has done great mischief among the lower and middling classes of people in this country. This is probably true; but not because man is without rights, or that these rights ought not to be known; but because Mr. Paine has fallen into some fundamental errors respecting the principles of government, and in many important points has shown himself totally unacquainted with the structure of society, and the different moral effects to be expected from the physical difference between this country and

America. Mobs of the same description as those collections of people known by this name in Europe could not exist in America. The number of people without property is there, from the physical state of the country, comparatively small; and therefore the civil power, which is to protect property, cannot require the same degree of strength. Mr. Paine very justly observes, that whatever the apparent cause of any riots may be, the real one is always want of happiness; but when he goes on to say, it shows that something is wrong in the system of government, that injures the felicity by which society is to be preserved, he falls into the common error of attributing all want of happiness to government. It is evident that this want of happiness might have existed, and from ignorance might have been the principal cause of the riots; and yet be almost wholly unconnected with any of the proceedings of government. The redundant population of an old state furnishes materials of unhappiness, unknown to such a state as that of America; and if an attempt were to be made to remedy this unhappiness by distributing the produce of the taxes to the poorer classes of society, according to the plan proposed by Mr. Paine, the evil would be aggravated a hundred fold, and in a very short time no sum that the society could possibly raise would be adequate to the proposed object.

Nothing would so effectually counteract the mischiefs occasioned by Mr. Paine's *Rights of Man*, as a general knowledge of the real rights of man. What these rights are it is not my business at present to explain; but there is one right which man has generally been thought to possess, which I am confident he neither does nor can possess—a right to subsistence when his labour will not fairly purchase it. Our laws indeed say that he has this right, and bind the society to furnish employment and food to those who cannot get them in the regular market; but in so doing they attempt to reverse the laws of nature; and it is in consequence to be expected, not only that they should fail in their object, but that the poor, who were intended to be benefited, should suffer most cruelly from the inhuman deceit thus practised upon them.

The Abbé Raynal has said, that "Avant toutes les loix sociales l'homme avoit le droit de subsister."[2] He might with just as much propriety have said that, before the institution of social laws, every man had a right to live a hundred years. Undoubtedly he had then, and has still, a good right to live a hundred years, nay a thousand if he can, without interfering with the right of others to live; but the affair in both cases is principally an affair of power not of right. Social laws very greatly increase this power, by enabling a much greater number to subsist than could subsist without them, and so far very greatly enlarge *le droit de subsister*; but, neither before nor after the institution of social laws, could an unlimited number subsist; and before as well as since, he who ceased to have the power ceased to have the right.

If the great truths on these subjects were more generally circulated, and the lower classes of people could be convinced that by the laws of nature, independently of any particular institutions, except the great one of property, which is absolutely necessary in order to attain any considerable produce, no person has any claim of right on society for subsistence, if his labour will not purchase it, the greatest part of the mischievous declamation on the unjust institutions of society would fall powerless to the ground. The poor are by no means inclined to be visionary. Their distresses are always real, though they are not attributed to the real causes. If these causes were properly explained to them, and they were taught to know what part of their present distress was attributable to government, and what part to causes totally unconnected with it, discontent and irritation among the lower classes of people would show themselves much less frequently than at present; and when they did show themselves, would be much less to be dreaded. The efforts of turbulent and discontented men in the middle classes of society might safely be disregarded, if the poor were so far enlightened respecting the real nature of their situation, as to be aware that by aiding them in their schemes of renovation, they would probably be promoting the ambitious views of others, without in any respect benefiting themselves. The country gentlemen and men of property in England might securely return to a wholesome jealousy of the encroachments of power; and instead of daily sacrificing the liberties of the subject on the altar of public safety, might, without any just apprehension from the people, not only tread back their late steps, but firmly insist upon those gradual reforms, which the lapse of time and the storms of the political world have rendered necessary, to prevent the gradual destruction of the British constitution.

All improvements in governments must necessarily originate with persons of some education; and these will of course be found among the people of property. Whatever may be said of a few, it is impossible to suppose that the great mass of the people of property should be really interested in the abuses of government. They merely submit to them from the fear that an endeavour to remove them might be productive of greater evils. Could we but take away this fear, reform and improvement would proceed with as much facility as the removal of nuisances, or the paving and lighting of the streets. In human life we are continually called upon to submit to a lesser evil in order to avoid a greater; and it is the part of a wise man to do this readily and cheerfully; but no wise man will submit to any evil, if he can get rid of it without danger. Remove all apprehension from the tyranny or folly of the people, and the tyranny of government could not stand a moment. It would then appear in its proper deformity, without palliation, without pretext, without protector. Naturally feeble in itself, when it was once stripped naked, and deprived of the support of public opinion and of the great plea of necessity, it would fall without a struggle. Its few interested defenders would hide their heads abashed, and would be ashamed any longer to support a cause, for which no human ingenuity could invent a plausible argument.

The most successful supporters of tyranny are without doubt those general declaimers, who attribute the distresses of the poor, and almost all the evils to which society is subject, to human institutions and the iniquity of governments. The falsity of these accusations, and the dreadful consequences that would result from their being generally admitted and acted upon, make it absolutely necessary that they should at all events be resisted; not only on account of the immediate revolutionary horrors to be expected from a movement of the people acting under such impressions (a consideration which must at all times have very great weight); but also on account of the extreme probability that such a revolution would terminate in a much worse despotism than that which it had destroyed. On these grounds a genuine friend of freedom, a zealous advocate for the real rights of man, might be found among the defenders of a considerable degree of tyranny. A cause bad in itself might be supported by the good and the virtuous, merely because that which was opposed to it was much worse; and because it was absolutely necessary at the moment to make a choice between the two. Whatever therefore may be the intention of those indiscriminate accusations against governments, their real effect undoubtedly is, to add a weight of talents and principles to the prevailing power, which it never would have received otherwise.

It is a truth, which I trust has been sufficiently proved in the course of this work, that under a government constructed upon the best and purest principles, and executed by men of the highest talents and integrity, the most squalid poverty and wretchedness might universally prevail from an inattention to the prudential check to population. And as this cause of unhappiness has hitherto been so little understood, that the efforts of society have always tended rather to aggravate than to lessen it, we have the strongest reasons for supposing that, in all the governments with which we are acquainted, a great part of the misery to be observed among the lower classes of the people arises from this cause.

The inference therefore which Mr. Paine and others have drawn against governments from the unhappiness of the people, is palpably unfair; and before we give a sanction to such accusations, it is a debt we owe to truth and justice, to ascertain how much of this unhappiness arises from the principle of population, and how much is fairly to be attributed to government. When this distinction has been properly made, and all the vague, indefinite and false accusations removed, government would remain, as it ought to be, clearly responsible for the rest; and the amount of this would still be such as to make the responsibility very considerable. Though government has but little power in the direct and immediate relief of poverty, yet its indirect influence on the prosperity of its subjects is striking and incontestable. And the reason is, that though it is comparatively impotent in its efforts to make the food of a country keep pace with an unrestricted increase of population, yet its influence is great in giving the best direction to those checks, which in some form or other must necessarily take place. It has clearly appeared in the former part of this work, that the most despotic and worst-governed countries, however low they might be in actual population, were uniformly the most populous in proportion to their means of subsistence; and the necessary effect of this state of things must of course be very low wages. In such countries the checks to population arise more from the sickness and mortality consequent on poverty, than from the prudence and foresight which restrain the frequency and universality of early marriages. The checks are more of the positive and less of the preventive kind.

The first grand requisite to the growth of prudential habits is the perfect security of property; and the next perhaps is that respectability and importance, which are given to the lower classes by equal laws, and the possession of some influence in the framing of them. The more excellent therefore is the government, the more does it tend to generate that prudence and elevation of sentiment, by which alone in the present state of our being poverty can be avoided.

It has been sometimes asserted that the only reason why it is advantageous that the people should have some share in the government, is that a representation of the people tends best to secure the framing of good and equal laws; but that, if the same object could be attained under a despotism, the same advantage would accrue to the community. If however the representative system, by securing to the lower classes of society a more equal and liberal mode of treatment from their superiors, gives to each individual a greater personal respectability, and a greater fear of personal degradation; it is evident that it will powerfully co-operate with the security of property in animating the exertions of industry, and in generating habits of prudence; and thus more powerfully tend to increase the riches and prosperity of the lower classes of the community, than if the same laws had existed under a despotism.

But though the tendency of a free constitution and a good government to diminish poverty be certain; yet their effect in this way must necessarily be indirect and slow, and very different from the direct and immediate relief, which the lower classes of people are too frequently in the habit of looking forward to as the consequence of a revolution. This habit of expecting too much, and the irritation occasioned by disappointment, continually give a wrong direction to their efforts in favour of liberty, and constantly tend to defeat the accomplishment of those gradual reforms in government, and that slow melioration of the condition of the lower classes of society, which are really attainable. It is of the very highest importance therefore, to know distinctly what government cannot do, as well as what it can. If I were called upon to name the cause, which, in my conception, had more than any other contributed to the very slow progress of freedom, so disheartening to every liberal mind, I should say that it was the confusion that had existed respecting the causes of the unhappiness and discontents which prevail in society; and the advantage which governments had been able to take, and indeed had been compelled to take, of this confusion, to confirm and strengthen their power. I cannot help thinking, therefore, that a knowledge generally circulated, that the principal cause of want and unhappiness is only indirectly connected with government, and totally beyond its power directly to remove, and that it depends upon the conduct of the poor themselves, would, instead of giving any advantage to governments, give a great additional weight to the popular side of the question, by removing the dangers with which from ignorance it is at present accompanied, and thus tend, in a very powerful manner, to promote the cause of rational freedom.

NOTES

1. 1800 and 1801.
2. Raynal, *Hist. des Indes*, vol. x. s. x. p. 322, 8vo.

7

Continuation of the Same Subject[1]

The reasonings of the foregoing chapter have been strikingly confirmed by the events of the last two or three years. Perhaps there never was a period when more erroneous views were formed by the lower classes of society of the effects to be expected from reforms in the government, when these erroneous views were more immediately founded on a total misapprehension of the principal cause of poverty, and when they more directly led to results unfavourable to liberty.

One of the main causes of complaint against the government has been, that a considerable number of labourers, who are both able and willing to work, are wholly out of employment, and unable consequently to command the necessaries of life. That this state of things is one of the most afflicting events that can occur in civilized life, that it is a natural and pardonable cause of discontent among the lower classes of society, and that every effort should be made by the higher classes to mitigate it, consistently with a proper care not to render it permanent, no man of humanity can doubt. But that such a state of things may occur in the best-conducted and most economical government that ever existed is as certain, as that governments have not the power of commanding with effect the resources of a country to be progressive, when they are naturally stationary or declining.

It will be allowed that periods of prosperity may occur in any well-governed state, during which an extraordinary stimulus may be given to its wealth and population, which cannot in its nature be permanent. If, for instance, new channels of trade are opened, new colonies are possessed, new inventions take place in machinery, and new and great improvements are made in agriculture, it is quite obvious that while the markets at home and abroad will readily take off at advantageous prices the increasing produce, there must be a rapid increase of capital, and an unusual stimulus given to the population. On the other hand, if subsequently these channels of trade are either closed by accident, or contracted by foreign competition; if colonies are lost, or the same produce is supplied from other quarters; if the markets, either from glut or competition, cease to extend with the extension of the new machinery; and if the improvements in agriculture from any cause whatever cease to be progressive, it is as obvious that, just at the time when the stimulus to population has produced its greatest effect, the means of employing and supporting this population may, in the natural course of things, and without any fault whatever in the government, become deficient. This failure must unavoidably produce great distress among the labouring classes of society; but it is quite clear that no inference can be drawn from this distress, that a radical change is required in the government; and the attempt to accomplish such a change might only aggravate the evil.

It has been supposed in this case, that the government has in no respect by its conduct contributed to the pressure in question, a supposition which in practice perhaps will rarely be borne out by the fact. It is unquestionably in the power of a government to produce great distress by war and taxation, and it requires some skill to distinguish the distress which is the natural result of these causes, from that which is occasioned in the way just described. In our own case unquestionably both descriptions of causes have combined, but the former in a greater degree than the latter. War and taxation, as far as they operate directly and simply, tend to destroy or retard the progress of capital, produce, and population; but during the late war these checks to prosperity have been much more than overbalanced by a combination of circumstances which has given an extraordinary stimulus to production. That for this overbalance of advantages the country cannot be considered as much indebted to the government, is most certain. The government during the last twenty-five years has shown no very great love either of peace or liberty; and no particular economy in the use of the national resources. It has proceeded in a very straightforward manner to spend great sums in war, and to raise them by very heavy taxes. It has no doubt done its part towards the dilapidation of the national resources. But still the broad fact must stare every impartial observer in the face, that at the end of the war in 1814 the national resources were not dilapidated; and that not only were the wealth and population of the country considerably greater than they were at the commencement of the war, but that they had increased in the interval at a more rapid rate than was ever experienced before.

Perhaps this may justly be considered as one of the most extraordinary facts in history; and it certainly follows from it, that the sufferings of the country since the peace have not been occasioned so much by the usual and most natural effects to be expected from war and taxation, as by the sudden ceasing of an extraordinary stimulus to production, the distresses consequent upon which, though increased no doubt by the weight of taxation, do not essentially arise from it, and are not directly, therefore, and immediately, to be relieved by its removal.

That the labouring classes of society should not be fully aware that the main causes of their distress are, to a certain extent and for a certain time, irremediable, is natural enough; and that they should listen much more readily and willingly to those who confidently promise immediate relief, rather than to those who can only tell them unpalatable truths, is by no means surprising. But it must be allowed that full advantage has been taken by the popular orators and writers of a crisis which has given them so much power. Partly from ignorance, and partly from design, every thing that could tend to enlighten the labouring classes as to the real nature of their situation, and encourage them to bear an unavoidable pressure with patience, has been either sedulously kept out of their view, or clamorously reprobated; and every thing that could tend to deceive them, to aggravate and encourage their discontents, and to raise unreasonable and extravagant expectations as to the relief to be expected from reform, has been as sedulously brought forward. If under these circumstances the reforms proposed had been accomplished, it is impossible that the people should not have been most cruelly disappointed; and under a system of universal suffrage and annual parliaments, a general disappointment of the people would probably lead to every sort of experiment in government, till the career of change was stopped by a military despotism. The warmest friends of genuine liberty might justly feel alarmed at such a prospect. To a cause conducted upon such principles, and likely to be attended with such results, they could not of course, consistently with their duty, lend any assistance. And if with great difficulty, and against the sense of the great mass of petitioners, they were to effect a more moderate and more really useful reform, they could not but feel certain that the unavoidable disappointment of the people would be attributed to the half-measures which had been pursued; and that they would be either forced to proceed to more radical changes, or submit to a total loss of their influence and popularity by stopping short while the distresses of the people were unrelieved, their discontents unallayed, and the great panacea on which they had built their sanguine expectations untried.

These considerations have naturally paralyzed the exertions of the best friends of liberty; and those salutary reforms which are acknowledged to be necessary in order to repair the breaches of time, and improve the fabric of our constitution, are thus rendered much more difficult, and consequently much less probable.

But not only have the false expectations and extravagant demands suggested by the leaders of the people given an easy victory to government over every proposition for reform, whether violent or moderate, but they have furnished the most fatal instruments of offensive attack against the constitution itself. They are naturally calculated to excite some alarm, and to check moderate reform; but alarm, when once excited, seldom knows where to stop, and the causes of it are particularly liable to be exaggerated. There is reason to believe that it has been under the influence of exaggerated statements, and of inferences drawn by exaggerated fears from these statements, that acts unfavourable to liberty have been passed without an adequate necessity. But the power of creating these exaggerated fears, and of passing these acts, has been unquestionably furnished by the extravagant expectations of the people. And it must be allowed that the present times furnish a very striking illustration of the doctrine, that an ignorance of the principal cause of poverty is peculiarly unfavourable, and that a knowledge of it must be peculiarly favourable, to the cause of civil liberty.

NOTE

1. Written in 1817.

8

Plan of the Gradual Abolition of the Poor-Laws Proposed

If the principles in the preceding chapters should stand the test of examination, and we should ever feel the obligation of endeavouring to act upon them, the next inquiry would be, in what way we ought practically to proceed. The first grand obstacle which presents itself in this country is the system of the poor-laws, which has been justly stated to be an evil, in comparison of which the national debt, with all its magnitude of terror, is of little moment.[1] The rapidity with which the poor's rates have increased of late years presents us indeed with the prospect of such an extraordinary proportion of paupers in the society, as would seem to be incredible in a nation flourishing in arts, agriculture and commerce, and with a government which has generally been allowed to be the best that has hitherto stood the test of experience.[2]

Greatly as we may be shocked at such a prospect, and ardently as we may wish to remove it, the evil is now so deeply seated, and the relief given by the poor-laws so widely extended, that no man of humanity could venture to propose their immediate abolition. To mitigate their effects however and stop their future increase, to which, if left to continue upon their present plan, we can see no probable termination, it has been proposed to fix the whole sum to be raised at its present rate, or any other that might be determined upon; and to make a law, that on no account this sum should be exceeded. The objection to this plan is, that a very large sum would be still to be raised, and a great number of people to be supported; the consequence of which would be, that the poor would not be easily able to distinguish the alteration that had been made. Each individual would think that he had as good a right to be supported when he was in want as any other person; and those who unfortunately chanced to be in distress, when the fixed sum had been collected, would think themselves particularly ill-used on being excluded from all assistance, while so many others were enjoying this advantage. If the sum collected were divided among all that were in want, however their numbers might increase, though such a plan would not be so unfair with regard to those who became dependent after the sum had been fixed, it would undoubtedly be very hard upon those who had been in the habit of receiving a more liberal supply, and had done nothing to justify its being taken from them: and in both cases it would certainly be unjust in the society to undertake the support of the poor, and yet, if their numbers increased, to feed them so sparingly, that they must necessarily die of hunger and disease.

I have reflected much on the subject of the poor-laws, and hope therefore that I shall be excused in venturing to suggest a mode of their gradual abolition, to which I confess that at present I can see no material objection. Of this indeed I feel nearly convinced, that, should we ever become so fully sensible of the widespreading tyranny, dependence, indolence and unhappiness which they create, as seriously to make an effort to abolish them, we shall be compelled by a sense of justice to adopt the principle, if not the plan, which I shall mention. It seems impossible to get rid of so extensive a system of support, consistently with humanity, without applying ourselves directly to its vital principle, and endeavouring to counteract that deeply-seated cause which occasions the rapid growth of all such establishments, and invariably renders them inadequate to their object.

As a previous step even to any considerable alteration in the present system, which would contract or stop the increase of the relief to be given, it appears to me that we are bound in justice and honour formally to disclaim the right of the poor to support.

To this end, I should propose a regulation to be made, declaring, that no child born from any marriage, taking place after the expiration of a year from the date of the law, and no illegitimate child born two years from the same date, should ever be entitled to parish assistance. And to give a more general knowledge of this law, and to enforce it more strongly on the minds of the lower classes of people, the clergyman of each parish should, after the publication of bans, read a short address, stating the strong obligation on every man to support his own children; the impropriety, and even immorality, of marrying without a prospect of being able to do this; the evils which had resulted to the poor themselves from the attempt which had been made to assist by public institutions in a duty which ought to be exclusively appropriated to parents; and the absolute necessity which had at length appeared of abandoning all such institutions, on account of their producing effects totally opposite to those which were intended.

This would operate as a fair, distinct and precise notice, which no man could well mistake; and, without pressing hard on any particular individuals, would at once throw off the rising generation from that miserable and helpless dependence upon the government and the rich, the moral as well as physical consequences of which are almost incalculable.

After the public notice which I have proposed had been given, and the system of poor-laws had ceased with regard to the rising generation, if any man chose to marry, without a prospect of being able to support a family, he should have the most perfect liberty so to do. Though to marry, in this case, is, in my opinion, clearly an immoral act, yet it is not one which society can justly take upon itself to prevent or punish; because the punishment provided for it by the laws of nature falls directly and most severely upon the individual who commits the act, and through him, only more remotely and feebly, on the society. When nature will govern and punish for us, it is a very miserable ambition to wish to snatch the rod from her hands, and draw upon ourselves the odium of executioner. To the punishment therefore of nature he should be left, the punishment of want. He has erred in the face of a most clear and precise warning, and can have no just reason to complain of any person but himself when he feels the consequences of his error. All parish assistance should be denied him; and he should be left to the uncertain support of private charity. He should be taught to know, that the laws of nature, which are the laws of God, had doomed him and his family to suffer for disobeying their repeated admonitions; that he had no claim of right on society for the smallest portion of food, beyond that which his labour would fairly purchase; and that if he and his family were saved from feeling the natural consequences of his imprudence, he would owe it to the pity of some kind benefactor, to whom, therefore, he ought to be bound by the strongest ties of gratitude.

If this system were pursued, we need be under no apprehensions that the number of persons in extreme want would be beyond the power and the will of the benevolent to supply. The sphere for the exercise of private charity would, probably, not be greater than it is at present; and the principal difficulty would be, to restrain the hand of benevolence from assisting those in, distress in so indiscriminate a manner as to encourage indolence and want of foresight in others.

With regard to illegitimate children, after the proper notice had been given, they should not be allowed to have any claim to parish assistance, but be left entirely to the support of private charity. If the parents desert their child, they ought to be made answerable for the crime. The infant is, comparatively speaking, of little value to the society, as others will immediately supply its place. Its principal value is on account of its being the object of one of the most delightful passions in human nature—parental affection. But if this value be disregarded by those who are alone in a capacity to feel it, the society cannot be called upon to put itself in their place; and has no further business in its protection than to punish the crime of desertion or intentional ill treatment in the persons whose duty it is to provide for it.

At present the child is taken under the protection of the parish,[3] and generally dies, at least in London, within the first year. The loss to the society is the same; but the crime is diluted by the number of people concerned, and the death passes as a visitation of Providence, instead of being considered as the necessary consequence of the conduct of its parents, for which they ought to be held responsible to God and to society.

The desertion of both parents, however, is not so common as the desertion of one. When a servant or labouring man has an illegitimate child, his running away is perfectly a matter of course; and it is by no means uncommon for a man who has a wife and large family to withdraw into a distant county, and leave them to the parish; indeed I once heard a hard-working good sort of man propose to do this, as the best mode of providing for a wife and six children.[4] If the simple fact of these frequent desertions were related in some countries, a strange inference would be drawn against the English character; but the wonder would cease when our public institutions were explained.

By the laws of nature, a child is confided directly and exclusively to the protection of its parents. By the laws of nature, the mother of a child is confided almost as strongly and exclusively to the man who is the father of it. If these ties were suffered to remain in the state in which nature has left them, and the man were convinced that the woman and the child depended solely upon him for support, I scarcely believe that there are ten men breathing so atrocious as to desert them. But our laws, in opposition to the laws of nature, say, that if the parents forsake their child, other persons will undertake to support it; or, if the man forsake the woman, that she shall still meet with protection elsewhere; that is, we take all possible pains to weaken and render null the ties of nature, and then say that men are unnatural. But the fact is, that the society itself, in its body politic, is the unnatural character, for framing laws that thus counteract the laws of nature, and give premiums to the violation of the best and most honourable feelings of the human heart.

It is a common thing in most parishes, when the father of an illegitimate child can be seized, to endeavour to frighten him into marriage by the terrors of a jail; but such a proceeding cannot surely be too strongly reprobated. In the first place, it is a most shallow policy in the parish officers; for, if they succeed, the effect upon the present system will generally be, that of having three or four children to provide for, instead of one. And in the next place it is difficult to conceive a more gross and scandalous profanation of a religious ceremony. Those who believe that the character of a woman is restored by such a forced engagement, or that the moral worth of the man is enhanced by affirming a lie before God, have, I confess, very different ideas of delicacy and morality from those which I have been taught to consider as just. If a man deceive a woman into a connexion with him under a promise of marriage, he has undoubtedly been guilty of a most atrocious act, and there are few crimes which merit a more severe punishment; but the last that I should choose is that which will oblige him to affirm another falsehood, which will probably render the woman that he is to be joined to miserable, and will burden the society with a family of paupers.

The obligation on every man to support his children, whether legitimate or illegitimate, is so clear and strong, that it would be just to arm society with any power to enforce it, which would be likely to answer the purpose. But I am inclined to believe that no exercise of the civil power, however rigorous, would be half so effectual as a knowledge generally circulated, that children were in future to depend solely for support upon their parents, and would be left only to casual charity if they were deserted.

It may appear to be hard that a mother and her children, who have been guilty of no particular crime themselves, should suffer for the ill conduct of the father; but this is one of the invariable laws of nature; and, knowing this, we should think twice upon the subject, and be very sure of the ground on which we go, before we presume systematically to counteract it.

I have often heard the goodness of the Deity impeached on account of that part of the Decalogue in which he declares that he will visit the sins of the father upon the children; but the objection has not perhaps been sufficiently considered. Without a most complete and fundamental change in the whole constitution of human nature; without making man an angel, or at least something totally different from what he is at present; it seems absolutely necessary that such a law should prevail. Would it not require a perpetual miracle, which is perhaps a contradiction in terms, to prevent children from being affected in their moral and civil condition by the conduct of their parents? What man is there, that has been brought up by his parents, who is not at the present moment enjoying something from their virtues, or suffering something from their vices; who, in his moral character, has not been elevated in some degree by their prudence, their justice, their benevolence, their temperance, or depressed by the contraries; who, in his civil condition, has not been raised by their reputation, their foresight, their industry, their good fortune, or lowered by their want of character, their imprudence, their indolence, and their adversity? And how much does a knowledge of this transmission of blessings contribute to excite and invigorate virtuous exertion? Proceeding upon this certainty, how ardent and incessant are the efforts of parents to give their children a good education, and to provide for their future situation in the world! If a man could neglect or desert his wife and children without their suffering any injury, how many individuals there are, who, not being very fond of their wives, or being tired of the shackles of matrimony, would withdraw from household cares and difficulties, and resume their liberty and independence as single men! But the consideration that children may suffer for the faults of their parents has a strong hold even upon vice; and many who are in such a state of mind, as to disregard the consequence of their habitual course of life, as far as relates to themselves, are yet greatly anxious that their children should not suffer from their vices and follies. In the moral government of the world, it seems evidently necessary, that the sins of the fathers should be visited upon the children; and if in our overweening vanity we imagine, that we can govern a private society better by endeavouring systematically to counteract this law, I am inclined to believe, that we shall find ourselves very greatly mistaken.

If the plan which I have proposed were adopted, the poor's rates in a few years would begin very rapidly to decrease, and in no great length of time would be completely extinguished; and yet, as far as it appears to me at present, no individual would be either deceived or injured, and consequently no person could have a just right to complain.

The abolition of the poor-laws however is not of itself sufficient; and the obvious answer to those who lay too much stress on this system is, to desire them to look at the state of the poor in some other countries where such laws do not prevail, and to compare it with their condition in England. But this comparison, it must be acknowledged, is in many respects unfair; and would by no means decide the question of the utility or inutility of such a system. England possesses very great natural and political advantages, in which perhaps the countries, that we should in this case compare with her, would be found to be palpably deficient. The nature of her soil and climate is such, that those almost universal failures in the crops of grain, which are known in some countries, never occur in England. Her insular situation and extended commerce are peculiarly favourable for importation. Her numerous manufactures employ nearly all the hands that are not engaged in agriculture, and afford the means of a regular distribution of the annual produce of the land and labour to the whole of her inhabitants. But, above all, throughout a very large class of people, a decided taste for the conveniences and comforts of life, a strong desire of bettering their condition (that master-spring of public prosperity), and, in consequence, a most laudable spirit of industry and foresight, are observed to prevail. These dispositions, so contrary to the hopeless indolence remarked in despotic countries, are generated by the constitution of the English government, and the excellence of its laws, which secure to every individual the produce of his industry. When, therefore, on a comparison with other countries, England appears to have the advantage in the state of her poor, the superiority is entirely to be attributed to these favourable circumstances, and not to the poor-laws. A woman with one bad feature, may greatly excel in beauty some other, who may have this individual feature tolerably good; but it would be rather strange to assert, in consequence, that the superior beauty of the former was occasioned by this particular deformity. The poor-laws have constantly tended to counteract the natural and acquired advantages of this country. Fortunately these disadvantages have been so considerable, that though weakened they could not be overcome; and to these advantages, together with the checks to marriage, which the laws themselves create, it is owing that England has been able to bear up so long against this pernicious system. Probably there is not any other country in the world, except perhaps Holland before the revolution, which could have acted upon it so completely for the same period of time, without utter ruin.

It has been proposed by some to establish poor-laws in Ireland; but from the depressed state of the common people, there is little reason to doubt, that, on the establishment of such laws, the whole of the landed property would very soon be absorbed, or the system be given up in despair.

In Sweden, from the dearths which are not unfrequent, owing to the general failure of crops in an unpropitious climate and the impossibility of great importations in a poor country, an attempt to establish a system of parochial relief such as that in England (if it were not speedily abandoned from the physical impossibility of executing it) would level the property of the kingdom from one end to the other, and convulse the social system in such a manner, as absolutely to prevent it from recovering its former state on the return of plenty.

Even in France, with all her advantages of situation and climate, the tendency to population is so great, and the want of foresight among the lower classes of the people so remarkable, that if poor-laws were established, the landed property would soon sink under the burden, and the wretchedness of the people at the same time be increased. On these considerations the committee de Mendicité, at the beginning of the revolution, very properly and judiciously rejected the establishment of such a system, which had been proposed.

The exception of Holland, if it were an exception, would arise from very particular circumstances—her extensive foreign trade and her numerous colonial emigrations, compared with the smallness of her territory, together with the extreme unhealthiness of a great part of the country, which occasions a much greater average mortality than is common in other states. These, I conceive, were the unobserved causes which principally contributed to render Holland so famous for the management of her poor, and able to employ and support all who applied for relief.

No part of Germany is sufficiently rich to support an extensive system of parochial relief; but I am inclined to think, that from the absence of it the lower classes of the people, in some parts of Germany, are in a better situation than those of the same class in England. In Switzerland, for the same reason, their condition, before the late troubles, was perhaps universally superior: and in a journey through the duchies of Holstein and Sleswick belonging to Denmark, the houses of the lower classes of people appeared to me to be neater and better, and in general there were fewer indications of poverty and wretchedness among them than among the same ranks in this country.

Even in Norway, notwithstanding the disadvantage of a severe and uncertain climate, from the little that I saw in a few weeks' residence in the country, and the information that I could collect from others, I am inclined to think that the poor are, on the average, better off than in England. Their houses and clothing are often superior; and though they have no white bread, they have much more meat, fish and milk than our labourers; and I particularly remarked, that the farmers' boys were much stouter and healthier looking lads than those of the same description in England. This degree of happiness, superior to what could be expected from the soil and climate, arises almost exclusively from the degree in which the preventive check to population operates. The establishment of a system of poor-laws, which would destroy this check, would at once sink the lower classes of the people into a state of the most miserable poverty and wretchedness; would diminish their industry, and consequently the produce of the land and labour of the country; would weaken the resources of ingenuity in times of scarcity; and ultimately involve the country in all the horrors of continual famines.

If, as in Ireland, Spain, and many countries of the more southern climates, the people are in so degraded a state, as to propagate their species without regard to consequences, it matters little whether they have poor-laws or not. Misery in all its various forms must be the predominant check to their increase. Poor-laws, indeed, will always tend to aggravate the evil, by diminishing the general resources of the country; and in such a state of things can exist only for a very short time; but with or without them, no stretch of human ingenuity and exertion can rescue the people from the most extreme poverty and wretchedness.

NOTES

1. Reports of the Society for bettering the Condition of the Poor, vol. iii, p. 21.
2. If the poor's rates continue increasing as rapidly as they have done on the average of the last ten years, how melancholy are our future prospects! The system of the poor-laws bus been justly stated by the French to be *la plaie politique de l'Angleterre la plus devorante.* (Comité de Mendicité.)
3. I fully agree with Sir F.M. Eden, in thinking that the constant public support which deserted children receive is the cause of their very great numbers in the two most opulent countries of Europe, France and England. *State of the Poor*, vol. i, p. 339.
4. "That many of the poorer classes of the community avail themselves of the liberality of the law, and leave their wives and children on the parish, the reader will find abundant proof in the subsequent part of this work." Sir F.M. Eden on the *State of the Poor*, vol. i, p. 339.

9

Of the Modes of Correcting the Prevailing Opinions on Population

It is not enough to abolish all the positive institutions which encourage population; but we must endeavour, at the same time, to correct the prevailing opinions which have the same, or perhaps even a more powerful effect. This must necessarily be a work of time; and can only be done by circulating juster notions on these subjects in writings and conversation; and by endeavouring to impress as strongly as possible on the public mind, that it is not the duty of man simply to propagate his species, but to propagate virtue and happiness; and that, if he has not a tolerably fair prospect of doing this, he is by no means called upon to leave descendants.

Among the higher ranks of society, we have not much reason to apprehend the too great frequency of marriage. Though the circulation of juster notions on this subject might, even in this part of the community, do much good, and prevent many unhappy marriages; yet whether we make particular exertions for this purpose or not, we may rest assured that the degree of proper pride and spirit of independence almost invariably connected with education and a certain rank in life will secure the operation of the prudential check to marriage to a considerable extent. All that the society can reasonably require of its members is, that they should not have families without being able to support them. This may be fairly enjoined as a positive duty. Every restraint beyond this must be considered as a matter of choice and taste; but from what we already know of the habits which prevail among the higher ranks of life, we have reason to think that little more is wanted to attain the object required, than to award a greater degree of respect and of personal liberty to single women, and to place them nearer upon a level with married women;—a change, which, independently of any particular purpose in view, the plainest principles of equity seem to demand.

If, among the higher classes of society, the object of securing the operation of the prudential check to marriage to a sufficient degree appear to be attainable without much difficulty, the obvious mode of proceeding with the lower classes of society, where the point is of the principal importance, is to endeavour to infuse into them a portion of that knowledge and foresight, which so much facilitates the attainment of this object in the educated part of the community.

The fairest chance of accomplishing this end would probably be by the establishment of a system of parochial education upon a plan similar to that proposed by Adam Smith.[1] In addition to the usual subjects of instruction, and those which he has mentioned, I should be disposed to lay considerable stress on the frequent explanation of the real state of the lower classes of society, as affected by the principle of population, and their consequent dependence on themselves for the chief part of their happiness or misery. It would be by no means necessary or proper in these explanations to underrate, in the smallest degree, the desirableness of marriage. It should always be represented as, what it really is, a state peculiarly suited to the nature of man, and calculated greatly to advance his happiness and remove the temptations to vice; but, like property or any other desirable object, its advantages should be shown to be unattainable, except under certain conditions. And a strong conviction in a young man of the great desirableness of marriage, with a conviction at the same time that the power of supporting a family was the only condition which would enable him really to enjoy its blessings, would be the most effectual motive imaginable to industry and sobriety before marriage, and would powerfully urge him to save that superfluity of income which single labourers necessarily possess, for the accomplishment of a rational and desirable object, instead of dissipating it, as is now usually done, in idleness and vice.

If in the course of time a few of the simplest principles of political economy could be added to the instructions given in these schools, the benefit to society would be almost incalculable.[2] In some conversations with labouring men, during the late scarcities,[3] I confess that I was to the last degree disheartened, at observing their inveterate prejudices on the subject of grain; and I felt very strongly the almost absolute incompatibility of a government really free with such a degree of ignorance. The delusions are of such a nature, that, if acted upon, they must at all events be repressed by force; and it is extremely difficult to give such a power to the government as will be sufficient at all times for this purpose, without the risk of its being employed improperly, and endangering the liberty of the subject.

We have lavished immense sums on the poor, which we have every reason to think have constantly tended to aggravate their misery. But in their education and in the circulation of those important political truths that most nearly concern them, which are perhaps the only means in our power of really raising their condition, and of making them happier men and more peaceable subjects, the have been miserably deficient. It is surely a great national disgrace, that the education of the lower classes of people in England should be left merely to a few Sunday schools, supported by a subscription from individuals, who can give to the course of instruction in them any kind of bias which they please. And even the improvement of Sunday schools (for, objectionable as they are in some points of view, and imperfect in all, I cannot but consider them as an improvement) is of very late date.[4]

The arguments which have been urged against instructing the people appear to me to be not only illiberal, but to the last degree feeble; and they ought, on the contrary, to be extremely forcible, and to be supported by the most obvious and striking necessity, to warrant us in withholding the means of raising the condition of the lower classes of people, when they are, in our power. Those who will not listen to any answer to these arguments drawn from theory, cannot, I think, refuse the testimony of experience; and I would ask, whether the advantage of superior instruction which the lower classes of people in Scotland are known to possess, has appeared to have any tendency towards creating a spirit of tumult and discontent amongst them. And yet, from the natural inferiority of its soil and climate, the pressure of want is more constant, and the dearths are not only more frequent, but more dreadful than in England. In the case of Scotland, the knowledge circulated among the common people, though not sufficient essentially to better their condition by increasing, in an adequate degree, their habits of prudence and foresight, has yet the effect of making them bear with patience the evils which they suffer, from being aware of the folly and inefficacy of turbulence. The quiet and peaceable habits of the instructed Scotch peasant, compared with the turbulent disposition of the ignorant Irishman, ought not to be without effect upon every impartial reasoner.

The principal argument which I have heard advanced against a system of national education in England is, that the common people would be put in a capacity to read such works as those of Paine, and that the consequences would probably be fatal to government. But on this subject I agree most cordially with Adam Smith[5] in thinking, that an instructed and well-informed people would be much less likely to be led away by inflammatory writings, and much better able to detect the false declamation of interested and ambitious demagogues, than an ignorant people. One or two readers in a parish are sufficient to circulate any quantity of sedition; and if these be gained to the democratic side, they will probably have the power of doing much more mischief, by selecting the passages best suited to their hearers, and choosing the moments when their oratory is likely to have the most effect, than if each individual in the parish had been in a capacity to read and judge of the whole work himself; and at the same time to read and judge of the opposing arguments, which we may suppose would also reach him.

But in addition to this, a double weight would undoubtedly be added to the observation of Adam Smith, if these schools were made the means of instructing the people in the real nature of their situation; if they were taught, what is really true, that without an increase of their own industry and prudence no change of government could essentially better their condition; that, though they might get rid of some particular grievance, yet in the great point of supporting their families they would be but little, or perhaps not at all benefited; that a revolution would not alter in their favour the proportion of the supply of labour to the demand, or the quantity of food to the number of the consumers; and that if the supply of labour were greater than the demand, and the demand for food greater than the supply, they might suffer the utmost severity of want, under the freest, the most perfect, and best executed government, that the human imagination could conceive.

A knowledge of these truths so obviously tends to promote peace and quietness, to weaken the effect of inflammatory writings and to prevent all unreasonable and ill-directed opposition to the constituted authorities, that those who would still object to the instruction of the people may fairly be suspected of a wish to encourage their ignorance, as a pretext for tyranny, and an opportunity of increasing the power and the influence of the executive government.

Besides explaining the real situation of the lower classes of society, as depending principally upon themselves for their happiness or misery, the parochial schools would, by early instruction and the judicious distribution of rewards, have the fairest chance of training up the rising generation in habits of sobriety, industry, independence and prudence, and in a proper discharge of their religious duties; which would raise them from their present degraded state, and approximate them, in some degree, to the middle classes of society, whose habits, generally speaking, are certainly superior.

In most countries, among the lower classes of people, there appears to be something like a standard of wretchedness, a point below which they will not continue to marry and propagate their species. This standard is different in different countries, and is formed by various concurring circumstances of soil, climate, government, degree of knowledge, and civilization, etc. The principal circumstances which contribute to raise it are liberty, security of property, the diffusion of knowledge, and a taste for the conveniences and the comforts of life. Those which contribute principally to lower it are despotism and ignorance.

In an attempt to better the condition of the labouring classes of society, our object should be to raise this standard as high as possible, by cultivating a spirit of independence, a decent pride, and a taste for cleanliness and comfort. The effect of a good government in increasing the prudential habits and personal respectability of the lower classes of society has already been insisted on; but certainly this effect will always be incomplete without a good system of education; and, indeed, it may be said that no government can approach to perfection, that does not provide for the instruction of the people. The benefits derived from education are among those, which may be enjoyed without restriction of numbers; and, as it is in the power of governments to confer these benefits, it is undoubtedly their duty to do it.

NOTES

1. *Wealth of Nations*, vol. iii. b. v. c. i. p. 187.
2. Adam Smith proposes, that the elementary parts of geometry and mechanics should be taught in these parish schools; and I cannot help thinking, that the common principles by which markets are regulated might be made sufficiently clear, to be of considerable use. It is certainly a subject that, as it interests the lower classes of people very nearly, would be likely to attract their attention. At the same time it must be confessed, that it is impossible to be in any degree sanguine on this point, recollecting how very ignorant in general the educated part of the community is of these principles. If, however, political economy cannot be taught to the common people, I really think that it ought to form a branch of university education. Scotland has set us an example in this respect, which we ought not to be so slow to imitate. It is of the utmost importance, that the gentlemen of the country, and particularly the clergy, should not from ignorance aggravate the evils of scarcity, every time that it unfortunately occurs. During the late dearths, half of the gentlemen and clergymen in the kingdom richly deserved to have been prosecuted for sedition. After inflaming the minds of the common people against the farmers and corn dealers, by the manner in which they talked of them or preached about them, it was but a feeble antidote to the poison which they had infused, coldly to observe that, however the poor might be oppressed or cheated, it was their duty to keep the peace. It was little better than Antony's repeated declaration, that the conspirators were all honourable men; which did not save either their houses or their

persons from the attacks of the mob. Political economy is perhaps the only science, of which it may be said that the ignorance of it is not merely a deprivation of good, but produces great positive evil.

This note was written in 1803; and it is particularly gratifying to me, at the end of the year 1825, to see that what I stated as so desirable twenty-two years ago, seems to be now on the eve of its accomplishment. The increasing attention which in the interval has been paid generally to the science of political economy; the lectures which have been given at Cambridge, London, and Liverpool; the chair which has lately been established at Oxford; the projected University in the Metropolis; and, above all, the Mechanics Institution, open the fairest prospect that, within a moderate period of time, the fundamental principles of political economy will, to a very useful extent, be known to the higher, middle, and a most important portion of the working classes of society in England.

3. 1800 and 1801.
4. Written in 1803.
5. *Wealth of Nations*, vol. iii. b. v. c. i. p. 193.

10

Of the Directions of Our Charity

An important and interesting inquiry yet remains, relating to the mode of directing our private charity, so as not to interfere with the great object in view, of meliorating the condition of the labouring classes of people, by preventing the population from pressing too hard against the limits of the means of subsistence.

The emotion which prompts us to relieve our fellow-creatures in distress is, like all our other natural passions, general, and, in some degree, indiscriminate and blind. Our feelings of compassion may be worked up to a higher pitch by a well-wrought scene in a play, or a fictitious tale in a novel, than by almost any events in real life: and if among ten petitioners we were to listen only to the first impulses of our feelings without making further inquiries, we should undoubtedly give our assistance to the best actor of the party. It is evident, therefore, that the impulse of benevolence, like the impulses of love, of anger, of ambition, the desire of eating and drinking, or any other of our natural propensities, must be regulated by experience, and frequently brought to the test of utility, or it will defeat its intended purpose.

The apparent object of the passion between the sexes is the continuation of the species, and the formation of such an intimate union of views and interests between two persons as will best promote their happiness, and, at the name time, secure the proper degree of attention to the helplessness of infancy and the education of the rising generation; but if every man were to obey at all times the impulses of nature in the gratification of this passion, without regard to consequences, the principal part of these important objects would not be attained, and even the continuation of the species might be defeated by a promiscuous intercourse.

The apparent end of the impulse of benevolence is, to draw the whole human race together, but more particularly that part of it which is of our own nation and kindred, in the bonds of brotherly love; and by giving men an interest in the happiness and misery of their fellow-creatures, to prompt them, as they have power, to mitigate the partial evils arising from general laws, and thus to increase the sum of human happiness; but if our benevolence be indiscriminate, and the degree of apparent distress be made the sole measure of our liberality, it is evident that it will be exercised almost exclusively upon common beggars, while modest unobtrusive merit, struggling with unavoidable difficulties, yet still maintaining some slight appearances of decency and cleanliness, will be totally neglected. We shall raise the worthless above the worthy; we shall encourage indolence and check industry; and in the most marked manner subtract from the sum of human happiness.

Our experience has, indeed, informed us that the impulse of benevolence is not so strong as the passion between the sexes and that, generally speaking, there is much less danger to be apprehended from the indulgence of the former than of the latter; but independently of this experience and of the moral codes founded upon it, we should be as much justified in a general indulgence of the former passion as in following indiscriminately every impulse of our benevolence. They are both natural passions, excited by their appropriate objects, and to the gratification of which we are prompted by the pleasurable sensations which accompany them. As animals, or till we know their consequences, our only business is to follow these dictates of nature; but, as reasonable beings, we are under the strongest obligations to attend to their consequences; and if they be evil to ourselves or others, we may justly consider it as an indication, that such a mode of indulging these passions is not suited to our state or conformable to the will of God. As moral agents, therefore, it is clearly our duty to restrain their indulgence in these particular directions; and by thus carefully examining the consequences of our natural passions, and frequently bringing them to the test of utility, gradually to acquire a habit of gratifying them only in that way, which, being unattended with evil, will clearly add to the sum of human happiness, and fulfil the apparent purpose of the Creator.

Though utility, therefore, can never be the immediate excitement to the gratification of any passion, it is the test by which alone we can know, independently of the revealed will of God, whether it ought or ought not to be indulged; and is therefore the surest criterion of moral rules which can be collected from the light of nature. All the moral codes, which have inculcated the subjection of the passions to reason, have been, as I conceive, really built upon this foundation, whether the promulgators of them were aware of it or not.

I remind the reader of these truths, in order to apply them to the habitual direction of our charity; and if we keep the criterion of utility constantly in view, we may find ample room for the exercise of our benevolence, without interfering with the great purpose which we have to accomplish.

One of the most valuable parts of charity is its effect upon the giver. It is more blessed to give than to receive. Supposing it to be allowed that the exercise of our benevolence in acts of charity is not, upon the whole, really beneficial to the poor; yet we could never sanction any endeavour to extinguish an impulse, the proper gratification of which has so evident a tendency to purify and exalt the human mind. But it is particularly satisfactory and pleasing to find that the mode of exercising our charity, which, when brought to the test of utility, will appear to be most beneficial to the poor, is precisely that, which will have the best and most improving effect on the mind of the donor.

The quality of charity, like that of mercy,
is not strained;
It droppeth as the gentle rain from Heav'n
Upon the earth beneath.

The immense sums distributed to the poor in this country by the parochial laws are improperly called charity. They want its most distinguishing attribute; and, as might be expected from an attempt to force that which loses its essence the moment it ceases to be voluntary, their effects upon those from whom they are collected are as prejudicial as on those to whom they are distributed. On the side of the receivers of this miscalled charity, instead of real relief, we find accumulated distress and more extended poverty; on the side of the givers, instead of pleasurable sensations, unceasing discontent and irritation.

In the great charitable institutions supported by voluntary contributions, some of which are certainly of a prejudicial tendency, the subscriptions, I am inclined to fear, are sometimes given grudgingly, and rather because they are expected by the world from certain stations and certain fortunes, than because they are prompted by motives of genuine benevolence; and as the greater part of the subscribers do not interest themselves in the management of the funds or in the fate of the particular objects relieved, it is not to be expected that this kind of charity should have any strikingly beneficial influence on the minds of the majority who exercise it.

Even in the relief of common beggars, we shall find that we are often as much influenced by the desire of getting rid of the importunities of a disgusting object, as by the pleasure of relieving it. We wish that it had not fallen in our way, rather than rejoice in the opportunity given us of assisting a fellow-creature. We feel a painful emotion at the sight of so much apparent misery; but the pittance we give does not relieve it. We know that it is totally inadequate to produce any essential effect. We know besides, that we shall be addressed in the same manner at the corner of the next street; and we know that we are liable to the grossest impositions. We hurry therefore sometimes by such objects, and shut our ears to their importunate demands. We give no more than we can help giving without doing actual violence to our feelings. Our charity is in some degree forced; and, like forced charity, it leaves no satisfactory impression on the mind, and cannot therefore have any very beneficial and improving effect on the heart and affections.

But it is far otherwise with that voluntary and active charity, which makes itself acquainted with the objects which it relieves; which seems to feel, and to be proud of the bond that unites the rich with the poor; which enters into their houses, informs itself not only of their wants, but of their habits and dispositions; checks the hopes of clamorous and obtrusive poverty, with no other recommendation but rags; and encourages, with adequate relief, the silent and retiring sufferer, labouring under unmerited difficulties. This mode of exercising our clarity presents a very different picture from that of any other; and its contrast with the common mode of parish relief cannot be better described than in the words of Mr. Townsend, in the conclusion of his admirable dissertation on the Poor-Laws. "Nothing in nature can be more disgusting than a parish pay-table, attendant upon which, in the same objects of misery, are too often found combined, snuff, gin, rags, vermin, insolence, and abusive language; nor in nature can any thing be more beautiful than the mild complacency of benevolence hastening to the humble cottage to relieve the wants of industry and virtue, to feed the hungry, to clothe the naked, and to soothe the sorrows of the widow with her tender orphans; nothing can be more pleasing, unless it be their sparkling eyes, their bursting tears, and their uplifted hands, the artless expressions of unfeigned gratitude for unexpected favours. Such scenes will frequently occur, whenever men shall have power to dispose of their own property."

I conceive it to be almost impossible that any person could be much engaged in such scenes without daily making advances in virtue. No exercise of our affections can have a more evident tendency to purify and exalt the human mind. It is almost exclusively this species of charity that blesseth him that gives; and, in a general view, it is almost exclusively this species of charity which blesseth him that takes; at least it may be asserted that there are but few other modes of exercising our charity, in which large sums can be distributed, without a greater chance of producing evil than good.

The discretionary power of giving or withholding relief; which is, to a certain extent, vested in parish officers and justices, is of a very different nature, and will have a very different effect, from the discrimination which may be exercised by voluntary charity. Every man in this country, under certain circumstances, is entitled by law to parish assistance; and unless his disqualification is clearly proved, has a right to complain if it be withheld. The inquiries necessary to settle this point, and the extent of the relief to be granted, too often produce evasion and lying on the part of the petitioner, and afford an opening to partiality and oppression in the overseer. If the proposed relief be given, it is of course received with unthankfulness; and, if it be denied, the party generally thinks himself severely aggrieved, and feels resentment and indignation at his treatment.

In the distribution of voluntary charity nothing of this kind can take place. The person who receives it is made the proper subject of the pleasurable sensation of gratitude; and those who do not receive it cannot possibly conceive themselves in the slightest degree injured. Every man has a right to do what he will with his own, and cannot, in justice, be called upon to render a reason why he gives in the one case, and abstains from it in the other. This kind of despotic power, essential to voluntary charity, gives the greatest facility to the selection of worthy objects of relief, without being accompanied by any ill consequences; and has further a most beneficial effect from the degree of uncertainty which must necessarily be attached to it. It is in the highest degree important to the general happiness of the poor, that no man should look to charity as a fund on which he may confidently depend. He should be taught that his own exertions, his own industry and foresight, are his only just ground of dependence; that if these fail, assistance in his distresses can only be the subject of rational hope; and that even the foundation of this hope will depend in a considerable degree on his own good conduct and the consciousness that he has not involved himself in these difficulties by his indolence or imprudence.

That in the distribution of our charity we are under a strong moral obligation to inculcate this lesson on the poor by a proper discrimination, is a truth of which I cannot feel a doubt. If all could be completely relieved, and poverty banished from the country, even at the expense of three-fourths of the fortunes of the rich, I would be the last person to say a single syllable against relieving all, and making the degree of distress alone the measure of our bounty. But as experience has proved, I believe, without a single exception, that poverty and misery have always increased in proportion to the quantity of indiscriminate charity, are we not bound to infer, reasoning as we usually do from the laws of nature, that it is an intimation that such a mode of distribution is not the proper office of benevolence?

The laws of nature say, with St. Paul, "If a man will not work, neither shall he eat." They also say that he is not rashly to trust to Providence. They appear indeed to be constant and uniform for the express purpose of telling him what he is to trust to, and that, if he marry without a reasonable prospect of supporting a family, he must expect to suffer want. These intimations appear from the constitution of human nature to be absolutely necessary, and to have a strikingly beneficial tendency. If in the direction either of our public or our private charity we say that though a man will not work, yet he shall eat; and though he marry without being able to support a family, yet his family shall be supported; it is evident that we do not merely endeavour to mitigate the partial evils arising from general laws, but regularly and systematically to counteract the obviously beneficial effects of these general laws themselves. And we cannot easily conceive, that the Deity should implant any passion in the human breast for such a purpose.

In the great course of human events, the best-founded expectations will sometimes be disappointed; and industry, prudence, and virtue not only fail of their just reward, but be involved in unmerited calamities. Those who are thus suffering in spite of the best-directed endeavours to avoid it, and from causes which they could not be expected to foresee, are the genuine objects of charity. In relieving these, we exercise the appropriate office of benevolence, that of mitigating the partial evils arising from general laws; and in this direction of our charity therefore we need not apprehend any ill consequences. Such objects ought to be relieved, according to our means, liberally and adequately, even though the worthless were in much more severe distress.

When indeed this first claim on our benevolence was satisfied, we might then turn our attention to the idle and improvident; but the interests of human happiness most clearly require, that the relief which we afford them should not be abundant. We may perhaps take upon ourselves, with great caution, to mitigate the punishments which they are suffering from the laws of nature, but on no account to remove them entirely. They are deservedly at the bottom in the scale of society; and if we raise them from this situation, we not only palpably defeat the end of benevolence, but commit a most glaring injustice to those who are above them. They should on no account be enabled to command so much of the necessaries of life as can be obtained by the wages of common labour.

It is evident that these reasonings do not apply to those cases of urgent distress arising from disastrous accidents, unconnected with habits indolence and improvidence. If a man break a leg or an arm, we are not to stop to inquire into his moral character before we lend him our assistance; but in this case we are perfectly consistent, and the touchstone of utility completely justifies our conduct. By affording the most indiscriminate assistance in this way, we are in little danger of encouraging people to break their arms and legs. According to the touchstone of utility, the high approbation which Christ gave to the conduct of the good Samaritan, who followed the immediate impulse of his benevolence in relieving a stranger in the urgent distress of an accident, does not, in the smallest degree, contradict the expression of St. Paul, "If a man will not work, neither shall he eat."

We are not, however, in any case, to lose a present opportunity of doing good, from the mere supposition that we may meet possibly with a worthier object. In all doubtful cases it may safely be laid down as our duty to follow the natural impulse of our benevolence; but when, in fulfilling our obligations as reasonable beings to attend to the consequences of our actions, we have, from our own experience and that of others, drawn the conclusion that the exercise of our benevolence in one mode is prejudicial, and in another is beneficial in its effects; we are certainly bound, as moral agents, to check our natural propensities in the one direction, and to encourage them and acquire the habits of exercising them in the other.

11

Different Plans of Improving the Condition of the Poor Considered

In the distribution of our charity, or in any efforts which we may make to better the condition of the lower classes of society, there is another point relating to the main argument of this work, to which we must be particularly attentive. We must on no account do any thing which tends directly to encourage marriage, or to remove, in any regular and systematic manner, that inequality of circumstances which ought always to exist between the single man and the man with a family. The writers who have best understood the principle of population appear to me all to have fallen into very important errors on this point.

Sir James Steuart, who was fully aware of what he calls vicious procreation, and of the misery that attends a redundant population, recommends, notwithstanding, the general establishment of foundling hospitals; the taking of children under certain circumstances from their parents, and supporting them at the expense of the state; and particularly laments the inequality of condition between the married and single man, so ill proportioned to their respective wants.[1] He forgets, in these instances, that if, without the encouragement to multiplication of foundling hospitals, or of public support for the children of some married persons, and under the discouragement of great pecuniary disadvantages on the side of the married man, population be still redundant, which is evinced by the inability of the poor to maintain all their children; it is a clear proof that the funds destined for the maintenance of labour cannot properly support a greater population; and that, if further encouragements to multiplication be given, and discouragements removed, the result must be, an increase somewhere or other of that vicious procreation, which he so justly reprobates.

Mr. Townsend, who in his Dissertation on the Poor Laws has treated this subject with great skill and perspicuity, appears to me to conclude with a proposal, which violates the principles on which he had reasoned so well. He wishes to make the benefit clubs, or friendly societies, which are now voluntarily established in many parishes, compulsory and universal; and proposes as a regulation that an unmarried man should pay a fourth part of his wages, and a married man with four children not more than a thirtieth part.[2]

I must first remark that the moment these subscriptions are made compulsory, they will necessarily operate exactly like a direct tax upon labour, which, as Adam Smith justly states, will always be paid, and in a more expensive manner, by the consumer. The landed interest therefore would receive little relief from this plan, but would pay the same sum as at present, only in the advanced price of labour and of commodities, instead of in the parish rates. A compulsory subscription of this kind would have almost all the bad effects of the present system of relief, and, though altered in name, would still possess the essential spirit of the poor-laws.

Dean Tucker, in some remarks on a plan of the same kind, proposed by Mr. Pew, observed that, after much talk and reflection on the subject, he had come to the conclusion, that they must be voluntary associations, and not compulsory assemblies. A voluntary subscription is like a tax upon a luxury, and does not necessarily raise the price of labour.

It should be recollected, also, that in a voluntary association of a small extent, over which each individual member can exercise a superintendence, it is highly probable that the original agreements will all be strictly fulfilled, or, if they be not, every man may at least have the redress of withdrawing himself from the club. But in an universal compulsory subscription, which must necessarily become a national concern, there would be no security whatever for the fulfilment of the original agreements; and when the funds failed, which they certainly would do, when all the idle and dissolute were included, instead of some of the most industrious and provident, as at present, a larger subscription would probably be demanded, and no man would have the right to refuse it. The evil would thus go on increasing as the poor-rates do now. If indeed the assistance given were always specific, and on no account to be increased, as in the present voluntary associations, this would certainly be a striking advantage; but the same advantage might be completely attained by a similar distribution of the sums collected by the parish rates. On the whole, therefore, it appears to me that, if the friendly societies were made universal and compulsory, it would be merely a different mode of collecting parish rates; and any particular mode of distribution might be as well adopted upon one system as upon the other.

With regard to the proposal of making single men pay a fourth part of their earnings weekly, and married men with families only a thirtieth part, it would evidently operate as a heavy fine upon bachelors, and a high bounty upon children; and is, therefore, directly adverse to the general spirit in which Mr. Townsend's excellent dissertation is written. Before he introduces this proposal, he lays it down as a general principle, that no system for the relief of the poor can be good, which does not regulate population by the demand for labour;[3] but this proposal clearly tends to encourage population without any reference to the demand for labour, and punishes a young man for his prudence in refraining from marriage, at a time, perhaps, when this demand may be so small, that the wages of labour are totally inadequate to the support of a family. I should be averse to any compulsory system whatever for the poor; but certainly if single men were compelled to pay a contribution for the future contingencies of the married state, they ought in justice to receive a benefit proportioned to the period of their privation; and the man who had contributed a fourth of his earnings for merely one year, ought not to be put upon a level with him who had contributed this proportion for ten years.

Mr. Arthur Young, in most of his works, appears clearly to understand the principle of population, and is fully aware of the evils which must necessarily result from an increase of people beyond the demand for labour, and the means of comfortable subsistence. In his Tour through France he has particularly laboured this point, and shewn most forcibly the misery which results in that country from the excess of population occasioned by the too great division of property. Such an increase he justly calls merely a multiplication of wretchedness. "Couples marry and procreate on the idea, not the reality, of a maintenance; they increase beyond the demand of towns and manufactures; and the consequence is, distress, and numbers dying of diseases arising from insufficient nourishment."[4]

In another place he quotes a very sensible passage from the Report of the Committee of Mendicity, which, alluding to the evils of overpopulation, concludes thus, "Il faudroit enfin nécessairement que le prix de travail baissât par la plus grande concurrence de travailleurs, d'où résulteroit une indigence complette pour ceux qui ne trouveroient pas de travail, et une subsistence incomplette pour ceux mêmes auxquels il ne seroit pas réfusé." And in remarking upon this passage, he observes, "France itself affords an irrefragable proof of the truth of these sentiments; for I am clearly of opinion, from the observations I made in every province of the kingdom, that her population is so much beyond the proportion of her industry and labour, that she would be much more powerful and infinitely more flourishing, if she had five or six millions less of inhabitants. From her too great population she presents in every quarter such spectacles of wretchedness, as are absolutely inconsistent with that degree of national felicity which she was capable of attaining, even under the old government. A traveller much less attentive than I was to objects of this kind must see at every turn most unequivocal signs of distress. That these should exist, no one can wonder, who considers the price of labour and of provisions, and the misery into which a small rise in the price of wheat throws the lower classes.[5]

"If you would see," he says, "a district with as little distress in it as is consistent with the political system of the old government of France, you must assuredly go where there are no little proprietors at all. You must visit the great farms in Beauce, Picardy, part of Normandy and Artois, and there you will find no more population than what is regularly employed, and regularly paid; and if in such districts you should, contrary to this rule, meet with much distress, it is twenty to one but that it is in a parish, which has some commons which tempt the poor to have cattle—to have property—and in consequence misery. When you are engaged in this political tour, finish it by seeing England, and I will show you a set of peasants well clothed, well nourished, tolerably drunken from superfluity, well lodged, and at their ease; and yet amongst them, not one in a thousand has either land or cattle."[6] A little farther on, alluding to encouragements to marriage, he says of France, "The predominant evil of the kingdom is the having so great a population, that she can neither employ nor feed it; why then encourage marriage? Would you breed more people, because you have more already than you know what to do with? You have so great a competition for food, that your people are starving or in misery; and you would encourage the production of more, to increase that competition. It may almost be questioned, whether the contrary policy ought not to be embraced; whether difficulties should not be laid on the marriage of those who cannot make it appear that they have the prospect of maintaining the children that shall be the fruit of it? But why encourage marriages, which are sure to take place in all situations in which they ought to take place? There is no instance to be found of plenty of regular employment being first established, where marriages have not followed in a proportionate degree. The policy therefore, at best, is useless, and may be pernicious."

After having once so clearly understood the principle of population, as to express these and many other sentiments on the subject, equally just and important, it is not a little surprising to find Mr. Young, in a pamphlet, entitled *The Question of Scarcity plainly stated, and Remedies considered* (published in 1800), observing, that "the means which would of all others perhaps tend most surely to prevent future scarcities so oppressive to the poor as the present, would be to secure to every country labourer in the kingdom, that has three children and upwards, half an acre of land for potatoes; and grass enough to feed one or two cows.[7] ...If each had his ample potato-ground and a cow, the price of wheat would be of little more consequence to them than it is to their brethren in Ireland."

"Every one admits the system to be good, but the question is how to enforce it."

I was by no means aware that the excellence of the system had been so generally admitted. For myself I strongly protest against being included in the general term of every one, as I should consider the adoption of this system as the most cruel and fatal blow to the happiness of the lower classes of people in this country that they had ever received.

Mr. Young, however, goes on to say, that "The magnitude of the object should make us disregard any difficulties, but such as are insuperable: none such would probably occur, if something like the following means were resorted to.

"I. Where there are common pastures, to give to a labouring man having children, a right to demand an allotment proportioned to the family, to be set out by the parish officers, etc., ...and a cow bought. Such labourer to have both for life, paying 40s. a year till the price of the cow, etc., was reimbursed: at his death to go to the labourer having the most numerous family, for life, paying shillings a week to the widow of his predecessor."

"II. Labourers thus demanding allotments by reason of their families to have land assigned and cows bought, till the proportion so allotted amounts to one of the extent of the common."

"III. In parishes where there are no commons, and the quality of the land adequate, every cottager having children, to whose cottage there is not within a given time land sufficient for a cow, and half an acre of potatoes, assigned at a fair average rent, subject to appeal to the sessions, to have a right to demand shillings per week of the parish for every child, till such land be assigned; leaving to landlords and tenants the means of doing it. Cows to be found by the parish under an annual reimbursement."[8]

"The great object is, by means of milk and potatoes, to take the mass of the country poor front the consumption of wheat, and to give them substitutes equally wholesome and nourishing, and as independent of scarcities, natural and artificial, as the providence of the Almighty will admit.""[9]

Would not this plan operate, in the most direct manner, as an encouragement to marriage and a bounty on children, which Mr. Young has with so much justice reprobated in his travels in France? and does he seriously think that it would be an eligible thing to feed the mass of the people in this country on milk and potatoes, and make them as independent of the price of corn and demand for labour as their brethren in Ireland?

The specific cause of the poverty and misery of the lower classes of people in France and Ireland is, that from the extreme subdivision of property in the one country, and the facility of obtaining a cabin and potatoes in the other, a population is brought into existence, which is not demanded by the quantity of capital and employment in the country; and the consequence of which must therefore necessarily be, as is very justly expressed in the Report of the Committee of Mendicity before mentioned, to lower in general the price of labour by too great competition; from which must result complete indigence to those who cannot find employment, and an incomplete subsistence even to those who can.

The obvious tendency of Mr. Young's plan is, by encouraging marriage and furnishing a cheap food, independent of the price of corn, and of course of the demand for labour, to place the lower classes of people exactly in this situation.

It may perhaps be said, that our poor-laws at present regularly encourage marriage and children, by distributing relief in proportion to the size of families; and that this plan, which is proposed as a substitute, would merely do the same thing in a less objectionable manner. But surely, in endeavouring to get rid of the evil of the poor-laws, we ought not to retain their most pernicious quality; and Mr. Young must know as well as I do, that the principal reason why poor-laws have invariably been found ineffectual in the relief of the poor is, that they tend to encourage a population, which is not regulated by the demand for labour. Mr. Young himself, indeed, expressly takes notice of this effect in England, and observes that, notwithstanding the unrivalled prosperity of her manufactures, "population is sometimes too active, as we see clearly by the dangerous increase of poor's rates in country villages."[10]

But the fact is, that Mr. Young's plan would be incomparably more powerful in encouraging a population beyond the demand for labour, than our present poor-laws. A laudable repugnance to the receiving of parish relief, arising partly from a spirit of independence not yet extinct, and partly from the disagreeable mode in which the relief is given, undoubtedly deters many from marrying with a certainty of falling on the parish; and the proportion of births and marriages to the whole population, which has before been noticed, clearly proves that the poor-laws do not encourage marriage so much as might be expected from theory. But the case would be very different, if, when a labourer had an early marriage in contemplation, the terrific forms of workhouses and parish officers, which might disturb his resolution, were to be exchanged for the fascinating visions of land and cows. If the love of property, as Mr. Young has repeatedly said, will make a man do much, it would be rather strange if it would not make him marry; an action to which, it appears from experience, that he is by no means disinclined.

The population, which would be thus called into being, would be supported by the extended cultivation of potatoes, and would of course go on without any reference to the demand for labour. In the present state of things, notwithstanding the flourishing condition of our manufactures and the numerous chocks to our population, there is no practical problem so difficult, as to find employment for the poor; but this difficulty would evidently be aggravated a hundredfold, under the circumstances here supposed.

In Ireland, or in any other country, where the common food is potatoes, and every man who wishes to marry may obtain a piece of ground sufficient, when planted with this root, to support a family, prizes may be given till the treasury is exhausted for essays on the best means of employing the poor; but till some stop to the progress of population naturally arising from this state of things takes place, the object in view is really a physical impossibility.[11]

Mr. Young has intimated, that, if the people were fed upon milk and potatoes, they would be more independent of scarcities than at present; but why this should be the case I really cannot comprehend. Undoubtedly people who live upon potatoes will not be much affected by a scarcity of wheat; but is there any contradiction in the supposition of a failure in the crops of potatoes? I believe it is generally understood that they are more liable to suffer damage during the winter than grain. From the much greater quantity of food yielded by a given piece of land when planted with potatoes, than under any other kind of cultivation, it would naturally happen that, for some time after the introduction of this root as the general food of the labouring classes of people, a greater quantity would be grown than was demanded, and they would live in plenty. Mr. Young, in his Travels through France, observes, that, "In districts which contain immense quantities of waste land of a certain degree of fertility, as in the roots of the Pyrenees, belonging to communities ready to sell them, economy and industry, animated with the views of settling and marrying, flourish greatly; in such neighbourhoods something like an American increase takes place, and if the land be cheap little distress is found. But as procreation goes on rapidly under such circumstances, the least check to subsistence is attended with great misery; as wastes becoming dearer, or the best portions being sold, or difficulties arising in the acquisition; all which circumstances I met with in those mountains. The moment that any impediment happens, the distress of such a people will be proportioned to the activity and vigour, which had animated population."[12]

This description will apply exactly to what would take place in this country, on the distribution of small portions of land to the common people, and the introduction of potatoes as their general food. For a time the change might appear beneficial, and of course the idea of property would make it, at first, highly acceptable to the poor; but, as Mr. Young in another place says, "You presently arrive at the limit, beyond which the earth, cultivate it as you please, will feed no more mouths; yet those simple manners, which instigate to marriage still continue; what then is the consequence, but the most dreadful misery imaginable?"[13]

When the commons were all divided, and difficulties began to occur in procuring potato-grounds, the habit of early marriages, which had been introduced, would occasion the most complicated distress; and when, from the increasing population, and diminishing sources of subsistence, the average growth of potatoes was not more than the average consumption, a scarcity of potatoes would be, in every respect, as probable as a scarcity of wheat at present; and, when it did arrive, it would be beyond all comparison more dreadful.

When the common people of a country live principally upon the dearest grain, as they do in England on wheat, they have great resources in a scarcity; and barley, oats, rice, cheap soups, and potatoes, all present themselves as less expensive, yet at the same time wholesome means of nourishment; but when their habitual food is the lowest in this scale, they appear to be absolutely without resource, except in the bark of trees, like the poor Swedes; and a great portion of them must necessarily be starved.

The wages of labour will always be regulated mainly by the proportion of the supply of labour to the demand. And as, upon the potato system, a supply more than adequate to the demand would very soon take place, and this supply might be continued at a very cheap rate, on account of the cheapness of the food which would furnish it, the common price of labour would soon be regulated principally by the price of potatoes instead of the price of wheat, as at present; and the rags and wretched cabins of Ireland would follow of course.

When the demand for labour occasionally exceeds the supply, and wages are regulated by the price of the dearest grain, they will generally be such as to yield something besides mere food, and the common people may be able to obtain decent houses and decent clothing. If the contrast between the state of the French and English labourers, which Mr. Young has drawn, be in any degree near the truth, the advantage on the side of England has been occasioned precisely and exclusively by these two circumstances; and if, by the adoption of milk and potatoes as the general food of the common people, these circumstances were totally altered, so as to make the supply of labour constantly in a great excess above the demand for it, and regulate wages by the price of the cheapest food, the advantage would be immediately lost, and no efforts of benevolence could prevent the most general and abject poverty.

Upon the same principle it would by no means be eligible that the cheap soups of Count Rumford should be adopted as the general food of the common people. They are excellent inventions for the public institutions, and as occasional resources; but if they were once universally adopted by the poor, it would be impossible to prevent the price of labour from being regulated by them; and the labourer, though at first he might have more to spare for other expenses, besides food, would ultimately have much less to spare than before.

The desirable thing, with a view to the happiness of the common people, seems to be, that their habitual food should be dear, and their wages regulated by it; but that, in a scarcity, or other occasional distress, the cheaper food should be readily and cheerfully adopted.[14] With a view of rendering this transition easier, and at the same time of making an useful distinction between those who are dependent on parish relief and those who are not, I should think that one plan, which Mr. Young proposes, would be extremely eligible. This is, "to pass an act prohibiting relief, so far as subsistence is concerned, in any other manner than by potatoes, rice and soup; not merely as a measure of the moment, but permanently."[15] I do not think that this plan would necessarily introduce these articles as the common food of the lower classes; and if it merely made the transition to them in periods of distress easier, and at the same time drew a more marked line than at present between dependence and independence, it would have a very beneficial effect.

As it is acknowledged that the introduction of milk and potatoes, or of cheap soups, as the general food of the lower classes of people, would lower the price of labour, perhaps some cold politician might propose to adopt the system, with a view of underselling foreigners in the markets of Europe. I should not envy the feelings which could suggest such a proposal. I really cannot conceive any thing much more detestable than the idea of knowingly condemning the labourers of this country to the rags and wretched cabins of Ireland, for the purpose of selling a few more broadcloths and calicoes.[16] The wealth and power of nations are, after all, only desirable as they contribute to happiness. In this point of view, I should be very far from undervaluing them, considering them, in general, as absolutely necessary means to attain the end; but if any particular case should occur, where they appear to be in direct opposition to each other, we cannot rationally doubt which ought to be preferred.

Fortunately, however, even on the narrowest political principles, the adoption of such a system would not answer. It has always been observed that those, who work chiefly on their own property, work very indolently and unwillingly when employed for others; and it must necessarily happen, when, from the general adoption of a very cheap food, the population of a country increases considerably beyond the demand for labour, that habits of idleness and turbulence will be generated, most peculiarly unfavourable to a flourishing state of manufactures. In spite of the cheapness of labour in Ireland, there are few manufactures which can be prepared in that country for foreign sale so cheap as in England: and this is in a great measure owing to the want of those industrious habits which can only be produced by regular employment.

NOTES

1. *Political Economy*, vol. i. b. i. c. xiii.
2. *Dissertation on the Poor-Laws*, p. 89, 2nd edit. 1787.
3. P. 84.
4. *Travels in France*, vol. i. c. xii. p. 408.
5. *Id.* c. xvii. p. 469.
6. *Id.* p. 471.
7. P. 77.
8. P. 78.
9. P. 79.
10. *Travels in France*, vol. i. c. xvii. p. 470.
11. Mr. Crumpe's Prize Essay on the best means of finding employment for the people is an excellent treatise, and contains most valuable information; but till the capital of the country is better proportioned to its population, it is perfectly chimerical to expect success in any project of the kind. I am also strongly disposed to believe that the

indolent and turbulent habits of the lower Irish can never be corrected, while the potato system enables them to increase so much beyond the regular demand for labour.

12. Travels in France, vol. i. c. xvii. p. 409.

13. *Id.*

14. It is certainly to be wished that every cottage in England should have a garden to it well stocked with vegetables. A little variety of food is in every point of view highly useful. Potatoes are undoubtedly a most valuable assistance, though I should be very sorry ever to see them the principal dependence of our labourers.

15. Question of Scarcity, etc., p. 80. This might be done, at least with regard to workhouses. In assisting the poor at their own homes, it might be subject to some practical difficulties.

16. In this observation I have not the least idea of alluding to Mr. Young, who, I firmly believe, ardently wishes to improve the condition of the lower classes of people; though I do not think that his plan would effect the object in view. He either did not see those consequences which I apprehend from it; or he has a better opinion of the happiness of the common people in Ireland than I have. In his his Irish Tour he seemed much struck with the plenty of potatoes which they possessed, and the absence of all apprehension of want. Had he travelled in 1800 and 1801, his impressions would by all accounts have been very different. From the facility which has hitherto prevailed in Ireland of procuring potato-grounds, scarcities have certainly been rare, and all the effects of the system have not yet been felt, though certainly enough to make it appear very far from desirable.

    Mr. Young has since pursued his idea more in detail, in a pamphlet entitled, *An Inquiry into the Propriety of applying Wastes to the better Maintenance and Support of the Poor.* But the impression on my mind is still the same; and it appears to be calculated to assimilate the condition of the labourers of this country to that of the lower classes of the Irish. Mr. Young seems, in a most unaccountable manner, to have forgotten all his general principles on this subject. He has treated the question of a provision for the poor, as if it was merely, How to provide in the cheapest and best manner for a given number of people. If this had been the sole question, it would never have taken so many hundred years to resolve. But the real question is, How to provide for those who are in want, in such a manner as to prevent a continual accumulation of their numbers? and it will readily occur to the reader, that a plan of giving them land and cows cannot promise much success in this respect. If, after all the commons had been divided, the poor-laws were still to continue in force, no good reason can be assigned why the rates should not in a few years be as high as they are at present, independently of all that had been expended in the purchase of land and stock.

12

Continuation of the Same Subject[1]

The increasing portion of the society which has of late years become either wholly or partially dependent upon parish assistance, together with the increasing burden of the poor's rates on the landed property, has for some time been working a gradual change in the public opinion respecting the benefits resulting to the labouring classes of society, and to society in general, from a legal provision for the poor. But the distress which has followed the peace of 1814, and the great and sudden pressure which it has occasioned on the parish rates, have accelerated this change in a very marked manner. More just and enlightened views on the subject are daily gaining ground; the difficulties attending a legal provision for the poor are better understood, and more generally acknowledged; and opinions are now seen in print, and heard in conversation, which twenty years ago would almost have been considered as treason to the interests of the state.

This change of public opinion, stimulated by the severe pressure of the moment, has directed an unusual portion of attention to the subject of the poor-laws; and as it is acknowledged that the present system has essentially failed, various plans have been proposed either as substitutes or improvements. It may be useful to inquire shortly how far the plans which have already been published are calculated to accomplish the ends which they propose. It is generally thought that some measure of importance will be the result of the present state of public opinion. To the permanent success of any such measure, it is absolutely necessary that it should apply itself in some degree to the real source of the difficulty. Yet there is reason to fear, that, notwithstanding the present improved knowledge on the subject, this point may be too much overlooked.

Among the plans which appear to have excited a considerable degree of the public attention, is one of Mr. Owen. I have already adverted to some views of Mr. Owen in a chapter on Systems of Equality, and spoken of his experience with the respect which is justly due to it. If the question were merely how to accommodate, support and train, in the best manner, societies of 1200 people, there are perhaps few persons more entitled to attention than Mr. Owen: but in the plan which he has proposed, he seems totally to have overlooked the nature of the problem to be solved. This problem is, How to provide for those who are in want, in such a manner as to prevent a continual increase of their numbers, and of the proportion which they bear to the whole society. And it must be allowed that Mr. Owen's plan not only does not make the slightest approach towards accomplishing this object, but seems to be peculiarly calculated to effect an object exactly the reverse of it, that is, to increase and multiply the number of paupers.

If the establishments which he recommends could really be conducted according to his apparent intentions, the order of nature and the lessons of providence would indeed be in the most marked manner reversed; and the idle and profligate would be placed in a situation which might justly be the envy of the industrious and virtuous. The labourer or manufacturer who is now ill lodged and ill clothed, and obliged to work twelve hours a day to maintain his family, could have no motive to continue his exertions, if the reward for slackening them, and seeking parish assistance, was good lodging, good clothing, the maintenance and education of all his children, and the exchange of twelve hours hard work in an unwholesome manufactory for four or five hours of easy agricultural labour on a pleasant farm. Under these temptations, the numbers yearly falling into the new establishments from the labouring and manufacturing classes, together with the rapid increase by procreation of the societies themselves, would very soon render the first purchases of land utterly incompetent to their support. More land must then be purchased and fresh settlements made; and if the higher classes of society were bound to proceed in the system according to its apparent spirit and intention, there cannot be a doubt that the whole nation would shortly become a nation of paupers with a community of goods.

Such a result might not perhaps be alarming to Mr. Owen. It is just possible indeed that he may have had this result in contemplation when he proposed this plan, and have thought that it was the best mode of quietly introducing that community of goods which he believes is necessary to complete the virtue and happiness of society. But to those who totally dissent from him as to the effects to be expected from a community of goods; to those who are convinced that even his favourite doctrine, that a man can be trained to produce more than he consumes, which is no doubt true at present, may easily cease to be true, when cultivation is pushed beyond the bounds prescribed to it by private property;[2] the approaches towards a system of this kind will be considered as approaches towards a system of universal indolence, poverty, and wretchedness.

Upon the supposition, then, that Mr. Owen's plan could be effectively executed, and that the various pauper societies scattered over the country could at first be made to realize his most sanguine wishes, such might be expected to be their termination in a moderately short time, from the natural and necessary action of the principle of population.

But it is probable that the other grand objection to all systems of common propriety would even at the very outset confound the experience of Mr. Owen, and destroy the happiness to which he looks forward. In the society at the Lanerk Mills, two powerful stimulants to industry and good conduct are in action, which would be totally wanting in the societies proposed. At Lanerk, the whole of every man's earnings is his own; and his power of maintaining himself, his wife and children, in decency and comfort, will be in exact proportion to his industry, sobriety, and economy. At Lanerk, also, if any workman be perseveringly indolent and negligent, if he get drunk and spoil his work, or if in any way he conduct himself essentially ill, he not only naturally suffers by the diminution of his earnings, but he may at any time be turned off, and the society be relieved from the influence and example of a profligate and dangerous member. On the other hand, in the pauper establishments proposed in the present plan, the industry, sobriety, and good conduct of each individual, would be very feebly indeed connected with his power of maintaining himself and family comfortably; and in the case of persevering idleness and misconduct, instead of the simple and effective remedy of dismission, recourse must be had to a system of direct punishment of some kind or other, determined and enforced by authority, which is always painful and distressing, and generally inefficient.

I confess it appears to me that the most successful experience in such an establishment as that of Lanerk, furnishes no ground whatever to say what could be done towards the improvement of society in an establishment where the produce of all the labour employed would go to a common stock, and dismissal, from the very nature and object of the institution, would be impossible, if under such disadvantages the proper management of these establishments were within the limits of possibility, what judgment, what firmness, what patience, would be required for the purpose! But where are such qualities to be found in sufficient abundance to manage one or two millions of people?

On the whole, then, it may be concluded, that Mr. Owen's plan would have to encounter obstacles that really appear to be insuperable, even at its first outset; and that if these could by any possible means be overcome, and the most complete success attained, the system would, without some most unnatural and unjust laws to prevent the progress of population, lead to a state of universal poverty and distress, in which, though all the rich might be made poor, none of the poor could be made rich,—not even so rich as a common labourer at present.

The plan for bettering the condition of the labouring classes of the community, published by Mr. Curwen, is professedly a slight sketch: but principles, not details, are what it is our present object to consider; and the principles on which he would proceed are declared with sufficient distinctness, when he states the great objects of his design to be:

1. Meliorating the present wretched condition of the lower orders of the people.

2. Equalizing by a new tax the present poor's rates, which must be raised for their relief.
3. And giving to all those who may think proper to place themselves under its protection, a voice in the local management and distribution of the fund destined for their support.

The first proposition is, of course, or ought to he, the object of every plan proposed. And the two last may be considered as the modes by which it is intended to accomplish it.

But it is obvious that these two propositions, though they may be both desirable on other accounts, not only do not really touch, but do not even propose to touch, the great problem. We wish to check the increase and diminish the proportion of paupers, in order to give greater wealth, happiness, and independence to the mass of the labouring classes. But the equalization of the poor's rates, simply considered, would have a very strong tendency to increase rather than to diminish the number of the dependent poor. At present the parochial rates fall so very heavily upon one particular species of property, that the persons, whose business it is to allow them, have in general a very strong interest indeed to keep them low; but if they fell equally on all sorts of property, and particularly if they were collected from large districts, or from counties, the local distributors would have comparatively but very feeble motives to reduce them, and they might be expected to increase with great rapidity.

It may be readily allowed, however, that the peculiar weight with which the poor's rates press upon land is essentially unfair. It is particularly hard upon some country parishes, where the births greatly exceed the deaths, owing to the constant emigrations which are taking place to towns and manufactories, that, under any circumstances, a great portion of these emigrants should be returned upon them when old, disabled, or out of work. Such parishes may be totally without the power of furnishing either work or support for all the persons born within their precincts. In fact, the same number would not have been born in them unless these emigrations had taken place. And it is certainly hard, therefore, that parishes so circumstanced should be obliged to receive and maintain all who may return to them in distress. Yet, in the present state of the country, the most pressing evil is not the weight upon the land, but the increasing proportion of paupers. And, as the equalization of the rates would certainly have a tendency to increase this proportion, I should be sorry to see such a measure introduced, even if it were easily practicable, unless accompanied by some very strong and decisive limitations to the continued increase of the rates so equalized.

The other proposition of Mr. Curwen will, in like manner, be found to afford no security against the increase of pauperism. We know perfectly well that the funds of the friendly societies, as they are at present constituted, though managed by the contributors themselves, are seldom distributed with the economy necessary to their permanent efficiency; and in the national societies proposed, as a considerable part of the fund would be derived from the poor's rates, there is certainly reason to expect that every question which could be influenced by the contributors would be determined on principles still more indulgent, and less economical.

On this account it may well be doubted, whether it would ever be advisable to mix any public money, derived from assessments, with the subscriptions of the labouring classes. The probable result would be, that in the case of any failure in the funds of such societies, arising from erroneous calculations and too liberal allowances, it would be expected that the whole of the deficiency should be made up by the assessments. And any rules which might have been made to limit the amount applied in this way would probably be but a feeble barrier against claims founded on a plan brought forward by the higher classes of society.

Another strong objection to this sort of union of parochial and private contributions is, that from the first the members of such societies could not justly feel themselves independent. If one-half or one-third of the fund were to be subscribed from the parish, they would stand upon a very different footing from the members of the present benefit-clubs. While so considerable a part of the allowances to which they might be entitled in sickness or in age would really come from the poor's rates, they would be apt to consider the plan as what, in many respects, it really would be,—only a different mode of raising the rates. If the system were to become general, the contributions of the labouring classes would have nearly the effects of a tax on labour, and such a tax has been generally considered as more unfavourable to industry and production than most other taxes.

The best part of Mr. Curwen's plan is that which proposes to give a credit to each contributor in proportion to the amount of his contributions, and to make his allowance in sickness, and his annuity in old age, dependent upon this amount; but this object could easily be accomplished without the objectionable accompaniments. It is also very properly observed, that "want of employment must furnish no claims on the society; for, if this excuse were to be admitted, it would most probably be attended with the most pernicious consequences." Yet it is at the same time rather rashly intimated, that employment must be found for all who are able to work; and in another place it is observed, that timely assistance would be afforded by these societies, without degradation, on all temporary occasions of suspended labour.

On the whole, when it is considered that a large and probably increasing amount of poor's rates would be subscribed to these societies; that on this account their members could hardly be considered as independent of parish assistance; and that the usual poor's rates would still remain to be applied as they are now, without any proposed limitations, there is little hope that Mr. Curwen's plan would be successful in diminishing the whole amount of the rates, and the proportion of dependent poor.

There are two errors respecting the management of the poor, into which the public seem inclined to fall at the present moment. The first is a disposition to attach too much importance to the effects of subscriptions from the poor themselves, without sufficient attention to the mode in which they are distributed. But the mode of distribution is much the more important point of the two; and if this be radically bad, it is of little consequence in what manner the subscriptions are raised, whether from the poor themselves, or from any other quarter. If the labouring classes were universally to contribute what might at first appear a very ample proportion of their earnings, for their own support in sickness and in old age, when out of work, and when the family consisted of more than two children; it is quite certain that the funds would become deficient. Such a mode of distribution implies a power of supporting a rapidly increasing and unlimited population on a limited territory, and must therefore terminate in aggravated poverty. Our present friendly societies or benefit-clubs aim at only limited objects, which are susceptible of calculation; yet many have failed, and many more it is understood are likely to fail from the insufficiency of their funds. If any society were to attempt to give much more extensive assistance to its members; if it were to endeavour to imitate what is partially effected by the poor-laws, or to accomplish those objects which Condorcet thought were within the power of proper calculations; the failure of its funds, however large at first, and from whatever sources derived, would be absolutely inevitable. In short, it cannot be too often or too strongly impressed upon the public, especially when any question for the improvement of the condition of the poor is in agitation, that no application of knowledge and ingenuity to this subject, no efforts either of the poor or of the rich, or both, in the form of contributions, or in any other way, can possibly place the labouring classes of society in such a state as to enable them to marry generally at the same age in an old and fully peopled country as they may do with perfect safety and advantage in a new one.

The other error towards which the public seems to incline at present is that of laying too much stress upon the employment of the poor. It seems to be thought that one of the principal causes of the failure of our present system is the not having properly executed that part of the 43rd of Elizabeth which enjoins the purchase of materials to set the poor to work. It is certainly desirable, on many accounts, to employ the poor, when it is practicable, though it will always be extremely difficult to make people work actively who are without the usual and most natural motives to such exertions; and a system of coercion involves the necessity of placing great power in the hands of persons very likely to abuse it. Still however it is probable that the poor might be employed more than they have hitherto been, in a way to be advantageous to their habits and morals, without being prejudicial in other respects. But we should fall into the grossest error if we were to imagine that any essential part of the evils of the poor-laws, or of the difficulties under which we are at present labouring, has arisen from not employing the poor; or if we were to suppose that any possible scheme for giving work to all who are out of employment can ever in any degree apply to the source of these evils and difficulties, so as to prevent their recurrence. In no conceivable case can the forced employment of the poor, though managed in the most judicious manner, have any direct tendency to proportion more accurately the supply of labour to the natural demand for it. And without great care and caution it is obvious that it may have a pernicious effect of an opposite kind. When, for instance, from deficient demand or deficient capital, labour has a strong tendency to fall, if we keep it up to its usual price by creating an artificial demand by public subscriptions or advances from the government, we evidently prevent the population of the country from adjusting itself gradually to its diminished resources, and act much in the same manner as those who would prevent the price of corn from rising in a scarcity, which must necessarily terminate in increased distress.

Without then meaning to object to all plans for employing the poor, some of which, at certain times and with proper restrictions, may be useful as temporary measures, it is of great importance, in order to prevent ineffectual efforts and continued disappointments, to be fully aware that the permanent remedy which we are seeking cannot possibly come from this quarter.

It may indeed be affirmed with the most perfect confidence that there is only one class of causes from which any approaches towards a remedy can be rationally expected; and that consists of whatever has a tendency to increase the prudence and foresight of the labouring classes. This is the touchstone to which every plan proposed for the improvement of the condition of the poor should be applied. If the plan be such as to co-operate with the lessons of Nature and Providence, and to encourage and promote habits of prudence and foresight, essential and permanent benefit may be expected from it; if it has no tendency of this kind, it may possibly still be good as a temporary measure, and on other accounts, but we may be quite certain that it does not apply to the source of the specific evil for which we are seeking a remedy.

Of all the plans which have yet been proposed for the assistance of the labouring classes, the saving-banks, as far as they go, appear to me much the best, and the most likely, if they should become general, to effect a permanent improvement in the condition of the lower classes of society. By giving to each individual the full and entire benefit of his own industry and prudence, they are calculated greatly to strengthen the lessons of Nature and Providence; and a young man, who had been saving from fourteen or fifteen with a view to marriage at four or five and twenty, or perhaps much earlier, would probably be induced to wait two or three years longer if the times were unfavourable; if corn were high; if wages were low; or if the sum he had saved had been found by experience not to be sufficient to furnish a tolerable security against want. A habit of saving a portion of present earnings for future contingencies can scarcely be supposed to exist without general habits of prudence and foresight; and if the opportunity furnished by provident banks to individuals, of reaping the full benefit of saving, should render the practice general, it might rationally be expected that, under the varying resources of the country, the population would be adjusted to the actual demand for labour, at the expense of less pain and less poverty; and the remedy thus appears, so far as it goes, to apply to the very root of the evil.

The great object of saving-banks, however, is to prevent want and dependence by enabling the poor to provide against contingencies themselves. And in a natural state of society, such institutions, with the aid of private charity well directed, would probably be all the means necessary to produce the best practicable effects. In the present state of things in this country the case is essentially different. With so very large a body of poor habitually dependent upon public funds, the institution of saving-banks cannot be considered in the light of substitutes for the poor's rates. The problem how to support those who are in want in such a manner as not continually to increase the proportion which they bear to the whole society will still remain to be solved. But if any plan should be adopted either of gradually abolishing or gradually reducing and fixing the amount of the poor's rates, saving-banks would essentially assist it; at the same time that they would receive a most powerful aid in return.

In the actual state of things, they have been established at a period likely to be particularly unfavourable to them—a period of very general distress, and of the most extensive parochial assistance; and the success which has attended them, even under these disadvantages, seems clearly to show, that in a period of prosperity and good wages, combined with a prospect of diminished parochial assistance, they might spread very extensively, and have a considerable effect on the general habits of a people.

With a view to give them greater encouragement at the present moment, an act has been passed allowing persons to receive parish assistance at the discretion of the justices, although they may have funds of their own under a certain amount in a saving-bank. But this is probably a shortsighted policy. It is sacrificing the principle for which saving-banks are established, to obtain an advantage which, on this very account, will be comparatively of little value. We wish to teach the labouring classes to rely more upon their own exertions and resources, as the only way of really improving their condition; yet we reward their saving by making them still dependent upon that very species of assistance which it is our object that they should avoid. The progress of saving-banks under such a regulation will be but an equivocal and uncertain symptom of good; whereas without such a regulation every step would tell, every fresh deposit would prove the growth of a desire to become independent of parish assistance; and both the great extension of the friendly societies and the success of the saving-banks in proportion to the time they have been established, clearly show that much progress might be expected in these institutions under favourable circumstances, without resorting to a measure which is evidently calculated to sacrifice the end to the means.

With regard to the plans which have been talked of for reducing and limiting the poor's rates, they are certainly of a kind to apply to the root of the evil; but they would be obviously unjust without a formal retraction of the right of the poor to support; and for many years they would unquestionably be much more harsh in their operation than the plan of abolition which I have ventured to propose in a preceding chapter. At the same tune, if it be thought that this country cannot entirely get rid of a system which has been so long interwoven in its frame, a limitation of the amount of the poor's rates, or rather of their proportion to the wealth and population of the country which would be more rational and just, accompanied with a very full and fair notice of the nature of the change to be made, might be productive of essential benefit, and do much towards improving the habits and happiness of the poor.

NOTES

1. Written in 1817.
2. See vol. ii, c. x. b. iii. p. 154.

13

Of the Necessity of General Principles on this Subject

It has been observed by Hume, that of all sciences there is none where first appearances are more deceitful than in politics.[1] The remark is undoubtedly very just, and is most peculiarly applicable to that department of the science which relates to the modes of improving the condition of the lower classes of society.

We are continually hearing declamations against theory and theorists, by men who pride themselves upon the distinction of being practical. It must be acknowledged that bad theories are very bad things, and the authors of them useless and sometimes pernicious members of society. But these advocates of practice do not seem to be aware that they themselves very often come under this description, and that a great part of them may be classed among the most mischievous theorists of their time. When a man faithfully relates any facts which have come within the scope of his own observation, however confined it may have been, he undoubtedly adds to the sum of general knowledge, and confers a benefit on society. But when from this confined experience, from the management of his own little farm, or the details of the workhouse in his neighbourhood, he draws a general inference, as is frequently the case, he then at once erects himself into a theorist; and is the more dangerous, because, experience being the only just foundation for theory, people are often caught merely by the sound of the word, and do not stop to make the distinction between that partial experience which, on such subjects, is no foundation whatever for a just theory, and that general experience on which alone a just theory can be founded.

There are perhaps few subjects on which human ingenuity has been more exerted than the endeavour to meliorate the condition of the poor; and there is certainly no subject in which it has so completely failed. The question between the theorist who calls himself practical, and the genuine theorist, is, whether this should prompt us to look into all the holes and corners of workhouses, and content ourselves with mulcting the parish officers for their waste of cheese-parings and candle-ends, and with distributing more soups and potatoes; or to recur to general principles, which show us at once the cause of the failure, and prove that the system has been from the beginning radically erroneous. There is no subject to which general principles have been so seldom applied; and yet, in the whole compass of human knowledge, I doubt if there be one in which it is so dangerous to lose sight of them; because the partial and immediate effects of a particular mode of giving assistance are so often directly opposite to the general and permanent effects.

It has been observed in particular districts, where cottagers are possessed of small pieces of land, and are in the habit of keeping cows, that during the late scarcities some of them were able to support themselves without parish assistance, and others with comparatively little.[2]

According to the partial view in which this subject has been always contemplated, a general inference has been drawn from such instances, that, if we could place all our labourers in a similar situation, they would all be equally comfortable, and equally independent of the parish. This is an inference, however, that by no means follows. The advantage, which cottagers who at present keep cows enjoy, arises in a great measure from its being peculiar, and would be considerably diminished if it were made general.

A farmer or gentleman has, we will suppose, a certain number of cottages on his farm. Being a liberal man, and liking to see all the people about him comfortable, he may join a piece of land to each cottage sufficient to keep one or two cows, and give besides high wages. His labourers will of course live in plenty, and be able to rear up large families; but his farm may not require many hands; and though he may choose to pay those which he employs well, he will not probably wish to have more labourers on his land than his work requires. He does not therefore build more houses; and the children of the labourers whom he employs must evidently emigrate, and settle in other countries. While such a system continues peculiar to certain families or certain districts, the emigrants would easily be able to find work in other places; and it cannot be doubted that the individual labourers employed on these farms are in an enviable situation, and such as we might naturally wish was the lot of all our labourers. But it is perfectly clear that such a system could not, in the nature of things, possess the same advantages, if it were made general; because there would then be no countries to which the children could emigrate with the same prospect of finding work. Population would evidently increase beyond the demand of towns and manufactories, and the price of labour would universally fall.

It should be observed also, that one of the reasons why the labourers who at present keep cows are so comfortable, is, that they are able to make considerable profit of the milk which they do not use themselves; an advantage which would evidently be very much diminished, if the system were universal. And though they were certainly able to struggle through the late scarcities with less assistance than their neighbours, as might naturally be expected, from their having other resources besides the article which in those individual years was scarce; yet if the system were universal, there can be no reason assigned why they would not be subject to suffer as much from a scarcity of grass and a mortality among cows[3] as our common labourers do now from a scarcity of wheat. We should be extremely cautious therefore of trusting to such appearances, and of drawing a general inference from this kind of partial experience.

The main principle, on which the society for increasing the comforts and bettering the condition of the poor professes to proceed, is excellent. To give effect to that master-spring of industry, the desire of bettering our condition[4] is the true mode of improving the state of the lower classes; and we may safely agree with Sir Thomas Bernard, in one of his able prefaces, that whatever encourages and promotes habits of industry, prudence, foresight, virtue and cleanliness, among the poor, is beneficial to them and to the country; and whatever removes or diminishes the incitements to any of these qualities is detrimental to the state, and pernicious to the individual.[5]

Sir Thomas Bernard indeed himself seems in general to be fully aware of the difficulties, which the society has to contend with in the accomplishment of its object. But still it appears to be in some danger of falling into the error before alluded to, of drawing general inferences from insufficient experience. Without adverting to the plans respecting cheaper foods and parish shops, recommended by individuals, the beneficial effects of which depend entirely upon their being peculiar to certain families or certain parishes, and would be lost if they were general, by lowering the wages of labour; I shall only notice one observation of a more comprehensive nature, which occurs in the preface to the second volume of the Reports. It is there remarked that the experience of the society seemed to warrant the conclusion, that the best mode of relieving the poor was, by assisting them at their own homes, and placing out their children as soon as possible in different employments, apprenticeships, etc. I really believe that this is the best, and it is certainly the most agreeable, mode in which occasional and discriminate assistance can be given. But it is evident that it must be done with caution, and cannot be adopted as a general principle, and made the foundation of universal practice. It is open exactly to the same objection as the cow system, which has just been noticed, and that part of the act of the 43rd of Elizabeth, which directs the overseers to employ and provide for the children of the poor. A particular parish, where all the children, as soon as they were of a proper age, were taken from their parents, and placed out in proper situations, might be very comfortable; but if the system were general, and the poor saw that all their children would be thus provided for, every employment would presently be overstocked with hands, and the consequences need not be again repeated.

Nothing can be more clear than that it is within the power of money, and of the exertions of the rich, adequately to relieve a particular family, a particular parish, and even a particular district. But it will be equally clear, if we reflect a moment on the subject, that it is totally out of their power to relieve the whole country in the same way; at least without providing a regular vent for the overflowing numbers in emigration, or without the prevalence of a particular virtue among the poor, which the distribution of this assistance tends obviously to discourage.

Even industry itself is, in this respect, not very different from money. A man who possesses a certain portion of it, above what is usually possessed by his neighbours, will, in the actual state of things, be almost sure of a competent livelihood; but if all his neighbours were to become at once as industrious as himself, the absolute portion of industry which he before possessed would no longer be a security against want. Hume fell into a great error, when he asserted that "almost all the moral as well as natural evils of human life arise from idleness;" and for the cure of these ills required only that the whole species should possess naturally an equal diligence with that, which many individuals are able to attain by habit and reflection.[6] It is evident that this given degree of industry possessed by the whole species, if not combined with another virtue of which he takes no notice, would totally fail of rescuing society from want and misery, and would scarcely remove a single moral or physical evil of all those to which he alludes.

I am aware of an objection, which will, with great appearance of justice, be urged against the general scope of these reasonings. It will be said that to argue thus is at once to object to every mode of assisting the poor, as it is impossible, in the nature of things, to assist people individually, without altering their relative situation in society, and proportionally depressing others; and that as those who have families are the persons naturally most subject to distress, and as we are certainly not called upon to assist those who do not want our aid, we must necessarily, if we act at all, relieve those who have children, and thus encourage marriage and population.

I have already observed, however, and I here repeat it again, that the general principles on these subjects ought not to be pushed too far, though they should always be kept in view; and that many cases may occur, in which the good resulting from the relief of the present distress may more than overbalance the evil to be apprehended from the remote consequence.

All relief in instances of distress, not arising from idle and improvident habits, clearly comes under this description; and in general it may be observed, that it is only that kind of systematic and certain relief, on which the poor can confidently depend, whatever may be their conduct, that violates general principles in such a manner as to make it clear that the general consequence is worse than the particular evil.

Independently of this discriminate and occasional assistance, the beneficial effects of which I have fully allowed in a preceding chapter, I have before endeavoured to show, that much might be expected from a better and more general system of education. Every thing that can be done in this way has indeed a very peculiar value; because education is one of those advantages, which not only all may share without interfering with each other, but the raising of one person may actually contribute to the raising of others. If, for instance, a man by education acquires that decent kind of pride and those juster habits of thinking, which will prevent him from burdening society with a family of children which he cannot support, his conduct, as far as an individual instance can go, tends evidently to improve the condition of his fellow-labourers; and a contrary conduct from ignorance would tend as evidently to depress it.

I cannot help thinking also, that something might be done towards bettering the situation of the poor by a general improvement of their cottages, if care were taken, at the same time, not to make them so large as to allow of two families settling in them; and not to increase their number faster than the demand for labour required. One of the most salutary and least pernicious checks to the frequency of early marriages in this country is the difficulty of procuring a cottage, and the laudable habits which prompt a labourer rather to defer his marriage some years in the expectation of a vacancy, than to content himself with a wretched mud cabin, like those in Ireland.[7]

Even the cow system, upon a more confined plan, might not to be open to objection. With any view of making if a substitute for the poor-laws, and of giving labourers a right to demand land and cows in proportion to their families; or of taking the common people from the consumption of wheat, and feeding them on milk and potatoes; it appears to me, I confess, truly preposterous: but if it were so ordered as merely to provide a comfortable situation for the better and more industrious labourers, and to supply at the same time a very important want among the poor in general, that of milk for their children; I think that it would be extremely beneficial, and might be made a very powerful incitement to habits of industry, economy and prudence. With this view, however, it is evident that only a certain portion of labourers in each parish could be included in the plan; that good conduct, and not mere distress, should have the most valid claim to preference; that too much attention should not be paid to the number of children; and that universally, those who had saved money enough for the purchase of a cow, should be preferred to those who required to be furnished with one by the parish.[8]

One should undoubtedly be extremely unwilling not to make as much use as possible of that known stimulus to industry and economy, the desire of, and attachment to, property: but it should be recollected that the good effects of this stimulus show themselves principally when this property is to be procured or preserved by personal exertions; and that they are by no means so general under other circumstances. If any idle man with a family could demand and obtain a cow and some land, I should expect to see both very often neglected.

It has been observed that those cottagers, who keep cows, are more industrious and more regular in their conduct, than those who do not. This is probably true, and what might naturally be expected; but the inference that the way to make all people industrious is to give them cows, may by no means be quite so certain. Most of those who keep cows at present have purchased them with the fruits of their own industry. It is therefore more just to say that their industry has given them a cow, than that a cow has given them their industry; though I would by no means be understood to imply that the sudden possession of property never generates industrious habits.

The practical good effects, which have been already experienced from cottagers keeping cows,[9] arise in fact from the system being nearly such as the confined plan which I have mentioned. In the districts where cottagers of this description most abound, they do not bear a very large proportion to the population of the whole parish; they consist in general of the better sort of labourers, who have been able to purchase their own cows; and the peculiar comforts of their situation arise as much from the relative as the positive advantages which they possess.

From observing therefore their industry and comforts, we should be very cautious of inferring that we could give the same industry and comforts to all the lower classes of people, by giving them the same possessions. There is nothing, that has given rise to such a cloud of errors, as a confusion between relative and positive, and between cause and effect.

It may be said, however, that any plan of generally improving the cottages of the poor, or of enabling more of them to keep cows, would evidently give them the power of rearing a greater number of children, and, by thus encouraging population, violate the principles which I have endeavoured to establish. But if I have been successful in making the reader comprehend the principal bent of this work, he will be aware that the precise reason why I think that more children ought not to be born than the country can support is, that the greatest possible number of those that are born may be supported. We cannot, in the nature of things, assist the poor in any way, without enabling them to rear up to manhood a greater number of their children. But this is, of all other things, the most desirable, both with regard to individuals and the public. Every loss of a child from the consequences of poverty must evidently be preceded and accompanied by great misery to individuals; and in a public view, every child that dies under ten years of age is a loss to the nation of all that had been expended in its subsistence till that period. Consequently, in every point of view, a decrease of mortality at all ages is what we ought to aim at. We cannot however effect this object, without first crowding the population in some degree by making more children grow up to manhood;

but we shall do no harm in this respect, if, at the same time, we can impress these children with the idea, that, to possess the same advantages as their parents, they must defer marriage till they have a fair prospect of being able to maintain a family. And it must be candidly confessed that, if we cannot do this, all our former efforts will have been thrown away. It is not in the nature of things that any permanent and general improvement in the condition of the poor can be effected without an increase in the preventive check; and unless this take place, either with or without our efforts, every thing that is done for the poor must be temporary and partial: a diminution of mortality at present will be balanced by an increased mortality in future; and the improvement of their condition in one place will proportionally depress it in another. This is a truth so important, and so little understood, that it can scarcely be too often insisted on.

Paley, in a chapter on population, provision, etc., in his *Moral Philosophy*, observes, that the condition most favourable to the population of a country, and at the same time to its general happiness, is, "that of a laborious frugal people ministering to the demands of an opulent luxurious nation."[10] Such a form of society has not, it must be confessed, an inviting aspect. Nothing but the conviction of its being absolutely necessary could reconcile us to the idea of ten millions of people condemned to incessant toil, and to the privation of every thing but absolute necessaries, in order to minister to the excessive luxuries of the other million. But the fact is, that such a form of society is by no means necessary. It is by no means necessary that the rich should be excessively luxurious, in order to support the manufactures of a country; or that the poor should be deprived of all luxuries, in order to make them sufficiently numerous. The best, and in every point of view the most advantageous manufactures in this country, are those which are consumed by the great body of the people. The manufactures which are confined exclusively to the rich are not only trivial, on account of the comparative smallness of their quantity, but are further liable to the great disadvantage of producing much occasional misery among those employed in them, from changes of fashion. It is the diffusion of luxury therefore among the mass of the people, and not an excess of it in a few, that seems to be most advantageous, both with regard to national wealth and national happiness; and what Paley considers as the true evil and proper danger of luxury, I should be disposed to consider as its true good and peculiar advantage. If, indeed, it be allowed that in every society, not in the state of a new colony, some powerful check to population must prevail; and if it be observed that a taste for the comforts and conveniences of life will prevent people from marrying, under the certainty of being deprived of these advantages; it must be allowed that we can hardly expect to find any check to marriage so little prejudicial to the happiness and virtue of society as the general prevalence of such a taste; and consequently, that the extension of luxury in this sense of the term is particularly desirable, and one of the best means of raising that standard of wretchedness alluded to in a former chapter.

It has been generally found that the middle parts of society are most favourable to virtuous and industrious habits, and to the growth of all kinds of talents. But it is evident that all cannot be in the middle. Superior and inferior parts are in the nature of things absolutely necessary; and not only necessary, but strikingly beneficial. If no man could hope to rise, or fear to fall in society; if industry did not bring with it its reward, and indolence its punishment; we could not expect to see that animated activity in bettering our condition, which now forms the master-spring of public prosperity. But in contemplating the different states of Europe, we observe a very considerable difference in the relative proportions of the superior, the middle and the inferior parts; and from the effect of these differences it seems probable, that our best-grounded expectations of an increase in the happiness of the mass of human society are founded in the prospect of an increase in the relative proportions of the middle parts. And if the lower classes of people had acquired the habit of proportioning the supplies of labour to a stationary or even decreasing demand, without an increase of misery and mortality, as at present, we might even venture to indulge a hope that at some future period the processes for abridging human labour, the progress of which has of late years been so rapid, might ultimately supply all the wants of the most wealthy society with less personal effort than at present; and if they did not diminish the severity of individual exertion, might, at least, diminish the number of those employed in severe toil. If the lowest classes of society were thus diminished, and the middle classes increased, each labourer might indulge a more rational hope of rising by diligence and exertion into a better station; the rewards of industry and virtue would be increased in number; the lottery of human society would appear to consist of fewer blanks and more prizes, and the sum of social happiness would be evidently augmented.

To indulge, however, in any distant views of this kind, unaccompanied by the evils usually attendant on a stationary or decreasing demand for labour, we must suppose the general prevalence of such prudential habits among the poor, as would prevent them from marrying, when the actual price of labour, joined to what they might have saved in their single state, would not give them the prospect of being able to support a wife and five or six children without assistance. And undoubtedly such a degree of prudential restraint would produce a very striking melioration in the condition of the lower classes of people.

It may be said, perhaps, that even this degree of prudence might not always avail, as when a man marries he cannot tell what number of children he shall have, and many have more than six. This is certainly true; and in this case I do not think that any evil would result from making a certain allowance to every child above this number; not with a view of rewarding a man for his large family, but merely of relieving him from a species of distress which it would be unreasonable in us to expect that he should calculate upon. And with this view, the relief should be merely such as to place him exactly in the same situation as if he had had six children. Montesquieu disapproves of an edict of Lewis the Fourteenth, which gives certain pensions to those who had ten and twelve children, as being of no use in encouraging population.[11] For the very reason that he disapproves of it, I should think that some law of the kind might be adopted without danger, and might relieve particular individuals from a very pressing and unlooked for distress, without operating in any respect as an encouragement to marriage.

If at some future period any approach should be made towards the more general prevalence of prudential habits with respect to marriage among the poor, from which alone any permanent and general improvement of their condition can arise; I do not think that the narrowest politician need be alarmed at it, from the fear of its occasioning such an advance in the price of labour, as will enable our commercial competitors to undersell us in foreign markets. There are four circumstances that might be expected to accompany it, which would probably either prevent, or fully counterbalance any effect of this kind. These are, 1st, the more equable and lower price of provisions, from the demand being less frequently above the supply. 2ndly, the removal of that heavy burden on agriculture, and that great addition to the present wages of labour, the poor's rates. 3rdly, the national saving of a great part of that sum, which is expended without return in the support of those children who die prematurely from the consequences of poverty. And, lastly, the more general prevalence of economical and industrious habits, particularly among unmarried men, which would prevent that indolence, drunkenness and waste of labour, which at present are too frequently a consequence of high wages.

NOTES

1. Essay xi. vol. i. p. 431. 8vo.
2. See an Inquiry into the state of Cottagers in the Counties of Lincoln and Rutland, by Robert Gourlay. *Annals of Agriculture*, vol. xxxvii. p. 514.
3. At present the loss of a cow, which must now and then happen, is generally remedied by a petition and subscription; and as the event is considered as a most serious misfortune to a labourer, these petitions are for the most part attended to; but if the cow system were universal, losses would occur so frequently, that they could not possibly be repaired in the same way, and families would be continually dropping from comparative plenty into want.
4. Preface to vol. ii. of the Reports.
5. Preface to vol. iii. of the Reports.
6. *Dialogues on Natural Religion*, part xi. p. 212.
7. Perhaps, however, this is not often left to his choice, on account of the fear which every parish has of increasing its poor. There are many

ways by which our poor-laws operate in counteracting their first obvious tendency to increase population, and this is one of them. I have little doubt that it is almost exclusively owing to these counteracting causes, that we have been able to persevere in this system so long, and that the condition of the poor has not been so much injured by it as might have been expected.

8. The act of Elizabeth, which prohibited the building of cottages, unless four acres of land were annexed to them, is probably impracticable in a manufacturing country like England; but, upon this principle, certainly the greatest part of the poor might possess land; because the difficulty of procuring such cottages would always operate as a powerful check to their increase. The effect of such a plan would be very different from that of Mr. Young.
9. Inquiry into the State of Cottagers in Counties of Lincoln and Rutland, by Robert Gourlay. *Annals of Agriculture*, vol. xxxvii. p. 514.
10. Vol. ii. c. xi. p. 359. From a passage in Paley's *Natural Theology*, I am inclined to think that subsequent reflection induced him to modify some of his former ideas on the subject of population. He states most justly (ch. xxv. p. 539) that mankind will in every country breed up to a certain point of distress. If this be allowed, that country will evidently be the happiest, where the degree of distress at this point is the least; and consequently, if the diffusion of luxury, by producing the check sooner, tend to diminish this degree of distress, it is certainly desirable.
11. *Esprit des Loix*, liv. xxiii. c. xxvii.

14

Of Our Rational Expectations Respecting the Future Improvement of Society

In taking a general and concluding view of our rational expectations respecting the mitigation of the evils arising from the principle of population, it may be observed that though the increase of population in a geometrical ratio be incontrovertible, and the period of doubling, when unchecked, has been uniformly stated in this work rather below than above the truth; yet there are some natural consequences of the progress of society and civilization, which necessarily repress its full effects. These are, more particularly, great towns and manufactures, in which we can scarcely hope, and certainly not expect, to see any very material change. It is undoubtedly our duty, and in every point of view highly desirable, to make towns and manufacturing employments as little injurious as possible to the duration of human life; but, after all our efforts, it is probable that they will always remain less healthy than country situations and country employments; and consequently, operating as positive checks, will diminish in some degree the necessity of the preventive check.

In every old state, it is observed that a considerable number of grown-up people remain for a time unmarried. The duty of practising the common and acknowledged rules of morality during this period has never been controverted in theory, however it may have been opposed in practice. This branch of the duty of moral restraint has scarcely been touched by the reasonings of this work. It rests on the same foundation as before, neither stronger nor weaker. And knowing how incompletely this duty has hitherto been fulfilled, it would certainly be visionary to expect that in future it would be completely fulfilled.

The part which has been affected by the reasonings of this work is not therefore that which relates to our conduct during the period of celibacy, but to the duty of extending this period till we have a prospect of being able to maintain our children. And it is by no means visionary to indulge a hope of some favourable change in this respect; because it is found by experience that the prevalence of this kind of prudential restraint is extremely different in different countries, and in the same countries at different periods.

It cannot be doubted that throughout Europe in general, and most particularly in the northern states, a decided change has taken place in the operation of prudential restraint, since the prevalence of those warlike and enterprising habits which destroyed so many people. In later times the gradual diminution and almost total extinction of the plagues, which so frequently visited Europe in the seventeenth and beginnings of the eighteenth centuries, produced a change of the same kind. And in this country, it is not to be doubted that the proportion of marriages has become smaller since the improvement of our towns, the less frequent returns of epidemics, and the adoption of habits of greater cleanliness. During the late scarcities it appears that the number of marriages diminished;[1] and the same motives which prevented many people from marrying during such a period, would operate precisely in the same way, if, in future, the additional number of children reared to manhood from the introduction of the cow-pox, were to be such as to crowd all employments, lower the price of labour, and make it more difficult to support a family.

Universally, the practice of mankind on the subject of marriage has been much superior to their theories; and however frequent may have been the declamations on the duty of entering into this state, and the advantage of early unions to prevent vice, each individual has practically found it necessary to consider of the means of supporting a family, before he ventured to take so important a step. That great *vis medicatrix reipublicae*, the desire of bettering our condition, and the fear of making it worse, has been constantly in action, and has been constantly directing people into the right road, in spite of all the declamations which tended to lead them aside. Owing to this powerful spring of health in every state, which is nothing more than an inference from the general course of the laws of nature, irresistibly forced on each man's attention, the prudential check to marriage has increased in Europe; and it cannot be unreasonable to conclude that it will still make further advances. If this take place without any marked and decided increase of a vicious intercourse with the sex, the happiness of society will evidently be promoted by it; and with regard to the danger of such increase, it is consolatory to remark that those countries in Europe, where marriages are the latest or least frequent, are by no means particularly distinguished by vices of this kind. It has appeared, that Norway, Switzerland, England, and Scotland, are above all the rest in the prevalence of the preventive check; and though I do not mean to insist particularly on the virtuous habits of these countries, yet I think that no person would select them as the countries most marked for profligacy of manners. Indeed, from the little that I know of the continent, I should have been inclined to select them as most distinguished for contrary habits, and as rather above than below their neighbours in the chastity of their women, and consequently in the virtuous habits of their men. Experience therefore seems to teach us that it is possible for moral and physical causes to counteract the effects that might at first be expected from an increase of the check to marriage; but allowing all the weight to these effects which is in any degree probable, it may be safely asserted, that the diminution of the vices arising from indigence would fully counterbalance them; and that all the advantages of diminished mortality and superior comforts, which would certainly result from an increase of the preventive check, may be placed entirely on the side of the gains to the cause of happiness and virtue.

It is less the object of the present work to propose new plans of improving society, than to inculcate the necessity of resting contented with that mode of improvement which already has in part been acted upon as dictated by the course of nature, and of not obstructing the advances which would otherwise be made in this way.

It would be undoubtedly highly advantageous that all our positive institutions, and the whole tenour of our conduct to the poor, should be such as actively to co-operate with that lesson of prudence inculcated by the common course of human events; and if we take upon ourselves sometimes to mitigate the natural punishments of imprudence, that we could balance it by increasing the rewards of an opposite conduct. But much would be done, if merely the institutions which directly tend to encourage marriage were gradually changed, and we ceased to circulate opinions and inculcate doctrines, which positively counteract the lessons of nature.

The limited good, which it is sometimes in our power to effect, is often lost by attempting too much, and by making the adoption of some particular plan essentially necessary even to a partial degree of success. In the practical application of the reasonings of this work, I hope that I have avoided this error. I wish to press on the recollection of the reader, that, though I may have given some new views of old facts, and may have indulged in the contemplation of a considerable degree of possible improvement, that I might not shut out that prime cheerer hope; yet in my expectations of probable improvement and in suggesting the means of accomplishing it, I have been very cautious. The gradual abolition of the poor-laws has already often been proposed, in consequence of the practical evils which have been found to flow from them, and the danger of their becoming a weight absolutely intolerable on the landed property of the kingdom. The establishment of a more extensive system of national education has neither the advantage of novelty with some, nor its disadvantages with others, to recommend it. The practical good effects of education have long been experienced in Scotland; and almost every person who has been placed in a situation to judge, has given his testimony that education appears to have a considerable effect in the prevention of crimes,[2] and the promotion of industry, morality and regular conduct. Yet these are the only plans which have been offered; and though the adoption of them in the modes suggested would very powerfully contribute to forward the object of this work and better the condition of the poor; yet if nothing be done in this way, I shall not absolutely despair of some partial good resulting from the general effects of the reasoning.

If the principles which I have endeavoured to establish be false, I most sincerely hope to see them completely refuted; but if they be true, the subject is so important, and interests the question of human happiness so nearly, that it is impossible they should not in time be more fully known and more generally circulated, whether any particular efforts be made for the purpose or not.

Among the higher and middle classes of society, the effect of this knowledge will, I hope, be to direct without relaxing their efforts in bettering the condition of the poor; to shew them what they can and what they cannot do; and that, although much may be done by advice and instruction, by encouraging habits of prudence and cleanliness, by discriminate charity, and by any mode of bettering the present condition of the poor which is followed by an increase of the preventive check; yet that, without this last effect, all the former efforts would be futile; and that, in any old and well-peopled state, to assist the poor in such a manner as to enable them to marry as early as they please, and rear up large families, is a physical impossibility. This knowledge, by tending to prevent the rich from destroying the good effects of their own exertions, and wasting their efforts in a direction where success is unattainable, would confine their attention to the proper objects, and thus enable them to do more good.

Among the poor themselves, its effects would be still more important. That the principal and most permanent cause of poverty has little or no direct relation to forms of government, or the unequal division of property; and that, as the rich do not in reality possess the power of finding employment and maintenance for the poor, the poor cannot, in the nature of things, possess the right to demand them; are important truths flowing from the principle of population, which, when, properly explained, would by no means be above the most ordinary comprehensions. And it is evident that every man in the lower classes of society, who became acquainted with these truths, would be disposed to bear the distresses in which he might be involved with more patience; would feel less discontent and irritation at the government and the higher classes of society, on account of his poverty; would be on all occasions less disposed to insubordination and turbulence; and if he received assistance, either from any public institution or from the hand of private charity, he would receive it with more thankfulness, and more justly appreciate its value.

If these truths were by degrees more generally known, (which in the course of time does not seem to be improbable from the natural effects of the mutual interchange of opinions), the lower classes of people, as a body, would become more peaceable and orderly, would be less inclined to tumultuous proceedings in seasons of scarcity, and would at all times be less influenced by inflammatory and seditious publications, from knowing how little the price of labour and the means of supporting a family depend upon a revolution. The mere knowledge of these truths, even if they did not operate sufficiently to produce any marked change in the prudential habits of the poor with regard to marriage, would still have a most beneficial effect on their conduct in a political light; and undoubtedly, one of the most valuable of these effects would be the power, that would result to the higher and middle classes of society, of gradually improving their governments,[3] without the apprehension of those revolutionary excesses, the fear of which, at present, threatens to deprive Europe even of that degree of liberty, which she had before experienced to be practicable, and the salutary effects of which she had long enjoyed.

From a review of the state of society in former periods, compared with the present, I should certainly say that the evils resulting from the principle of population have rather diminished than increased, even under the disadvantage of an almost total ignorance of the real cause. And if we can indulge the hope that this ignorance will be gradually dissipated, it does not seem unreasonable to expect that they will be still further diminished. The increase of absolute population, which will of course take place, will evidently tend but little to weaken this expectation, as every thing depends upon the relative proportion between population and food, and not on the absolute number of people. In the former part of this work it appeared that the countries, which possessed the fewest people, often suffered the most from the effects of the principle of population; and it can scarcely be doubted that, taking Europe throughout, fewer famines and fewer diseases arising from want have prevailed in the last century than in those which preceded it.

On the whole, therefore, though our future prospects respecting the mitigation of the evils arising from the principle of population may not be so bright as we could wish, yet they are far from being entirely disheartening, and by no means preclude that gradual and progressive improvement in human satiety, which, before the late wild speculations on this subject, was the object of rational expectation. To the laws of property and marriage, and to the apparently narrow principle of self-interest which prompts each individual to exert himself in bettering his condition, we are indebted for all the noblest exertions of human genius, for every thing that distinguishes the civilized from the savage state. A strict inquiry into the principle of population obliges us to conclude that we shall never be able to throw down the ladder, by which we have risen to this eminence; but it by no means proves, that we may not rise higher by the same means. The structure of society, in its great features, will probably always remain unchanged. We have every reason to believe that it will always consist of a class of proprietors and a class of labourers; but the condition of each, and the proportion which they bear to each other, may be so altered, as greatly to improve the harmony and beauty of the whole. It would indeed be a melancholy reflection that, while the views of physical science are daily enlarging, so as scarcely to be bounded by the most distant horizon, the science of moral and political philosophy should be confined within such narrow limits, or at best be so feeble in its influence, as to be unable to counteract the obstacles to human happiness arising from a single cause. But, however formidable these obstacles may have appeared in some parts of this work, it is hoped that the general result of the inquiry is such, as not to make us give up the improvement of human society in despair. The partial good which seems to be attainable is worthy of all our exertions; is sufficient to direct our efforts, and animate our prospects. And although we cannot expect that the virtue and happiness of mankind will keep pace with the brilliant career of physical discovery; yet, if we are not wanting to ourselves, we may confidently indulge the hope that, to no unimportant extent, they will be influenced by its progress and will partake in its success.

NOTES

1. 1800 and 1801.
2. Mr. Howard found fewer prisoners in Switzerland and Scotland than in other countries, which is attributed to a more regular education among the lower classes of the Swiss and the Scotch. During the number of years which the late Mr. Fielding presided at Bow Street, only six Scotchmen were brought before him. He used to say, that of the persons committed the greater part were Irish. Preface to vol. iii. of the Reports of the Society for bettering the Condition of the Poor, p. 32.
3. I cannot believe that the removal of all unjust grounds of discontent against constituted authorities would render the people torpid and indifferent to advantages, which are really attainable. The blessings of civil liberty are so great that they surely cannot need the aid of false colouring to make them desirable. I should be sorry to think that the lower classes of people could never be animated to assert their rights but by means of such illusory promises, as will generally make the remedy of resistance much worse than the disease which it was intended to cure.

Index

The Roman Numerals refer to the Volumes; the Figures to the Pages.